ETHICS, POLITICS, AND NATURAL LAW

CATHOLIC IDEAS FOR A SECULAR WORLD

Jennifer Newsome Martin, series editor

DE NICOLA CENTER
for ETHICS AND CULTURE

Under the sponsorship of the de Nicola Center for Ethics and Culture at the University of Notre Dame, the purpose of this interdisciplinary series is to feature authors from around the world who will expand the influence of Catholic thought on the most important conversations in academia and the public square. The series is "Catholic" in the sense that the books will emphasize and engage the enduring themes of human dignity and flourishing, the common good, truth, beauty, justice, and freedom in ways that reflect and deepen principles affirmed by the Catholic Church for millennia. It is not limited to Catholic authors or even works that explicitly take Catholic principles as a point of departure. Its books are intended to demonstrate the diversity and enhance the relevance of these enduring themes and principles in numerous subjects, ranging from the arts and humanities to the sciences.

ETHICS, POLITICS, AND NATURAL LAW

Principles for Human Flourishing

MELISSA MOSCHELLA

Foreword by Russell Hittinger

University of Notre Dame Press

Notre Dame, Indiana

Library of Congress Control Number: 2024947144

ISBN: 978-0-268-20926-1 (Hardback)
ISBN: 978-0-268-20928-5 (WebPDF)
ISBN: 978-0-268-20929-2 (Epub3)

GPSR Compliance Inquiries:
Lightning Source France, 1 Av. Johannes Gutenberg, 78310 Maurepas, France
compliance@lightningsource.fr　　|　　Phone: +33 1 30 49 23 42

To my husband

DAVID

with love and gratitude

Contents

Foreword

Germain Grisez, John Finnis, and Joseph Boyle were once dubbed the "New Natural Law" theorists, albeit by a callow philosopher who did not quite understand that the title of a book would be transferred to the persons themselves. Talented second-generation colleagues and students—Robert George, Gerry Bradley, Patrick Lee, and Christopher Tollefsen—continued their mentors' profound and fruitful scholarship across the disciplines of law, moral theology, and moral and political philosophy.

It is my pleasure to write this brief foreword for Melissa Moschella, a scholar in the third generation of new natural law theorists, and for her new book *Ethics, Politics, and Natural Law: Principles for Human Flourishing*. She endeavors to convey "a commonsense morality." Her terminology, examples, and arguments hew carefully to the criteria of common sense, and are carried out "from the first-person perspective, that is, the perspective of the deliberating, choosing, and acting agent." It is tailor-made for those who teach and learn in the classroom. I cannot say that there is not a wasted word, which is impossible in this life's glow of a screen, but there is no wasted paragraph.

I wish to flag a couple of highlights on my reading of *Human Flourishing*. She provides a remarkably prescient and indeed penetrating account of what she calls the "Vocation Principle." Prioritizing some goods that comport with one's vocation without derogation of other human goods is tricky business in real life, one that needs serious discernment. Above all it needs awareness that vocation can operate on the borderline of fanatical attachment to one's own story. Her use of Alasdair MacIntyre in this regard is enlightening.

Second, her social and political philosophy in chapters 3 and 4 attempt to "square the circle," that is to say tongue-in-cheek she argues that political community is subsidiary in the strict sense of assisting the social formations and goods nestled within the polity—beginning with marriage and family, but including also other civic association. As she puts it, polity is "mostly instrumental." But not entirely. The reader will appreciate her careful and subtle treatment of social formations and their classifications according to differing aspects of basic human goods. Most of all her account of polity as bestriding merely functional and truly basic goods allows a more traditional account of moral agency to align moral realism and at least some liberal understandings of principled limits on the coercive power of civil government.

Russell Hittinger
Research Professor Emeritus, School of Philosophy,
and Executive Director, Institute for Human Ecology,
at the Catholic University of America

Acknowledgments

Many people have contributed directly and indirectly to this book. It would be impossible to name them all, but I want to acknowledge at least a few of them here.

I owe a great intellectual debt to Germain Grisez, Joseph Boyle, and John Finnis, who developed the account of ethics that now (for better or worse) is known as "new natural law theory." I feel fortunate to have been able to talk personally with all three about their work, and I hope the book reflects at least a small portion of their wisdom. I have also learned a great deal from the work of other new natural law theorists—Christopher Tollefsen, Patrick Lee, Robert George, Fr. Peter Ryan, R. J. Matava, Gerard Bradley, Christian Brugger, Adam MacLeod, Sherif Girgis, Ryan Anderson, and others—and from my conversations with them throughout the years. Among those whose work has shaped and influenced my own, Robert ("Robby") George deserves special mention. If it weren't for Robby, I might never have come to understand and appreciate new natural law theory. In addition to directing my doctoral dissertation at Princeton, Robby graciously invited me to participate in gatherings of new natural law theorists even when I was critical of the theory, and he (along with others at those gatherings) respectfully and patiently welcomed and responded to my criticisms. His professional guidance, friendship, and example have been an ongoing source of inspiration and support throughout my academic career.

The motivation to write this book came primarily from my experience of regularly teaching new natural law theory to both undergraduate and graduate students. This experience convinced me of the need for a book presenting this topic in a rigorous but relatively brief and accessible way, and also gave me ample opportunities to refine my views and improve my explanations. I am grateful to the School of Philosophy at the Catholic University of America for these opportunities, and to the students I have had the privilege to teach—especially the graduate students—for the thought-provoking questions, criticisms, and comments to which this book might be considered an extended response. I am also grateful to the Catholic University of America for the sabbatical leave during which I drafted a significant portion of this book, and to my research assistants Joseph Gazaille and Ana Botelho.

I have been fortunate to have many opportunities to receive feedback on this project at various stages. I am grateful to the Institute for Human Ecology, to David Hershenov at the Romanell Center at the University of Buffalo, and to Patrick Toner at Wake Forest University for inviting me to present my draft chapters at workshops, and to all those who attended and offered comments and criticisms. Thanks especially to my colleague Marshall Bierson, who generously took the time to offer detailed written comments on several draft chapters and to meet with me to discuss them, and also to Steven Waldorf for meeting with me to discuss my draft of chapter 4. I am also grateful to Gerard Bradley for enabling me to present a draft manuscript during a gathering of new natural law theorists (and friends) at the University of Notre Dame in June 2023, and to all who were there for their valuable suggestions for improving the manuscript. In particular, I want to thank Dan Philpott for encouraging me to add the final chapter on God and morality, for his comments on the draft of that chapter, and also for his suggestion to add an appendix to the book with an annotated resource bibliography. Thanks also to John Finnis and R. J. Matava for their contributions to the annotated bibliography, and to the book's reviewers for their thoughtful comments.

I owe special thanks to Russell Hittinger. I am a great admirer of Russ's work in social and political philosophy, and am honored by his gracious willingness to write the foreword, which is particularly meaningful given his influential early criticisms of the new natural law theory.

Several sections of this book are adapted from previous articles, and I am grateful to the publishers for their permission to incorporate that work into this larger project. In particular, the section "The Doctrine of Double Effect" in chapter 2 draws on portions of Moschella, "Contextualizing, Clarifying and Defending the Doctrine of Double Effect," *Journal of Ethics and Social Philosophy* 26 (2023): 297–324. In chapter 4, some portions of the discussion regarding the substantive limits on government are taken (with revisions and additions) from a section of Moschella, "Natural Law, Parental Rights, and the Defense of 'Liberal' Limits on Government," *Notre Dame Law Review* 98 (Spring 2023): 1559–94, and the section on the rule of law includes some text from Moschella, "What a Pandemic Reveals about the Rule of Law," *Renovatio*, October 17, 2022, https://renovatio.zaytuna.edu /article/what-a-pandemic-reveals-about-the-rule-of-law.

Most of all, I want to thank my husband, David Cloutier, without whom I am not sure I would have managed to complete this book. David has not only provided unfailing encouragement and support throughout all the ups and downs of the writing process, but has also patiently read (and reread) drafts of all the chapters, and has been an invaluable conversation partner helping me to shape and refine my ideas. I dedicate this book to him, with much love.

Introduction

Natural Law Ethics as "Commonsense Morality"

I remember my first official introduction to moral philosophy as a freshman at Harvard. I was taking Ethics and International Relations, cotaught by the eminent professors Stanley Hoffmann and J. Bryan Hehir. Early in the course we were taught various moral theories we would then use to analyze ethical issues in international relations. I don't recall exactly what we read — the course had 300 to 500 pages of reading per week, so I suppose I can be forgiven for not remembering all the details — but I do clearly remember being dissatisfied with all of the moral theories presented. We were taught that there were basically two types of moral theories: deontological theories that define what is morally right independent of the consequences or considerations of what is good for human beings, and teleological or consequentialist theories that define what is right on the basis of consequences, with a view toward promoting (usually maximizing) the good, variously defined. Deontological theories, we were told, had moral absolutes — moral prohibitions on certain actions, such as rape or killing the innocent — that were binding in all circumstances. Consequentialist theories did not.

Yet neither of these options seemed appealing to me, and neither seemed compatible with my own moral convictions or what I thought of as "commonsense morality." Divorcing morality entirely from the good seemed problematic. According to my commonsense view of things, morality was concerned with promoting the good; being a good person and acting in morally upright ways meant trying to do good to people, or at least refrain from harming them. At the same time, it was clear to me that consequentialist theories had major problems. In fact, my first paper for the course (which I still have and still consider to be philosophically sound) was a critique of consequentialism. Further, the absence of moral absolutes in consequentialist theories seemed contrary to moral common sense. At least in my view, any theory that could not absolutely forbid actions such as rape or the torture of innocent children just had to be wrong. Clearly there had to be a third way?

In another course, I was reading Aristotle's *Nicomachean Ethics*. I found Aristotle's approach more attractive, but it did not fit into either of the categories I was learning about in my other class, and it seemed insufficient on its own to answer a number of important moral questions. Aristotle's emphasis on moral character and on ethics as fundamentally about *eudaimonia* or human flourishing seemed right to me, and he also clearly expressed a belief in certain moral absolutes, but the basis for those absolutes was left unexplained, as was the basis for determining what actually counts as a virtuous rather than a vicious action.[1] Aristotle tells us that the standard for a virtuous action is how the practically wise man would act in any given situation. This advice is not without merits as a practical rule of thumb for the moral life, at least if one is able to identify genuine moral exemplars, but in terms of actually providing a principled account of what makes an action right or wrong, it seems somewhat circular or at least insufficient. How can we identify a practically wise person to imitate if we do not already know what it means to act virtuously?

This book is the fruit of more than two decades spent trying to identify and articulate satisfying answers to these questions, both for myself and for my students. The book presents an ethical theory that is fundamentally Aristotelian in that it conceives of ethics as ultimately about promoting and respecting human flourishing, recognizes the centrality of character to the moral life, and understands ethics to be a distinctively practical inquiry that must therefore be carried out from the first-person perspective, that is, the

---

1. Aristotle, *Nicomachean Ethics* 1107a8–15.

perspective of the deliberating, choosing, and acting agent. What I mean by this will be explained more fully in chapter 1. At the same time, I recognize that significant advances in moral philosophy and in philosophy more generally have been made since Aristotle's time.

In particular, the work of Thomas Aquinas built upon and refined Aristotle's ethical theory in a number of important ways, including by incorporating it into an explicitly natural law approach to ethics. Among Aquinas's key contributions in this regard was his articulation of ethical first principles identifying a set of basic human goods as intrinsically choiceworthy, or "to-be-pursued": these goods are the basic purposes toward which all genuine human choices and actions are directed, and thus the foundations of all practical reasoning.[2] This articulation of the foundations of ethics as a set of practical principles identifying basic human goods as the basic reasons for action (something arguably implicit but never clearly articulated in Aristotle's work) is an important first step in overcoming the apparent circularity of Aristotle's account, and of grounding the moral absolutes that Aristotle presupposes but does not explain.[3] Yet Aquinas's account still leaves important logical gaps between the articulation of first principles and the specification of particular moral norms, such as moral rules prohibiting adultery, theft, or murder.

More recently, the work of Germain Grisez, Joseph Boyle, and John Finnis has sought to fill in these logical gaps, and more broadly to develop an ethical theory within the Aristotelian-Thomistic tradition that is articulated and defended with the precision and rigor characteristic of contemporary analytic philosophy. This approach was dubbed the "New Natural Law" (NNL) theory by Thomistic philosophers who criticized it as unfaithful to the Thomistic tradition. I believe these critics are wrong to see the theory as a departure from the tradition, but I will nonetheless adopt the label simply because it is so widely accepted that using any other label would likely cause confusion. No theory is perfect—refinements and corrections are always possible—but I have slowly become convinced that NNL theory provides the best account of ethics that has been developed up to this point, and that it offers a rigorous and satisfying alternative to deontology and consequentialism, largely resolving the questions I have had since I first began studying moral philosophy during my freshman year of college.

2. Aquinas, *Summa theologiae* I-II, q. 94, a. 2.
3. See Finnis, *Fundamentals of Ethics*, chap.1.

What makes this theory distinct—and enables it to provide what I consider the best account of ethics currently available—is that it coherently integrates three elements that all have a place in commonsense morality, but that tend to be isolated from one another in contemporary utilitarian, Kantian, or virtue theories. The three elements are goods, norms, and virtues.[4] NNL theorists recognize that ethics is ultimately about promoting and respecting human flourishing, capturing what I believe to be the basic intuition that makes utilitarianism attractive, but offering a vision of the human good that is much more varied and substantive than the one offered by most utilitarians, who tend to reduce the good to pleasure or preference satisfaction.[5] Like Kantians (and unlike utilitarians), NNL theorists recognize that morality is fundamentally about having a good will, that having a good will has something to do with respecting all persons, and that the requirements of respect for persons limit (in some respects absolutely and without exception) what it is morally permissible to choose and do. Yet by contrast with Kantianism, what rectifies the will on the NNL view is not a formal categorical imperative with no direct connection to a substantive account of human flourishing. Rather, what rectifies the will on the NNL account is precisely the ideal of integral human flourishing, the all-around flourishing of all human beings within a harmonious community. Thus there is an inherent connection between NNL theory's account of the human good—of the perfection of human nature—and its account of moral norms.[6] Finally, as with virtue ethics, the theory is agent-centered, recognizing the way in which choices and actions shape the character of the agent, and also offer-

---

4. MacIntyre, "Plain Persons and Moral Philosophy."

5. Also, unlike utilitarianism, natural law theory values human flourishing because it values human persons, whereas utilitarianism seeks to maximize "goodness" or "utility" in itself, in a way that neglects the separateness of persons and tends to treat human beings as mere receptacles of flourishing, as noted by John Rawls, *A Theory of Justice*, 23–24.

6. Particularly since many critics mistakenly view NNL theory as Kantian, it is worth highlighting that one of Germain Grisez's earliest articles (written as a graduate student) contrasts Kant's view of practical reason with Aquinas's, arguing that despite "some apparent resemblances," the differences between the two accounts "are differences of the greatest importance" (Grisez, "Kant and Aquinas," 75). Further, although this early essay is not meant to be evaluative, Grisez clearly agrees with Aquinas, and in developing his own ethical theory he draws on Aquinas's view of practical reason, not Kant's. (See the section on "History of New Natural Law Theory" in the appendix.)

ing an account of why virtue is necessary for the ability to make sound moral judgments and act upon them. Yet unlike most contemporary virtue ethicists, NNL theorists explicitly integrate virtues with an objective account of the human good and related moral principles. Such an integration is arguably implicit in Aquinas and in the work of many other contemporary Thomistic theories, but I believe that NNL theory offers the most explicit account of this integration.

Particularly for the sake of readers who consider themselves Thomists and who approach NNL theory with suspicion, it is worth noting here that my acceptance of the theory was a long and slow process. For—like perhaps many of you—I first heard about the theory from its critics, and before actually encountering NNL theory directly, I had spent a lot of time (particularly during my graduate studies at the Pontifical University of the Holy Cross in Rome) steeped in the study of Aristotle and Aquinas. I was also drawn particularly to Alasdair MacIntyre's interpretation and development of the Aristotelian-Thomistic tradition. As a result, the first time I actually read something by an NNL theorist—John Finnis's *Natural Law and Natural Rights*—I found the language and approach off-putting and confusing, quite different from what I had become accustomed to during my studies in Rome. Primed to be suspicious of the theory, I confess that I did not at first read the book with a truly open mind, but instead read it looking for evidence to confirm the criticisms I had been taught. I still learned a great deal from the book even in that first reading, and agreed with much of it, but nonetheless I believed that I had found the "evidence" I was looking for and considered my basic suspicions confirmed.

Thankfully, my encounter with NNL theory went beyond passing exposure in a graduate course. Working under Robert George at Princeton, I had the great good fortune to be invited to meetings at which NNL thinkers (often together with friendly critics) gathered to discuss various philosophical issues. I never hesitated to voice my criticisms and concerns at these meetings, and my comments were always welcomed and taken seriously. Over the course of several years, the dialogues I had with NNL theorists during these meetings slowly clarified and corrected my many misconceptions, until eventually I came to realize that my concerns about the theory had been resolved, and thus became convinced of the theory's fundamental soundness.

I relate this philosophical conversion story because I see one of the purposes of this book as articulating NNL theory in a way that can help to clarify some of the misconceptions that I believe underlie many if not most of the criticisms raised by those who consider themselves traditional Thomists. At the same time, the story is a reminder that we all approach philosophical arguments with certain biases that can lead us to misinterpret or prematurely dismiss these arguments, and that although authors have the responsibility to try to articulate their positions as clearly as possible, readers have the responsibility to consider those positions and the arguments for them with a genuinely open mind.

This book is, at any rate, not just for those who are already attracted to the Aristotelian-Thomistic approach to ethics, which unfortunately remains somewhat of an outlier in the contemporary academy. It is, rather, for anyone looking for a "commonsense" moral theory that can overcome the deontology/consequentialism dichotomy, recognizing the intrinsic connection between morality and human flourishing while also accounting for the existence of moral absolutes and the importance of moral character. It is also for those in the academy who are currently convinced of deontology or consequentialism (or some other moral theory) but are willing to consider an alternative viewpoint with an open mind, or who perhaps simply want to be able to offer an alternative viewpoint to their students. And since ethics is not merely an academic subject but is of vital importance to every human being—I believe that our flourishing as individuals and communities depends upon whether our choices and actions are in line with moral truth—I hope that the theory I present in this book will be a helpful resource for nonacademics seeking deeper answers to fundamental moral questions. With that end in mind, I have tried to present my claims and arguments in ways that, though rigorous, avoid unnecessary academic jargon and save most of the technical scholarly engagement for the footnotes. Those uninterested in the details of scholarly disputes will thus find that the main text offers a clean presentation of the theory, and academics and others interested in these disputes will find their scholarly questions attended to in the footnotes.

OVERVIEW

Over the course of five chapters, I will lay out an account of ethics and political philosophy based on new natural law theory. Chapter 1, "Basic

Human Goods: The First Principles of Ethics," explains the concept of human action as the subject of ethics, and then discusses the first principles of ethics (or first principles of practical reason), which identify the basic reasons or purposes that provide rational motivation for our actions. These basic reasons for action are fundamental aspects of human flourishing, called "basic human goods." The chapter will explain the concept of basic human goods in greater depth, identify what these goods are, respond to common objections about the list of goods, and explain the connection between basic goods and human nature. It will also clarify more broadly the role of "nature" in new natural law theory by discussing Aquinas's concept of the four orders (metaphysical/natural, logical, moral, and technical), and why it is crucial to recognize that ethics is a third-order, practical inquiry, rather than a first-order, speculative inquiry. Indeed, I believe that failure to appreciate the importance of this methodological point is a key source of critics' misunderstanding of the theory.

The first principles of practical reason (discussed in chapter 1) direct us to respect and promote each of the basic human goods, for all people, but we cannot pursue every good or benefit every person in every action—choices must be made. How can we distinguish morally right choices from morally wrong ones? This is the subject of chapter 2, "Moral Principles," principles that guide morally upright deliberation and choice. Morally upright choices are *fully reasonable* choices, choices in line not just with one or another of practical reason's first principles, but in line with *all* of them considered as a whole. Considered in their integral directiveness, practical reason's principles point us toward the ideal of *integral human fulfillment*, the all-around fulfillment of all human beings in a harmonious community. To choose and act in a way that is compatible with this ideal—in a way that is fully responsive to the intelligible appeal of all human goods, including community with all persons—is the most general moral requirement of natural law. This most general moral principle can be further specified through the articulation of intermediate moral norms, such as the prohibition on intentional damage or destruction of any basic human good, the requirement of fairness (i.e., the Golden Rule), the requirement to establish a reasonable order of priority among goods in accordance with one's vocation and commitments (which I call the Vocation Principle), and the related requirement to harmonize all of one's pursuits and commitments in view of an ultimate end (which I call the Unity of Life Principle). After presenting and explaining each of these moral norms and some of the more concrete moral rules they ground, the chapter goes on to present a version of the doctrine of double effect that serves as a synthesis of these intermediate moral norms. The final section of the chapter is dedicated to a discussion of moral virtues as the embodiment of moral principles, and an explanation of their importance for the moral life.

Chapter 3, "The Social Dimension of Human Flourishing," considers the nature of human community, its various basic forms (friendship, marriage and family, etc.), their importance for human flourishing, and their implications for the specification of our moral obligations toward others (and thus for the specification of many of the positive requirements of the virtue of justice). This chapter is limited to the discussion of subpolitical communities, but in explaining the nature and importance of such communities, it sets the stage for chapter 4's account of political community as a community composed not of atomistic individuals, but rather of prepolitical communities with their own proper spheres of competence and authority that the political community has an obligation to respect. The chapter first defines community as a unity of wills through common action for a common good, and also defines the concept of common good, connecting this concept to the account of basic human goods discussed in chapter 1. It then goes on to explain how communities can vary in breadth and depth, building on Aristotle's division of friendships into friendships of utility, friendships of pleasure, and friendships of virtue. To illustrate the importance of community for human flourishing, the second section of the chapter takes the reader through the hypothetical life of Susie, considering what sorts of communities Susie will need in order to flourish throughout her lifespan, with a particular focus on the family and intermediate associations. The third section discusses the virtue of justice and the ways in which special obligations (based in part on community ties) help to specify the positive requirements of justice. The argument here is that because genuine community requires partiality toward community members, and because community is intrinsic to and instrumentally necessary for human flourishing, justice not only allows but requires partiality toward those with whom we are in community. On the other hand, because practical reason directs us to respect and promote the good of all, such partiality has limits, and morally upright agents should use the Golden Rule to distinguish between reasonable partiality and the rationalization of selfishness.

Chapter 4, "The Political Dimension of Human Flourishing," considers the implications of the previous chapters for our understanding of the nature and purpose of political community, and our understanding of the justification, scope, and limits of political authority. In doing so, the chapter discusses the specifically political common good, the nature and importance of the rule of law, and the relationship between natural law and positive law. Particular emphasis is given to the nature of political authority as *limited* and *subsidiary*. Political authority is limited by its purpose, which is to remedy the lack of self-sufficiency of the subpolitical communities that compose it, resolving various coordination problems for the common good, and thereby facilitating the pursuit of flourishing by its members. The political community is subsidiary because it exists to assist individuals and subpolitical communities in achieving their ends, and has an obligation to respect the self-governance of those individuals and communities to the extent that is compatible with the common good. Various other limitations on political authority—including a defense of civil liberties, such as freedom of speech, association, and religion, and economic freedom and private property—will be explained as flowing from the natural law principles discussed in previous chapters. I will also explain how the natural law account of politics differs from liberal accounts, yet nonetheless offers an independent grounding for many of the civil liberties and aspects of limited government often associated with liberalism.

In chapter 5, "Human Flourishing, Morality, and God," I briefly consider the relationship between morality and God. I argue that although we can come to know moral norms and recognize our obligation to follow them without knowledge of or reference to the existence or will of God, questions about morality's ultimate metaphysical foundations can only be fully answered by recognizing that God is the source of the moral order. Further, coming to understand God as the ultimate source of the moral order—an understanding that is attainable through rational reflection—has practical relevance, for this understanding can deepen our sense of moral obligation and strengthen our motivation to act morally. In particular, this understanding can help us to overcome the difficulties for moral motivation that arise when acting morally requires considerable sacrifice, when the fruitfulness of our actions seems highly uncertain, or when it appears that human goods might be more effectively promoted by violating moral norms rather than by following them. After explaining how a purely reason-based belief in a benevolent and provident God can deepen our sense of moral obligation and bolster our moral motivation in the face of these difficulties, I close with a few reflections about how Christian revelation about the Kingdom of God is in line with the ideal of integral human flourishing, transforming that ideal into a promised reality and providing us with the fullest reassurance that our efforts to act morally will indeed ultimately contribute to the flourishing that we seek.

ONE

<hr>

Basic Human Goods

The First Principles of Ethics

WHAT ETHICS IS ABOUT:
HUMAN ACTION AND FREE CHOICE

Suppose a woman is killed while hiking because a loose boulder on the cliff above her just happens to become dislodged and fall on her. Even if the boulder that killed her can be clearly identified, no one would hold the boulder morally responsible for the killing, or propose putting the boulder in jail as punishment. We do not hold the boulder morally responsible because we know that the boulder's behavior is completely determined by physical causes. And if, upon further investigation, we learned that the loose boulder became dislodged because a deer ran into it, we would not hold the deer morally responsible either, because (as far as we know) the deer's behavior is determined by complex neurobiological causes. Yet if a mature human being had pushed the boulder off the cliff—either maliciously intending to kill the hiker below or recklessly failing to heed the warning signs saying "Lethal Danger: Loose Boulders. Keep Away!"—we would hold that person morally responsible, and probably put him in jail.

Why do we hold the human being morally responsible for the woman's death, but not the boulder or the deer? It is not just because the human being is human, for we would not hold a three-year-old child morally responsible for accidentally running into the boulder; nor would we hold an adult human responsible if she dislodged the boulder while suffering an epileptic fit. Rather, it is because we recognize that some human behaviors are *actions* in the strict sense, by which I mean that they are the executions of free choices.[1] In a free choice, no force external to our will—not the laws of physics or even complex neurobiological causes—determines our choice. Rather it is ultimately *the choice itself,* and nothing else, that determines what we do.[2]

Not everything we do is the execution of a free choice. Digesting my lunch, mindlessly playing with my fingernails as I think about what to write next, or reaching habitually for the glass of water on my desk when I feel thirsty are not human actions in this strict sense, precisely because they are not the product of deliberation and free choice. The same is true of the be-

---

1.   Throughout this book, I generally use the term "human action" (or sometimes just "action") in this strict sense to refer only to free choices and their execution. For this book is about practical and moral principles, principles that guide deliberation and choice, not principles such as the laws of physics that describe how things necessarily behave. This of course presumes that mature, healthy humans are indeed capable of genuinely free choices, a claim that many philosophers question. It is beyond the scope of this book to defend that claim here, but others have done so elsewhere (Boyle, Grisez, and Tollefsen, *Free Choice*). At any rate, given that our commonsense experience and widely shared judgments about the moral responsibility of adult humans (but not of deer or boulders) seems to support the existence of our capacity for free choice, it seems that the burden of proof falls on those who deny free choice rather than on those who affirm it.

2.   This does not mean, however, that choices are *arbitrary,* for acts of will are, by definition, responsive to *reasons.* On the Thomistic view, reason and will are two sides of the same coin. They are the understanding and appetitive aspects, respectively, of our intellectual powers. Practical reason *understands* certain things to be good (intelligibly choiceworthy), and will *responds* to that understanding with an inclination to pursue what reason grasps as good. On this view, genuine *rational motivation* is possible, in contrast to Hume's view that only (subrational) emotion can move us to act, and thus that practical reason is the slave of subrational desires; see Aquinas, *Summa theologiae* I-II, q. 17, a. 1, ad 2; Finnis, *Aquinas,* 70. For a defense of this view against contemporary noncognitivist accounts of motivation (along with a helpful explanation of the concept of basic goods), see Boyle, "Reasons for Action."

haviors of very young children. But when we are engaged in genuine human actions, those actions are, by definition, completely within our control to do or refrain from doing. When it comes to genuine human actions, in other words, I cannot say, "The laws of physics made me do it," or "My brain chemistry made me do it." Rather, I really am the cause of my own actions; the buck stops with me. It is because human beings are, in the sense just described, uncaused causes of their own actions that we hold human beings morally responsible for what they choose to do (or not do).[3]

The concept of human action is crucial because, when we are talking about morality, we are talking about principles and norms that govern free choices and the actions that execute those choices. We are morally responsible only for free choices, for unlike digestion or even compulsive or habitual behaviors, such as twiddling one's thumbs or reaching for a glass of water when thirsty, free choices and the actions that execute them are by definition entirely within our power. It is also worth noting here that although compulsive or habitual behaviors are not human actions insofar as they are not the execution of free choices, we may be indirectly morally responsible for them insofar as the compulsion or habit in question is itself the result of free choices in the past. If, for instance, previous choices had led me to develop an alcohol addiction, and the glass that I was habitually reaching for on my desk was filled with tequila rather than water, I would be morally responsible for this bad habit and its consequences, even if my current alcohol consumption was not the direct result of a free choice.

This brings me to another point about why free choice and the concept of human action are so important. In free choices, we sculpt our moral character, our identity as moral agents. A free choice sets our will and with it our whole self in the direction of the object of choice.[4] It is analogous to setting the destination in the GPS of a self-driving car. Unless and until you

3. I believe we have good reason to think that our free choices, our capacity for free choice, and our existence itself are contingent realities themselves metaphysically dependent on God, classically understood as the ultimate, uncaused cause of all being. Recognizing this dependency of our free choices on God does not, however, undermine the claim that (within the context of the created order of secondary causality dependent upon the primary causality of God) we are the uncaused causes of our actions; see Aquinas, *Summa theologiae*, I, q. 105, a. 5, q. 19, a. 8; q. 22, a. 2 and a. 4.

4. Finnis, "Human Acts," 149.

make a contrary choice (set a new destination that is not compatible with the previous one) or explicitly repent of the previous choice (delete the destination from the GPS), you remain directed to the object of your choice. For example, someone who chooses to kill an innocent person becomes a murderer, the sort of person willing to kill innocent people at least in certain circumstances, and thus the sort of person who is disrespectful of human life, unless and until that person repents of the choice. On the other hand, someone who makes choices respecting and promoting human life—such as aiding the needy, or caring for the sick—is a life-affirming person whose character is marked by a fundamentally positive disposition toward this basic aspect of human flourishing.

Our capacity for free choices is an aspect of our rationality. Because we are rational, we are capable of genuine knowledge of ourselves and of the world around us, knowledge that goes beyond mere sense perception. All knowledge begins with what we perceive through our senses, but human beings have *intellectual* powers that enable us to understand ourselves and the world *conceptually*. As Aristotle pointed out, we are able not only to see, feel, smell, touch, and taste water, but also to understand what water *is*.[5] We are also able to understand concepts that do not refer to any physical, sensible object at all, such as "freedom," "rationality," and "truth." We are capable not only of theoretical knowledge—knowledge aimed at understanding what *is*—but also of practical knowledge, knowledge directed to action. Just as theoretical knowledge is, most generally, about *being*—what *is* — practical knowledge is, most generally, about the *good*, what is intelligibly choiceworthy, or what *is-to-be-pursued*, that is, a state of affairs that is not yet, but might come to be through our actions, and that we recognize as worth bringing about.

Here is where we see the connection between our capacity for free choice and our rationality. For just as our understanding of being goes beyond the limits of sense perception, so too our grasp of what is good goes beyond what attracts us at the level of our senses and subrational desires (e.g., pleasure and the avoidance of pain). Because we are rational, we can grasp and be motivated to act for *intelligible* goods, such as knowledge or friendship, not just sensible goods, such as pleasure. I will say more in a moment about what these intelligible goods are and how we identify them. For

5. Aristotle, *De Anima* 3.4.

now, I simply want to point out that we are capable of free choice — and thus are morally responsible agents — precisely because we have the ability to grasp and act for intelligible goods, and because there are various intelligible goods we understand to be intrinsically choiceworthy, each providing a sufficient rational motivation for action.[6] For if we could act only on the basis of subrational motivation for sensible goods, our behavior would effectively be determined by complex neurobiological drives. And if there were ultimately only one intrinsic intelligible good (rather than a variety of distinct, irreducible intrinsic goods) we were rationally motivated to pursue, then there would be no real options to choose from.

BASIC HUMAN GOODS:
THE BASIC REASONS FOR ACTION

What, then, are the intelligible goods that rationally motivate genuine human action? Note that in asking this question, we are getting at the very foundations of ethics.[7] For ethics is about human action, and we have just seen that for something to count as a human action, it has to be aimed at some intelligible good. Intelligible goods are *reasons* for action (as opposed to *causes* of behavior, such as neurobiological drives). If, therefore, we can identify a set of reasons for action — goods — that are *basic* in the sense that they are in themselves sufficient to rationally motivate action and thus to make an action intelligible, we will have identified the first principles of ethics, sometimes called the "first principles of practical reason" or the "first principles of the natural law." A key part of what makes basic goods *basic* is that their goodness is *intrinsic* — they are constitutive aspects of the integral flourishing of human beings, not merely instrumentally or extrinsically related to human flourishing. Basic goods are sufficient reasons for action, which means that they must be intelligibly choiceworthy *in themselves* and *for their own sake*, not merely for the sake of or in relation to some other good. Merely extrinsic or instrumental goods, however, are by definition

6. Aquinas, *Summa theologiae* I-II, q. 17, a. 1, ad 2; Finnis, *Aquinas*, 70.

7. I use the term "ethics" to speak broadly about all of the practical principles that direct deliberation and choice, including principles that are not "moral" in the restricted, modern sense of offering norms for determining whether an action is morally right or wrong.

not intelligibly choiceworthy in themselves and for their own sake, but only insofar as they are related to a basic good.

Since intelligible goods are reasons for action, one way to identify basic goods—basic reasons for action—is to reflect on our own actions and the actions of others, and begin to ask why we are engaging in those actions, until we come up with reasons that require no further reason to make the actions intelligible. For instance, why are you reading this book? Why am I writing it? There are many possible answers to these questions. You might be reading this book because you are interested in learning about the subject, or perhaps because it has been assigned to you for a class, or because you do not want to disappoint a friend who recommended it to you. I might be writing it to develop my own and others' understanding of morality, to earn money (though philosophy books are not exactly big moneymakers), to advance my career, or because I believe that this is what God wants me to do.

Some of these answers are sufficient to make our actions intelligible, others are not. Reading in order to learn—to gain knowledge, to deepen our understanding of ourselves and the world around us—is intelligible without further explanation. We recognize knowledge as something good, worthy of pursuit, and personally enriching. We see the point of knowledge-seeking activity. I am not puzzled if you tell me you are reading simply because you want to learn, even if you do not think the knowledge will be useful for your present or future career, for impressing people with your intellectual sophistication, or for anything else. Of course, knowledge often is useful for the achievement of many other goods, but if you insisted that in this case you are simply interested in the subject and want to understand it better, that would be enough to make your action intelligible.

But what if I said that I was writing this book *just* to earn money, and claimed that I wanted the money purely for its own sake—not to be able to buy anything with it now or in the future, not to be able to give it away to worthy causes, not even for the sake of increasing my social status, but just for the money itself? You might respond: "Surely you must want the money for *something*. Maybe you just want the security of knowing you have extra cash in the bank for a rainy day?" But I might insist: "No. I am already financially secure. I really just want the money for its own sake." In the face of such insistence, you would find yourself genuinely baffled. You would either conclude that you must have misunderstood me—for how could such a seemingly reasonable person (a philosopher, no less) act so unreasonably?—or you might question whether I was really in my right mind. Being a charitable person, you might think: "Poor thing. She must be working too hard or under a lot of stress." You might even delicately suggest that I consider going on vacation, taking up yoga, or talking to a therapist. For money is a quintessential example of a *merely extrinsic and instrumental good*, something that is valuable not in itself, but only insofar as it can help you to get other things that are themselves *intrinsic and final goods* (worthy of pursuit in themselves), or to get other extrinsic and instrumental goods (such as medicine, food, or honor) that in turn are necessary for the promotion of an intrinsic and final good (such as health or friendship).[8]

So *knowledge* (understanding) is a basic reason for action—a basic good—but money is not. Let me say a bit more about knowledge before moving on to identify other basic goods. Knowledge, like all of the basic goods, is a category of good. For there are many, irreducibly distinct instantiations of the good of knowledge, each of which is intrinsically valuable. There is, for example, knowledge of Shakespeare, knowledge of chemistry, or knowledge of human psychology. Not all knowledge is equally deep or enriching, but there is always some intrinsic value to knowledge, even if, all things considered, some knowledge is so unimportant that your time and mental energy would be better spent seeking other goods (or other instantiations of knowledge), and some knowledge may involve such moral perils that it would be wrong to pursue it.[9]

I have described knowledge as *understanding* to avoid the problem of utterly trivial knowledge, such as how many blades of grass are in my front yard, or, to use Tal Brewer's example, how many things are less than a foot tall.[10]

---

8. For the sake of simplicity, and because basic goods are both intrinsic and final, in what follows I use the term "intrinsic" to mean both intrinsic and final, and I use the term "instrumental" to mean both instrumental and extrinsic, unless otherwise noted. On the differences between the intrinsic/extrinsic distinction and the final/instrumental distinction, see Korsgaard, "Two Distinctions in Goodness."

9. Recognizing that something is a basic good (or an instantiation of a basic good) only means that there is a reason to pursue it, not that that reason is decisive, for there may be many other, stronger reasons (including second-level reasons, such as moral norms) not to pursue it. In technical language, basic goods are *pro tanto* reasons for action, not decisive, all-things-considered reasons for action.

10. Brewer, *The Retrieval of Ethics*, 294.

It is not clear that there is any intrinsic value in such knowledge, and indeed most of us would be baffled by someone who spends her days counting blades of grass without any further purpose. Understanding, on the other hand, is the sort of knowledge that goes beyond mere facts to answer questions about why things are as they are, questions about the causes of things. Unlike merely factual knowledge, which in many cases seems to lack intrinsic value, I cannot think of any case in which we would find it utterly unintelligible for someone to want to understand something, to know why something is what it is or does what it does. This is why, departing slightly from the accounts of other new natural law theorists, I define the basic good of knowledge as understanding, and consider merely factual knowledge as having only instrumental, not intrinsic, value.[11]

Appreciation of beauty is a basic category of good that I combine with knowledge, insofar as appreciating beauty and seeking knowledge are both intentional activities, that is, activities in which our mind reaches out, as it were, to an object outside of itself, in order to understand that object (in the case of knowledge) or in order to appreciate the harmony and order of its form (in the case of appreciating beauty).

What other basic goods can we identify? I have already mentioned *health*, including *bodily integrity* and *life* itself. For we recognize the intelligibility of acting solely for the preservation and promotion of health and human life, as when we exercise to stay in shape, go to the doctor for a check-up, or look both ways before crossing the street. Because these actions are obviously related to the good of health, we are not baffled when people engage in them, as we would be if someone spent the afternoon pressing random keys on the computer keyboard. Many people's professional lives— healthcare professionals, rescue workers, firefighters, and so on— are dedicated to the promotion of this good, just as many people's professional lives are dedicated to knowledge or beauty. Obviously, life and health are also instrumentally necessary for the pursuit of any other good, but their value is not merely instrumental. I discuss this point further in the next section.

---

11. Finnis has argued that asserting skepticism about the intrinsic value of knowledge is performatively inconsistent or self-defeating, insofar as anyone who seriously argues that knowledge lacks intrinsic value is presumably committed to getting to the truth of the matter—and thus implicitly acknowledging that knowledge has intrinsic value (Finnis, *Natural Law and Natural Rights*, 74–75).

Skillful work and play are another category of basic good. We find it completely intelligible when people seek to develop their talents and skills in various ways, when teachers, writers, doctors, artists, electricians, and construction workers seek to perfect their craft; when chess players, musicians, athletes, and others practice day after day to improve their skills. Indeed, we admire and celebrate such people and their achievements.[12] Nor do we think it strange when people spend a Saturday afternoon playing a casual game of tennis or Scrabble, for we recognize the intrinsic value of skillful work and play.

These first three categories of good — (1) life and health, (2) knowledge and appreciation of beauty, and (3) skillful work and play — are substantive goods, meaning that our participation in them does not fundamentally depend on the choice or intention of the agent. A baby benefits from a life-saving surgery even though he is not capable of choosing the surgery and may not even be aware that it is happening. A child benefits by learning basic principles of biology, even if she fights her parents and teachers at every step. A baseball pitcher benefits from improving his fastball, even if he was not actually trying to do so.

The remaining goods, however, are not like this, for they are all forms of harmony or union between and within persons, and they are all reflexive in the sense that participation in them is constituted by a certain type of choice or intention.

One of these reflexive goods is *friendship*, broadly understood as an interpersonal harmony or union of mind and will, which, in its deepest and fullest form, involves shared activity and mutual and mutually recognized willing of the other's good. To participate in the good of friendship in its deepest sense, one's action must be for the sake of that interpersonal harmony, not merely for some ulterior end. Yet there are other, thinner forms of friendship that also have intrinsic value, such as harmonious relationships among colleagues, neighbors, or members of the same political community. We are, at any rate, not the least bit puzzled when someone does something — invites the neighbors over for dinner, calls a friend on her birthday, or strikes up a conversation with a classmate — precisely for the sake of building or maintaining a friendship,

---

12. Note that, like all of the goods, this good can be pursued immorally or for immoral ends. Even in these cases, however, we recognize the intelligible goodness of the skill, as when we admire the skill of an exceptionally stealthy thief, even if we lament that this skill is being used for immoral ends.

for we recognize that genuine friendships deeply enrich our lives, even apart from their many collateral benefits. Nor are we puzzled at actions aimed at promoting or maintaining peaceful relations among co-workers, team members, neighbors, classmates, fellow citizens, or indeed any of our fellow human beings, for we recognize that even apart from its instrumental value, such peace is choiceworthy for its own sake. Friendship and other forms of interpersonal harmony will be discussed further in chapter 3 on the social dimensions of human flourishing.

Another reflexive good is *marriage*, understood as an interpersonal union that is uniquely comprehensive (and thus different in type from friendship) because it involves all dimensions of the person: intellectual, volitional, psychological, and biological. Biological union between persons is only possible because of male–female sexual complementarity, enabling man and woman to unite bodily as a single organic unit with respect to the capacity for reproduction, and thus giving the marital union an intrinsic orientation toward procreation and child-rearing. This uniquely all-encompassing interpersonal union is something that we recognize as intelligibly choiceworthy, even in cases where that union will not actually result in procreation. Marriage is also unique among the goods in that it requires a comprehensive commitment that corresponds to the comprehensiveness of the union—a commitment to sexual exclusivity, to permanence, and to a broad sharing of life, including a sharing in child-rearing responsibilities—and this commitment may not always be compatible with other life commitments. Even for those who do not make this commitment, however, there are ways to participate in this good indirectly, supporting and benefiting from the marriages of others, and also participating in family relationships that are the outgrowth of marital relationships.[13] The

13. I recognize that this account of marriage is currently controversial, but its key elements were broadly accepted throughout human history and across a wide variety of cultures up until recent decades. It is beyond the scope of this book to defend this account, except to note that any definition of marriage that does not include genuine biological union (not just the overlapping of parts as in a handshake, but the actual union of two organisms, coordinating biologically toward the shared biological end of reproduction) will make marriage collapse into friendship, and thus be unable to account for its distinctiveness, or for the distinct norms and commitments that have generally been considered central to it. For more on this point, see Lee and George, *Conjugal Union*; Girgis, Anderson, and George, *What Is Marriage?*

basic human good of marriage and its importance for human flourishing will be discussed further in chapter 3.

Because human beings are complex, harmony is possible not only between and among persons, but also within persons. The goods of *integrity* and *authenticity*, sometimes jointly referred to as *practical reasonableness* or *virtue*, refer to this intrapersonal harmony.[14] Integrity is harmony between reason and emotions; authenticity is harmony between judgments and actions. We recognize the intrinsic desirability of the inner peace constituted by harmony among our judgments, emotions, and actions, and admire those who display the self-discipline and consistency of character that manifest this harmony, or who act in line with their principles even at the cost of considerable sacrifice.

Finally, as contingent beings in a universe of contingent beings—and as rational beings capable of recognizing that this is the case—we naturally wonder whether there might be some ultimate, transcendent source of existence and meaning. We recognize the importance of answering these ultimate questions correctly, and, if our quest reveals that there is such a "Source"—whom we conventionally call "God"—we also recognize the importance of being in harmony with that Source. Thus, *religion*, defined as knowledge of and harmony with God, understood as the transcendent source of existence and meaning, is also a basic human good. And, as is the case with all of the basic goods, its intrinsic choiceworthiness is attested to by the great importance given to it across time and culture.[15]

14. I prefer the terms "integrity" and "authenticity," however, because the term "practical reasonableness"—when it is understood to encompass the *integral directiveness* of practical reason, rather than to refer to a single basic good—can also be used as the standard for *morally right* actions, and thus can refer to second-level (moral) principles that govern our choices. Using the term to refer to one of the first-level practical principles—principles that direct and provide the intelligible point of all human action (including immoral action)—can therefore be confusing. The use of the term "virtue" to refer to this basic good is likewise potentially confusing and problematic, for true virtues are the embodiment of moral norms in one's character, formed through morally upright choices, and disposing one to act in line with moral truth, as will be further explained in chapter 2; see Grisez, Boyle, and Finnis, "Practical Principles."

15. For a defense of religion as a distinct basic good, knowable as such by reason, see Moschella, "Beyond Equal Liberty."

This brings us to what I believe to be a complete list of basic human goods: life and health, knowledge and appreciation of beauty, skillful performance in work and play, friendship, marriage and family, integrity and authenticity, and religion.[16]

RESPONSES TO COMMON OBJECTIONS

Some might argue that the list of basic goods is incorrect because it includes goods not actually intrinsically valuable, or excludes goods that do provide us with basic reasons for action. Here I respond to a few of these objections.

Does Human Life Really Have Intrinsic Value?

The intrinsic value of human life is often explicitly or implicitly denied, especially in the context of debates about such issues as euthanasia, assisted suicide, abortion, and embryo-destructive research. Peter Singer, for instance, argues for the permissibility of euthanasia in certain circumstances on the ground that "if the goods that life holds are, in general, reasons against killing, those reasons lose all their force when it is clear that those killed will not have such goods, or that the goods they have will be outweighed by bad things that will happen to them."[17] In other words, Singer sees human life as having value not in itself, but only insofar as being alive makes possible the enjoyment of other goods. Singer's approach has a certain intuitive plausibility. It is easy to see the value of the life of a relatively healthy, mature human being, capable of engaging in a broad range of meaningful pursuits, but it is harder to recognize the value of human life

---

16. Even if it turns out that the list is incomplete or partially incorrect, this would not undermine the basic soundness of the theory. In fact, the list originally presented by Grisez, Finnis, and Boyle did not include marriage. Marriage was added later when they realized this good is not reducible to the goods of life-in-transmission and friendship, but rather constitutes a distinct type of interpersonal union, uniting the spouses not only in mind and heart (as friendships do) but also in body (through the joining of the two complementary halves of the reproductive system in sexual intercourse), thus giving this union an inherent orientation to procreation (Finnis, *Natural Law and Natural Rights*, 447–48).

17. Singer, "Voluntary Euthanasia," 530.

when it is reduced to the exercise of the most basic vital functions, as in the case of someone who is in a coma or a persistent vegetative state.

Do the lives of such human beings—capable of only the most basic biological functions—really have intrinsic value? I believe that they do, and that many of our commonsense ethical judgments imply that they do. If we deny that such lives have value, this implies that the value of human life is merely instrumental, like the value of money. But if human life were only instrumentally good—good only to the extent that you can use it to pursue and enjoy intrinsically good things—then we should expect to find it baffling when doctors or rescue workers claim to do their jobs for the sole purpose of saving lives, without considering whether the people they save are going to do anything worthwhile with their lives, just as it would be baffling if I said I was writing this book solely for the money (not for any further good that the money might enable me to attain). Yet we do not find a doctor's indiscriminate commitment to saving lives baffling in the least.[18] This seems to be an indication that, at the most basic level of practical judgment, we recognize that such life-preserving acts have an intelligible point, even if they do not serve any further purpose, and this implies that we do recognize that human lives are intrinsically valuable.

Further, denying the intrinsic value of human life implies a problematic view of the human person, in which the body (except, on some views, the higher brain) is considered distinct from the person (often identified with a set of psychological states or mental capacities, such as self-consciousness and rationality).[19] On this view, which we can call "body-self dualism," my body, though instrumentally important as a vehicle for

18. Even those who recognize the intrinsic value of life do not think that life must be preserved at all costs. Natural law thinkers therefore generally agree that it is morally acceptable to refuse or withdraw care that is disproportionately burdensome, and that what counts as disproportionately burdensome will vary depending on the circumstances, because judgments of proportionality tend to come down to judgments about fairness and judgments about how to prioritize competing goods. In chapter 2, I discuss moral principles such as the Golden Rule and the Vocation Principle that can help to guide such judgments. For a more in-depth discussion of these issues in relation to judgments about medical care, see Keown, *Euthanasia, Ethics and Public Policy*, and Curlin and Tollefsen, *The Way of Medicine*.

19. See, e.g., McMahan, *The Ethics of Killing*.

self-expression and for engaging in activities I enjoy and benefit from at the conscious level, is not *me*. Why does denying the intrinsic value of life imply a dualist view of the person? Answering this question requires recalling that basic human goods are aspects of the flourishing or perfection of human persons. What makes basic goods good is that they are constitutive of the flourishing of human persons in some respect. In other words, what gives us a reason to act is not a "good" in the abstract, but the good *of a person* (or persons). This means that the center of value is the human person. To deny that bodily life is a basic good is therefore to deny that bodily life is itself a constitutive aspect of human flourishing. But to deny that bodily life is itself a constitutive aspect of human flourishing is to deny that bodily life is an intrinsic and essential aspect of our personhood. And to deny that bodily life is intrinsic to our personhood is to embrace body-self dualism.

I do not have space here to explain in detail why body-self dualism is problematic, but the most obvious difficulty is that it is contrary to our commonsense experience of ourselves as bodily beings. For example, consider the question, Who is typing this sentence? The commonsense answer is that I am typing it. Since the activity of typing a sentence is at once both bodily and rational, then I—the agent carrying out that activity—must be a being who is both bodily and rational. By contrast, body-self dualism cannot account for the seamless connection between bodily activities (e.g., typing or speaking this sentence) and mental activities (e.g. thinking about how to explain the problems with dualism), or for the unity of the agent whose actions almost always have both a bodily and a mental aspect.[20]

If, on the other hand, we reject this problematic dualist view of the human person and accept the commonsense view that bodily life is an essential and intrinsic aspect of the human person, then the only way to coherently deny the intrinsic value of bodily life is to deny the more basic premise that persons are centers of value—that the good of persons has intrinsic and ultimate ethical importance because *persons* have intrinsic and ultimate ethical importance. And although there are some who argue for

---

20. For an extended defense of the intrinsic value of human life, and a more detailed critique of body-self dualism, see Tollefsen and George, *Embryo*; Lee and George, *Body-Self Dualism*; Finnis, Boyle, and Grisez, *Nuclear Deterrence*, 304–9. David Oderberg, *Moral Theory*, chap. 4, also argues at length for the intrinsic value of life from the perspective of his own basic-goods-based moral theory.

expanding the sphere of ethical concern to include nonhuman animals—
thus arguing that persons are not the *only* center of value—there is widespread agreement that persons are at least *a* center of value. Denying the
premise that persons are centers of value seems even more implausible than
denying that bodily life is essential and intrinsic to personal identity. Since,
therefore, one cannot deny the intrinsic value of bodily life without either
embracing a problematic dualist view of the person or denying that persons
have intrinsic value, I conclude that bodily life is indeed a basic human
good, worthy of protection and promotion for its own sake, even when it
will not make possible the pursuit of any other good.

What about Pleasure?

Some would take issue with this account of basic human goods because
they believe that ultimately the only good is pleasure, and that all other
goods are valuable only insofar as the pursuit or achievement of them produces pleasure (or avoids pain). This view—that pleasure is the only intrinsic good, or that all other goods reduce to pleasure—is called hedonism.
Roger Crisp criticizes the new natural law account of basic goods from a he-
donist perspective. Going through the list of goods one by one, he questions whether these goods are truly valuable for their own sake, apart from
the conscious enjoyment (i.e., pleasure) they produce. He asks, for instance,
whether life is truly valuable for someone who never "experiences enjoyment of any kind," or whether the contemplation of beauty has value even
for someone who takes no pleasure in it.[21] In reducing the good to conscious enjoyment, hedonism also implicitly embraces a dualist, conscious-
ness-centered view of the person, and is therefore problematic for the reasons discussed in the previous section.[22]

Crisp also objects to the list of goods because "it makes no independent
room for the value of pleasure or enjoyment (and so also fails to recognize
the disvalue of pain or suffering)."[23] This is an objection even many non-
hedonists would share. Indeed, common sense and reflection on our own

21. Crisp, "Finnis on Well-being," 28, 31.
22. For an in-depth account of the relationship between hedonism and dualism,
and a general critique of hedonism, see Lee and George, *Body-Self Dualism*, chap. 3.
23. Crisp, "Finnis on Well-being," 33.

actions seem to reveal that we often do seek pleasure (or avoid pain) and that we are not the least bit baffled when people act for the sake of pleasure. According to the method I used earlier in this chapter to identify the basic goods, therefore, it appears that pleasure (together with avoidance of pain) belongs on the list.

There are several explanations for why pleasure appears to be a basic good, even though (as I will argue later in this section) it is not. First, pleasure is a *sensible* (as opposed to intelligible) good, meaning that it appeals to our subrational, sensory appetites. Because desire for pleasure and aversion to pain are such powerful and universal sense appetites, it does not baffle us when we see people acting in pursuit of these ends, for we too know the experience of being drawn toward pleasure or repulsed from pain. This does not necessarily mean, however, that pleasure in itself has any *intelligible* value—for if, for instance, I had a pathological drive to eat dirt, I would likewise not be baffled if I observed someone else eating dirt (recognizing that the person must have the same pathology), even though I would be fully aware that eating dirt has no intelligible value (but on the contrary causes intelligible harm to health).[24]

Second, pleasure can appear to be a basic good because pleasure (conscious enjoyment) is an aspect of the goodness of basic goods. If all is well with us physiologically, psychologically, and morally, participation in basic goods (which are constitutive of our flourishing) ought to be enjoyable. Finnis explains that "pleasure is not valueless; it is a valuable part of the reality and goodness of each of the basic goods and of full flourishing."[25] Although pleasure does have value, it is not itself a basic good because its value is not intrinsic. Instead, pleasure's value depends on the value of the activity that produces it.

24. It is possible to argue that pleasure has intelligible value, but that its goodness is extrinsic, depending upon the goodness of its object. (I am grateful to my colleague Marshall Bierson for pointing this out to me.) This view is compatible with the position I defend here. For what I aim to show here is simply that pleasure is not a basic good, and basic goods are not merely intelligible but intrinsic. For an influential discussion of the difference between the distinction between intrinsic and extrinsic goodness, and the distinction between final and instrumental goodness, see Korsgaard, "Two Distinctions in Goodness."

25. Finnis, "Reflections and Responses," 467.

Third, harmony between reason and emotion is itself a basic good—integrity—which accounts for the intelligible appeal of pleasure-seeking actions disconnected from (or even contrary to) other basic goods. When our emotions incline us toward pleasure—when you are salivating for a bite of the fresh-baked brownie on the table—this creates an inner tension or disharmony, particularly if those emotions are contrary to reason—for example, if you judge that eating the brownie would not be good for you. One way to resolve this tension and regain a (short-lived) inner harmony is to subordinate reason to emotion—give in to your desire and eat the brownie. Thus, it is always possible to *rationalize* purely pleasure-seeking activities by appeal to the basic good of integrity, even though in the long run giving in to unreasonable desires ultimately generates greater disharmony between reason and emotion, thus undermining the good of integrity. (I will say more about this in the section on virtues in chapter 2.)

Because pleasure is a sensible good and is so closely related to basic goods, it is therefore not surprising that it is often taken to be a basic good in itself. Similar things could be said about the avoidance of pain. Pain is a sensible evil, is often a sign of intrinsic, intelligible evils (such as illness), tends to impede our ability to pursue basic goods, and causes psychological disharmony. Pain's close connection to intrinsic evils thus often gives us a genuine reason to avoid it or alleviate it, and our repulsion from it as a sensible evil can easily lead us to rationalize avoiding it even when it is not fully reasonable to do so; for example, when enduring the pain is necessary for the achievement of goods that we ought to pursue.

This account shows why people might mistakenly believe that pleasure is a basic good even if it is not, but it still does not explain why pleasure is not actually a basic good. Many arguments have been given to defend this point.[26] Here I will limit myself to briefly articulating the argument that seems to me to be the most straightforward and decisive. That argument is based on the problem of morally evil pleasures. Some take pleasure in torturing cats, sexually abusing young children, making fun of the disabled, or engaging in myriad other morally reprehensible activities. If pleasure

---

26. See, e.g., Lee and George, *Body-Self Dualism*, chap. 3; Nozick, *Anarchy, State, and Utopia*, 42.

were a basic (intrinsic) good, we would have to say that, even though such activities are morally wrong, the pleasure that a person gains in pursuing them is nonetheless good. Yet this seems completely implausible. For we generally judge that taking pleasure in such activities is itself bad, a sign of a morally corrupt character. By contrast, though all the basic goods listed above can be pursued by immoral means — for example, one can seek knowledge through unethical experiments that seriously harm human subjects — in these cases it is not counterintuitive to claim that the knowledge itself is good, even if the means used to achieve it are immoral. This is because the goodness of knowledge (or of any of the basic goods) is intrinsic, whereas the goodness of pleasure is extrinsic, depending on the goodness of the activity that gives rise to it. Taking pleasure in a game of baseball, an insightful discussion, or the contemplation of a beautiful sunrise is good, because all of these activities are good, but the pleasure that accompanies bad or worthless activities has no value.[27]

What about Autonomy?

Particularly in contemporary Western liberal societies, the value of autonomy, understood broadly as the freedom to direct our own lives in accordance with our own values and goals, seems undeniable.[28] Further, it seems clear that people do act for the sake of preserving or promoting autonomy, even to the point of being willing to sacrifice their lives for this value, as ex-

---

27. Because the goodness of pleasure is extrinsic, any pleasure sought in isolation from the pursuit of intrinsic goods lacks value, and the pursuit of such "empty" pleasures is always at least indirectly harmful insofar as it involves prioritizing the feelings that tend to accompany genuinely fulfilling activities over those activities themselves. To use our limited time, energy, and resources in pursuit of empty pleasures (rather than genuinely fulfilling activities) would be unreasonable, akin to a long-distance hiker taking up precious space and weight in her backpack with boxes of Splenda rather than with nutritionally dense foods. This prioritization of sheer feeling over genuine fulfillment also involves a distorted attitude toward reality, treating something that lacks intrinsic value as if it were a basic good. For more on this point, see Pruss, *One Body*, 115–27.

28. Joseph Raz, for instance, defines the "ideal of personal autonomy" as "the vision of people controlling, to some degree, their own destiny, fashioning it through successive decisions throughout their lives" (Raz, *The Morality of Freedom*, 369).

pressed in the popular New Hampshire state motto, "Live Free or Die." Some philosophers, such as Joseph Raz, have argued that autonomy is intrinsically valuable, "a constituent element of the good life."[29] Why, then, is autonomy not on the list of basic goods?

New natural law theory does recognize the intelligible value of autonomy, but (as with pleasure) it denies the *intrinsic* nature of that value. The value of autonomy is extrinsic—it depends on how it is used. The autonomous choice to murder, for instance, is not valuable at all. If autonomy were intrinsically valuable, we would have to say that the choice to murder has value at least insofar as it is autonomous. Yet this seems implausible. Indeed, to the extent that the choice to murder is fully autonomous, that choice is actually morally *worse* than regretfully choosing to murder someone under duress.

Nonetheless, much like pleasure (though in a different way), autonomy is closely connected to intrinsic goods in several ways, which explains why autonomy may seem to be itself intrinsically valuable. Some goods, such as friendship, marriage, integrity and authenticity, and religion, can only be realized through free choices. Autonomy is therefore a crucial *condition* for participation in these goods. Further, even with regard to the substantive goods of life, knowledge, and skillful work and play, participating in these goods through a free choice contributes more to one's overall perfection as an agent than participating in them passively. For free choices in pursuit of the good can also contribute to one's perfection with regard to the goods of integrity and authenticity. And this can be true to a certain extent even when those choices are, all things considered, not fully reasonable. If, for instance, someone advocates for a cause he sincerely believes to be good, but that is in fact misguided and harmful, his action nonetheless has intelligible value as an instantiation of integrity and authenticity. It is therefore not autonomy per se that has intrinsic value, but the closely related basic goods of integrity and authenticity.[30]

---

29. Raz, *The Morality of Freedom*, 408.

30. I believe that similar things can be said about goods such as honor and self-respect, the goodness of which is extrinsic or dependent on certain conditions being met—e.g., that the honor and self-respect are deserved. Both of those goods also, like autonomy, seem closely related to the goods of integrity and authenticity.

HOW WE COME TO KNOW BASIC GOODS

The method used here to identify basic goods—reflecting upon the workings of our practical reason to make its first principles transparent—is not the way in which we actually first come to identify (usually inarticulately) these goods as reasons for action. I am presuming that you, the reader, have sufficient moral maturity and life experience to have participated in or at least been exposed to these goods, and thus to be capable of recognizing their intelligible appeal. But how do we initially come to know these goods as good, to grasp their intelligible appeal as to-be-pursued? Of course, the answer will be slightly different for each of us, but in general it goes something like this: As small children, we are exposed to various instances of these goods and experience a prerational attraction to them; for example, the child is curious, asks "Why?" and is given a satisfying answer; the child gets sick and desires to be healthy again; the child sees her parents fighting angrily and desires that family harmony be restored; the child enjoys the accomplishment of learning to catch a ball or ride a bike, and so on. As the child's cognitive powers mature and she begins to be able to fully exercise her rational capacities, such experiences provide data for practical reason's insight that attaining knowledge, being healthy, developing one's skills, having harmonious relationships, and so on are not merely subrationally appealing, but intelligibly good and to-be-pursued. It is not that the child ever necessarily explicitly articulates the proposition (even in her own head) that health, knowledge, or any other good is to-be-pursued. For this knowledge is not theoretical, but practical. Rather, what it means to say that the child has (at least inarticulately) come to know the basic goods—grasping their intrinsic choiceworthiness through an insight of practical reason into the data of her experience—is that the child can now be motivated to pursue these goods based not only on their emotional appeal, but also on their rational appeal.

Eventually, the child's parents and other educators will (or should) teach the child the language and concepts needed to make this knowledge more explicit and articulate, enabling the child to begin explicitly to distinguish what is *good* (intelligibly choiceworthy; genuinely fulfilling) from what she merely happens to desire at the subrational level: "No, dear, you can't have another cookie. I know you like them, but eating too many is not good for you. Remember the last time you ate too many cookies and got a tummy ache? We want you to grow up healthy and strong. If you are hungry, how about having a piece of fruit instead?" Or: "I heard that you had a fight with Jimmy at school today. I know you feel angry, but tomorrow you should try to work things out so that you can be friends again." In this way, the child comes to know the names—like health and friendship—of the goods she already finds intelligibly appealing, and slowly begins to deepen her understanding of what these goods consist in and how to pursue them.[31]

As the child's understanding of and motivation toward these goods shifts from the merely subrational (sensible/emotional) level to the rational (intellectual/volitional) level, the child also becomes capable of grasping these goods as good (intelligibly choiceworthy) not only for her, but for anyone who, like her, can benefit from them and be a potential partner with her in pursuit of them.[32] Once again, the child's ability to accurately grasp who counts as relevantly "like her" will depend in part on her social and cultural context, on what she learns from others by word and example, and on the experiences she is able to have. If, for instance, the child is a daughter of slave-owners in South Carolina in the early 1800s, living within a family and broader culture in which Black people are treated and spoken of as inferior and as radically "other," this may obscure her ability to recognize Black people as "like her" in the relevant sense. Even in such a corrupt culture, however, as

31. My focus here is on knowledge of the good, but the child's ability to actually act for the good even in the presence of conflicting desires will depend in large part on the extent to which parents and other educators have already begun to teach the child habits of self-discipline. Before the child is fully capable of exercising rationality, these habits will be taught by appealing to one emotional motivation—e.g., desire to please parents or fear of punishment—in order to overcome another emotional motivation leading to bad behavior, with the parents' (or other educators') reason in the driver's seat. As the child becomes capable of fully rational motivation, however, this same harnessing of one emotional motivation (in line with reason's judgment) to overcome a contrary emotional motivation (out of line with reason's judgment) can still occur (for there is always some element of emotional motivation in our action), but now with the child's own reason (and will) in the driver's seat.

32. "The direction the first practical principles give one's deliberation is towards goods one can share in along with others, and it has no rational stopping-place short of a universal *common good*: the fulfillment of all human persons" (Finnis, *Aquinas*, 132; emphasis original). For more on this point, see Lee and George, "The Nature and Basis of Human Dignity."

long as the child interacts enough with Black people to see that they are just like her in the relevant sense—for example, that Black children like to play, learn, and make friends just as she does, that Black families love and care for each other just as her family does, and so on—she has the relevant data to enable her to recognize this truth. Because of her corrupt culture and up-bringing, however, partiality, tribalism, or other subrational factors may lead her to willfully turn away from and fail to acknowledge this evidence.

Even though the focus here (and in the new natural law account more generally) is more on articulating ethical principles and norms than on dis-cussing the process of moral education, this account does not ignore the importance of social and cultural context for our development as practical reasoners.[33] Early moral education is crucial for a grasp of the basic goods in their full breadth and depth, and also for an accurate understanding of moral principles and their applications.[34] I will say more about moral edu-cation in chapter 3 on the social dimension of human flourishing.

SOME CLARIFICATIONS ABOUT BASIC GOODS

Incommensurability of Basic Goods

Each of the categories of good listed above is basic in two senses. First, any instantiation of any of these goods is a sufficient reason for action, meaning that no further reason needs to be given to make action for any of these goods intelligible, and nothing other than one of these goods is necessary to provide rational motivation for action. Second, the goods and their instan-tiations are basic in that they are distinct and irreducible to one another or to any other more general category of good. In other words, each offers a unique benefit that is not, just as such, reducible or comparable in value to any of the others. If, for example, I choose to spend the afternoon chatting

33. This point has been emphasized in the works of Alasdair MacIntyre, and, in a slightly different way, in the work of Jean Porter. See, e.g., MacIntyre, *Dependent Rational Animals*, and MacIntyre, *Ethics in the Conflicts of Modernity*; Porter, *Nature as Reason*, and Porter, "Does the Natural Law Provide a Universally Valid Morality?"

34. See, e.g., Tollefsen, "Basic Goods."

with a friend rather than working on this book, I really will have lost out on the distinct benefits (with regard to knowledge and skillful work) that would have come with the latter, even if my choice was reasonable, all things considered. To recognize the distinctiveness and irreducibility of each basic form of good (and each instantiation of these goods) is to recognize that basic goods (and their instantiations) are *incommensurable*, that is, that there is no common measure by which the value of the goods, just as such, can be compared or weighed against each other.[35]

Recognizing that the basic goods are incommensurable in value also implies that there is no single, objective hierarchy of basic value among the goods, considered just as such — that is, no good whose value always "outweighs" the others such that it includes all the goodness of the other goods *and more*, and thus must always take priority if we are to act rationally. If this were the case — for example, if, say, religion were at the top of a hierarchy of goods in the sense that any participation in the good of religion

35. This point is crucial for new natural law theorists' critique of utilitarianism, proportionalism, and other consequentialist moral theories, for all of these theories attempt to determine what is right by calculating which course of action will yield "the greatest good." But if basic goods and their instantiations are truly incommensurable in value, the notion of the "the greatest good" literally makes no sense, for the basic categories of good are basic, and cannot be reduced to any more general category of "goodness"; see Finnis, *Natural Law and Natural Rights*, 5.6.

Recognizing the incommensurability of basic goods is also necessary for the defense of free choice. Free choice requires that there be at least two incompatible options that each have a distinct intelligible appeal. But if the goods were commensurable, and thus if it were possible (at least in principle) to determine which choice would yield "the greatest good," all other options would simply lose their rational appeal. For, although subrational motivations or mistaken calculations could lead us to choose the "lesser good" rather than "greater good," there can be no reason for doing so. If goods are incommensurable in value, however, each offers a distinct reason for action. Even in cases where moral norms (which I will discuss in chapter 2) require choosing one option rather than another, e.g., canceling your golf game because your child needs to be taken to the hospital, the immoral option (going ahead with the game despite your child's medical emergency) nonetheless retains intelligible appeal, for it offers a distinct benefit that the morally required option (caring for your injured child) does not. If this were not the case, genuinely free immoral choices would be impossible, and immorality would instead be either a matter of miscalculation or of subrational motivations entirely overwhelming our capacity to choose. For more on the relationship between incommensurability of goods and free choice, see Boyle, "Free Choice."

always has more value than participation in any other good—this would lead to absurd conclusions. It would mean, for example, that in any situation in which it was not absolutely necessary for me to be doing something else, I would have to (on pain of irrationality) engage in some directly religious activity. For if religion simply had more value than all other goods, it would be irrational to, say, read a mystery novel (unless required to do so for work or school) rather than the Bible or some other religious book, or to go to an exercise class rather than a Bible study.

I should emphasize that this claim about the lack of a single hierarchy among the goods is a very limited and specific one. There is no *single, objective* hierarchy, and there is no hierarchy of *intelligible value* among the goods at the level of first practical principles. Chapter 2 will make clear, however, that when one considers the guidance of practical reasons in their *integral directiveness*—that is, when one considers the requirements of morality—one does discover objective hierarchies among the goods, including a special place for the good of religion as playing a uniquely pervasive and governing role in the life of a morally upright person who is fully aware of its demands.[36] There are also *subjective* hierarchies among goods that depend on a particular person's specific vocational commitments and obligations.[37]

---

36. This clarification is important for responding to the concerns of critics such as Russell Hittinger, who worries that new natural law theory's denial of a hierarchical ordering among the goods renders the theory unable to resolve important moral problems (Hittinger, *A Critique of the New Natural Law Theory*, 74–79). See chapter 2, especially the sections "The Vocation Principle" and "The Unity of Life Principle," for further discussion of this issue. For a more detailed response to Hittinger's critique, see George, "Recent Criticism of New Natural Law Theory."

37. Many critics fail to understand the specific and limited nature of the claim about incommensurability, i.e., that the basic goods are incommensurable *in intelligible value*, at the level of first practical principles; see, e.g., Richardson, "Incommensurability and Basic Goods"; Wright, "Does Free Speech Jurisprudence Rest on a Mistake?" However, second-level moral principles do commensurate the goods, not with respect to their intelligible value, but with respect to the requirements of practical reasons in their integral directiveness. This will be discussed in greater detail in chapter 2. For a response to Wright's critique, and a clarification of the claim that basic goods are incommensurable, see George, "Does the 'Incommensurability Thesis' Imperil Common Sense Moral Judgments?"

Basic Goods as First Principles of Practical Reason

This list of basic goods is also a list of first practical principles, for identifying something as intrinsically good is identifying it as inherently choiceworthy, to-be-pursued. There is therefore a set of first practical principles of the following form: X is good and to-be-pursued (and its opposite is bad and to-be-avoided), in which X stands for each of the basic goods. This list specifies and concretizes Aquinas's more general but largely formal first principle: "Good is to-be-done-and-pursued and evil is to-be-avoided."[38] What it means to say that these are first practical principles is that these principles are where all of our practical reasoning—our reasoning about how to act—begins. To put it another way, these principles are what get genuine human action—which is the fruit of deliberation and choice, and thus requires an intelligible purpose—off the ground.

The status of basic goods as first principles also explains why my account of how we identify these goods is simply an attempt to make transparent the practical judgments that underlie all of our actions and judgments about the actions of others. For, as first principles, they are self-evident and cannot be logically demonstrated, because every practical syllogism at least implicitly begins with them. Analogously, one cannot logically demonstrate the truth of the principle of noncontradiction—that a thing cannot both be and not be at the same time and in the same respect—because the truth of that principle is presupposed in every logical argument. One can show that any attempt to deny it leads to absurd conclusions or is performatively inconsistent,[39] but one cannot offer a strict demonstration. Likewise

---

38. Aquinas, *Summa theologiae* I-II, q. 94, a. 2: *Bonum est faciendum et prosequendum, et malum vitandum.* The hyphenations in my translation are meant to capture the meaning of the gerundive forms of *faciendum, prosequendum,* and *vitandum.* For the sake of brevity, I usually refer to basic goods simply as "to-be-pursued," as this seems sufficient to capture the meaning of "to-be-done-and-pursued."

39. A performatively inconsistent statement is one in which making the statement is inconsistent with the statement's meaning—"I cannot write a sentence." Arguably, any serious denial of the principle of noncontradiction is performatively inconsistent, for the person asserting that the principle is false is presuming that this assertion is incompatible with the contradictory assertion that the principle is true. But that assumption itself rests on the principle of noncontradiction.

with first practical principles, one can argue, for example, that denying them leads to absurd conclusions, is inconsistent with our actions and judgments,[40] rests on theoretical errors about human nature,[41] or makes it difficult to account for the overwhelming anthropological and sociological data supporting them.[42] But one cannot offer a strict demonstration.

Basic Goods and Human Nature

Further, although our knowledge of basic goods is not derived from speculative knowledge about human nature, upon reflection we can see that the basic goods correspond to the various aspects of our nature, and thus identify the *telos* (perfection) of our nature in its various dimensions.[43] The goods of life and health perfect us as bodily beings whose identity as animal organisms is essential and intrinsic to our overall personal identity.[44] The goods of knowledge and appreciation of beauty perfect us as *rational* animals. The goods of skillful work and play perfect us in our complex unity as rational

40. Finnis offers an extended argument in defense of the basic good of knowledge on the grounds that skepticism about this basic good is performatively inconsistent, for the person who advances a sincere argument against knowledge as a basic good is (if arguing in good faith) presumably, in that very act, seeking to get to the truth of the matter, i.e., seeking, for its own sake, the very good she is denying to be intrinsically choiceworthy; see Finnis, *Natural Law and Natural Rights*, chap. 3.

41. Denial that life is intrinsically valuable, for instance, implicitly rests on a false account of personal identity according to which the body (except perhaps the higher brain) is viewed as extrinsic to the person, which is identified with a conscious, thinking, willing "self."

42. See Finnis, *Natural Law and Natural Rights*, 81–84.

43. Stephen Brock criticizes Finnis and Grisez for "giv[ing] every appearance" of accepting the Humean view that "the notion of good does not contain the notion of what is according to nature" (Brock, *The Light That Binds*, 149). Yet in their "Practical Principles" article, which Brock cites in the book, and in most of their mature accounts of their theory, Grisez and Finnis clearly indicate—as I do here—that the basic goods are fulfillments of the various dimensions of human nature; see Grisez, Boyle, and Finnis, "Practical Principles," 107. I have also responded in detail to Brock's criticism on this point, which he articulated in an earlier article, in Moschella, "Sexual Ethics, Human Nature," 274–77.

44. See Lee and George, *Body-Self Dualism*.

animals who can act to develop and coordinate our physical and mental powers. Friendship perfects us as social beings whose rationality makes possible a unity of mind and will with others. Marriage perfects us as sexually complementary persons capable not only of creating new life through sexual intercourse, as other mammals do, but of doing so within the context of a comprehensive interpersonal union that encompasses all dimensions of the person and ensures (as far as possible) that the children conceived through that union will receive the united and stable love of their mother and father. Integrity and authenticity perfect us as complex beings capable of harmonizing our feelings, judgments, and actions. Finally, religion perfects us as spiritual beings whose rational powers go beyond the limits of materiality, opening us to recognition of and relationship with the transcendent source of existence and meaning. This correspondence between the basic goods and the various dimensions of human nature supports the plausibility and completeness of the proposed list, but of course one cannot strictly prove that the list is correct, for such a proof is impossible.

NATURE, NATURAL LAW, AND PRACTICAL RATIONALITY

The term "natural law" can easily give rise to confusion, for natural law theory understood as a set of principles and norms to guide deliberation and choice is fundamentally different from the "law of nature" understood as a set of physical laws that determine the behavior of material things (including humans insofar as we are animal organisms). From a metaphysical perspective, natural law thinkers have typically recognized that the existence of both the law of nature and the natural moral law are signs that the universe is ordered and intelligible, pointing to an ultimate transcendent source of that order and intelligibility. However, the law of nature and the natural moral law refer to two fundamentally distinct types of order, for the former *describes* the necessary workings of the material universe, but the latter *prescribes* how humans as rational and free agents ought to choose and act.

Aquinas recognizes (and adds to) this crucial distinction in his account of the "four orders":

Now order is related to reason in a fourfold way. There is one order that reason does not establish but only beholds, such is the order of things in nature. There is a second order that reason establishes in its own act of consideration, for example, when it arranges concepts among themselves. . . . There is a third order that reason in deliberating establishes in the operations of the will. There is a fourth order that reason in planning establishes in the external things which it causes, such as a chest and a house.[45]

This distinction is the basis for the different objects and methods of various fields of knowledge. Disciplines such as metaphysics and the natural sciences that study "things that human reason considers but does not establish" belong to the first order, often referred to as the natural order.[46] Logic belongs to the second order. Moral philosophy (including natural law theory) belongs to the third, or moral order, which is the existential order of choice and action.[47] The fourth order is the order of making, the technical order. Knowledge in the first two orders is speculative, aimed at consideration of the truth, and acquired through an examination of the subject from a third-person perspective (from the "outside"). Knowledge in the moral and technical orders is practical, directed toward action. This knowledge guides deliberation and choice, and thus needs to be considered from the perspective of the acting agent — this is especially crucial for the moral order, which is what primarily interests us here, but every deliberate making is also a human action in the third order.

The distinction among the four orders also helps us to clarify the sense in which natural law is natural, and how it differs from laws of nature. Laws of nature, including the law of gravity or laws governing chemical reactions, are in the first order, meaning that we can know them, but that they operate completely independently of our knowledge or choice. Natural law, however, is a set of norms that, though objective in the sense that they are dis-

45. Aquinas, *Commentary on the Nicomachean Ethics*, bk. 1, lect. 1.
46. Aquinas, *Commentary on the Nicomachean Ethics*, bk. 1, lect. 1.
47. Aquinas, *Commentary on the Nicomachean Ethics*, bk. 1, lect. 1. History and biography also belong to the third order, but by contrast with ethics and moral philosophy, they describe the deliberations, choices, and actions of human agents, rather than offer a normative account of how we should deliberate, choose, and act.

covered by reason, not created by our will, are operative only if we choose to follow them. Natural law is thus not "natural" in the sense that our feelings spontaneously incline us to follow it (for in many instances they do not), but rather in the sense that it directs us toward human flourishing, the perfection of our nature.

However, correctly interpreting what it means to say that natural law directs us toward the fulfillment of our nature requires further specification. For our nature is complex and encompasses each of the four orders: we are animals, thinkers, moral agents, and makers. Because of this complexity, the fulfillment of our nature in one respect may conflict with our fulfillment in another respect. If, for example, it is my moral duty to risk my life in order to defend my country from attack, my fulfillment *qua* moral agent will be in conflict with my fulfillment *qua* animal. Similarly, if I am a parent, fulfilling my duties toward my children will at certain times (when the children need my full attention) be incompatible with thinking through a philosophical argument (fulfilling myself *qua* thinker) or preparing a gourmet meal (fulfilling myself *qua* maker). The natural law (which is, after all, a *moral* law) directs us toward the fulfillment of our nature primarily *qua* moral agent—that is, toward the perfection of our will—even though, as the list of basic goods makes clear, our fulfillment *qua* animal, thinker, and maker cannot be entirely separated from our fulfillment *qua* agent, for human nature, though complex, is ultimately unified, and the perfection of our will requires respecting (and to the extent possible, promoting) the human good in all of its dimensions, not only for oneself but for all members of the human community.[48] Table 1 synthesizes the above account of the four orders.

48. Interestingly, MacIntyre's work never offers an in-depth account of basic human goods, but his account presupposes that there are such goods, and that we are directed toward them "by our nature *as rational agents*" —which, on my view, corresponds to our nature considered from a third-order perspective (as opposed to our nature understood as a first-order reality); see MacIntyre, *Ethics in the Conflicts of Modernity*, 216 (emphasis added). MacIntyre briefly notes that the first stage in articulating and defending an Aristotelian account of ethics "is a matter of identifying a set of goods whose contribution to a good life, whatever one's culture or social order, it would be difficult to deny." And though MacIntyre's list includes a mix of instrumental and intrinsic goods, it is nonetheless strikingly similar to the list proposed here, including health, family relationships, education, rewarding work, friends, athletic, aesthetic and intellectual activities, and practical reasonableness (222).

Table 1. The Four Orders

Order	Description	Discipline Examples	Type of Knowledge	Aspect of Human Nature
First (Natural)	Order that reason can know but does not establish	Metaphysics, natural sciences	Speculative— third-person perspective	Animal organism
Second (Logical)	Order that reason establishes in its own act of consideration	Logic	Speculative	Thinker
Third (Moral/ existential)	Order that reason establishes in the operations of the will	Ethics, political philosophy	Practical— first-person perspective	Agent
Fourth (Technical)	Order that reason establishes in external things	Architecture, engineering	Practical	Maker

In sum, ethics, and thus natural law theory, is a third-order inquiry, which means that its principles and norms are *practical*, known through practical reason (but informed by prior speculative knowledge).[49] This means that, contrary to the claims of some scholars, natural law does not derive moral

49. Thus, new natural law thinkers do not, as critics claim, deny the priority of speculative knowledge over practical knowledge, if this simply means that "practical knowledge presupposes and depends on a prior *speculum* or speculative truth" (Long, "Fundamental Errors of the New Natural Law Theory," 108; see also Jensen, *Knowing the Natural Law*, 18–20, 77–78). For the first principles of practical reason, though not derived from prior speculative knowledge, are intellectual insights into the relevant data of experience, including the data provided by prior speculative knowledge. Further, Finnis and others explicitly recognize that a faulty metaphysics or anthropology will interfere with one's ability to understand the basic goods: "A mistaken metaphysics or anthropology will block one's reflective understanding of the way in which one participates in the human goods (particularly the good of practical reasonableness itself). If, for example, one supposes that reason is the slave of the passions, a mere instrument for efficiently sorting out and attaining wants that are simply given prior to all understanding, one will find no reason to give the requirements of practical reasonableness their architectonic and conclusive force" (Finnis, *Fundamentals of Ethics*, 23). Further, Lee and George, in *Body-Self Dualism*, argue at length against dualism and claim that this false anthropology prevents many people from properly understanding and appreciating the basic human goods of life and marriage, leading to erroneous moral views about issues such as abortion, euthanasia, and sexual ethics.

norms from speculative knowledge of human nature.[50] Although some of our first-order inclinations as animals (such as the drive for self-preservation) might correspond to intelligible goods that perfect us as *rational* animals, others (such as drives toward aggression or conquest) do not, and even those drives that do correspond to intelligible goods do not always incline us to act in ways that are, all things considered, morally right.[51]

Rather, as Aquinas makes clear, practical reason has its own self-evident first principles, and these first principles are the first principles of natural law, identifying and directing us toward what is good (i.e., what fulfills or perfects us), and away from what is bad.[52] This implies that these first principles are

50. Some natural law theorists—who are critical of the approach I take here—argue that we do identify what is good on the basis of speculative knowledge about human nature. They might argue, for instance, that we know life is a good because we have a natural drive toward self-preservation, or that we know knowledge is a good because the purpose of our intellectual capacities is to discover the truth. Feser, for instance, writes the following: "When we consider that human beings have intellects and that the natural end or function of the intellect is to grasp the truth about things, it follows that it is good for us—it fulfills our nature—to pursue truth and avoid error. Consequently, a rational person apprised of the facts about human nature will see that this is what is good for us and thus strive to attain truth and avoid error. And so on for other human capacities" (Feser, *Neo-Scholastic Essays*, 386; see also Jensen, *Knowing the Natural Law*.). Yet for the reasons mentioned in this section (and developed at length elsewhere), we can only identify the ends of our natural capacities through our practical grasp of what is good. Our intellect, for instance, makes us capable not only of grasping the truth, but also of sophistry and deception. It is only practical reason's grasp of truth as good that enables us to identify truth, rather than sophistry or deception, as the fulfillment of this dimension of our nature. Further, attempting to derive moral norms directly from speculative knowledge of nature is logically problematic, for one cannot draw a prescriptive conclusion from purely descriptive premises, and doing so involves an illicit jump from first-order knowledge to third-order knowledge. For more on these points, see Moschella, "Sexual Ethics, Human Nature," and Tollefsen, "Aquinas's Four Orders."

51. Recognition that ethics is a third-order inquiry arguably helps to respond to an important problem in the Aristotelian tradition regarding the relationship between human nature and ethics. For a discussion of this problem and proposed solution that has many resonances with the account provided here, see Thompson, "Forms of Nature."

52. "The precepts of the natural law are to the practical reason, what first principles of demonstrations are to the speculative reason; because both are self-evident principles" (Aquinas, *Summa theologiae* I-II, q. 94, a. 2). Aquinas in the same article goes on to argue that the first principle of practical reason—"good is to be done and pursued, and evil is to

not derived or deduced from speculative knowledge; for if they were derived or deduced from speculative knowledge, they would not be self-evident. Unlike speculative knowledge, which is descriptive, the first principles of practical reason are inherently prescriptive, directing us toward goods as to-be-pursued and their opposites as to-be-avoided.[53] This does not mean, however, that this knowledge is unrelated to knowledge of human nature, for speculative knowledge about human nature makes us aware of what is possible for us, and provides the data for practical reason's grasp of some of those possibilities as intrinsically worthy of pursuit, that is, as good.[54]

Further, it is these principles that, by identifying what is intrinsically good for us, also identify the fully human (rational) end of the various dimensions of our nature.[55] According to Aquinas, we know the nature or essence of

---

be avoided"—plays the same foundational role in the practical order that the principle of noncontradiction—"the same thing cannot be affirmed and denied at the same time"—plays in the speculative order. Note that none of what I say here is contrary to Aquinas's claim that the first thing we know is "being," and thus that speculative knowledge has a certain priority. For we first have to know that something is possible for us before we can grasp it as good. Grisez's work on natural law theory began with a commentary on this article in the *Summa*; see Grisez, "The First Principle of Practical Reason." For more on the history of new natural law theory, see the appendix to this book.

53. The specific nature of third-order knowledge, knowledge considered from the first-person perspective of the deliberating and choosing agent, also explains the natural law account's focus on specifically human goods (rather than the goods of, say, cats or ecosystems). For practical reason directs us toward that which has intelligible appeal for us because fulfilling for us, i.e., me, and anyone whose nature makes possible fulfillment with respect to these goods, and cooperation with me in pursuit of them. This does not mean that human good is the only type of good, but only that, from a third-order perspective, human good is the only type of good toward which we are directed. (Indeed, from a metaphysical perspective, all good is a participation in divine goodness.) It does mean, however, that our knowledge of the good of nonhuman beings will always be knowledge by analogy with knowledge of our own good; see Tollefsen, "Aquinas's Four Orders," 252–53. Thus, Chappell's critique of the new natural law view as problematically anthropocentric involves a failure to appreciate the specific nature of third-order knowledge; see Chappell, "The Polymorphy of Practical Reason," 107.

54. See Boyle, "On the Most Fundamental Principle of Morality."

55. New natural law theory thus does not deny that nature is teleological, but distinguishes between natural teleology in the first order (which does not have direct normative force, though it of course has normative relevance), and teleology in the third order, which does have direct normative force. Further, the theory openly relies on certain metaphysical

a thing by knowing its capacities; we know its capacities through their acts; and we know their acts through their objects or ends.[56] For example, on a biological or first-order level, we come to understand the nature of different organs in our body by observing their ends. We know, for instance, that the stomach is a digestive organ, because we know that its end is the digestion of our food. But our ends as rational animals, as agents capable of deliberation and choice, are the ends of human acts, and the ends of human acts are the basic human goods. It is thus by coming to know the basic human goods that we come to know the ends of our nature in the moral order.

Recognizing that ethics is a third-order inquiry also has implications for understanding the nature of practical and moral truth.[57] Truth is an analogical term that has a slightly different meaning in each of the four orders. Truth in the first order (e.g., in metaphysics, philosophy of nature, natural sciences, etc.) is correspondence of the mind to reality. Truth in the third order, however, cannot be correspondence to an already-existing reality, for practical and moral truths guide deliberation and choice toward aspects of our fulfillment that do not exist prior to our willing and choosing them. Further, the fulfillment promised by participation in basic goods is essentially open-ended: opportunities for new and deeper realizations of the

---

and anthropological presuppositions, including the human capacity for free choice, the existence of God as the ultimate source of the moral order and deepest ground of moral obligation, and a nondualist view of the human person that recognizes the body as essential and intrinsic to personal identity, presuppositions that new natural lawyers have defended at length (see, e.g., Boyle, Grisez, and Tollefsen, *Free Choice*; Finnis, *Natural Law and Natural Rights*, chap. 13; Grisez, *Beyond the New Theism*; Lee and George, *Body-Self Dualism*). Thus, critics such as MacIntyre and McInerny are mistaken when they claim that the theory "aspire[s] to detach a Thomistic ethics from Aristotle's—and Aquinas's—teleology"; see MacIntyre, *Ethics in the Conflicts of Modernity*, 209n18, and McInerny, "The Primacy of Theoretical Knowledge." Likewise, Hittinger misunderstands the theory's account of the relationship between practical and speculative knowledge when he criticizes it for supposedly failing to acknowledge the relevance of metaphysics and philosophical anthropology to ethics, and thus for seeking "to recover natural law theory by way of shortcuts" (Hittinger, *A Critique of the New Natural Law Theory*, 198).

56. "So we proceed from objects to acts, from acts to faculties, and from faculties to essence" (Aquinas, *Commentary on Aristotle's "De Anima,"* bk. 2, lect. 6, no. 308).

57. For more on this point, and on the importance of the distinction between practical truth and speculative truth, see Moschella, "Practical Reason, Sexual Ethics," and Grisez, Boyle, and Finnis, "Practical Principles."

goods reveal themselves to us and are made possible for us only in the course of pursuing them.[58] Practical principles, such as the first principles of practical reason, *anticipate* a certain fulfillment that can be achieved through choice and action, and are true insofar as the fulfillment they anticipate is genuine, that is, insofar as they direct us toward genuine goods.[59] Moral principles are true insofar as they correspond to the *integral directiveness* of practical reasons, directing us to choose and act in ways that are fully responsive to all of practical reason's directives taken as a whole. This idea will be developed further in chapter 2.

Understanding the distinctive nature of moral truth helps to clarify some common misunderstandings about whether ethical claims—claims about what is good or about which actions are morally right—are *objective*. Most people recognize the existence of objective truth in such subjects as biology or chemistry, but it is common for people (including many of the students in my classes) to deny the existence of objective truths in ethics, arguing instead that what is good or right for one person or group depends on that person's subjective values, preferences, cultural background, upbringing, and so on. One of the most famous arguments against the existence of objective truth in the moral order is Mackie's "strangeness" argument.[60] Mackie states, in short,

---

58. "Basic goods . . . are achieved in their pursuit, which pursuit, if done well, always opens up a new horizon of pursuit, rather than bringing us closer to a shutting door" (Tollefsen, "Basic Goods," 38).

59. This point is also important for overcoming the dichotomy between what Bernard Williams calls "internal and external reasons" (Williams, "Internal and External Reasons," 101–2). Williams argues that a reason for action can only be operative for an agent if it can be related to a motivation that the agent already has, and he takes the Humean view that our motivations are subrational desires. This view makes reasons for action problematically subjective, for, as Tollefsen argues, it seems to deny "the existence of objective reasons, reasons not grounded in merely contingent desires" (Tollefsen, "Basic Goods," 33). Tollefsen explains that the natural law account of basic human goods is both internal and external, subjective and objective, for all agents who have had the relevant experience grasp (at least imperfectly) the intelligible point of acting for basic goods, and thus practical reason's directiveness toward the basic goods provides an internal/subjective source of motivation. At the same time, however, "since basic goods are objectively good, not grounded in contingent desires," they are in this sense "external" and objective (33).

60. It has often been referred to as the "queerness" argument, but because the word "queer" has now taken on a very different meaning in the broader culture, I will refer to it as the "strangeness" argument.

that if objective values and moral norms exist, they must be "qualities or relations of a very strange sort, utterly different from anything else in the universe," and thus that in order to track these strange entities we must have "some special faculty of moral perception or intuition, utterly different from our ordinary ways of knowing everything else."[61] Most people (my skeptical students included) might not state their objections to objective moral claims in quite this way, but the perhaps inarticulate sense that moral claims are somehow "very strange" seems to be a key factor in their skepticism.

I believe, however, that this sense of the "strangeness" of moral truth stems from living in a culture that exalts knowledge in the natural sciences as the paradigm case of all knowledge. As a result, we tend to think of first-order knowledge, and particularly knowledge in the natural sciences or other empirical knowledge, as "ordinary" knowledge. Yet awareness of the four orders helps us to see that there are different types of knowledge, attained through different methods and modes of knowing, each of which are also objective in their own way, and also subjective in their own way, for all knowledge is in some sense relative to the knower. Once we recognize this, the problem of "strangeness" falls away.

Consider, for instance, the rules of logic by which we can distinguish valid and invalid forms of argument—rules Mackie himself is relying upon in making his argument.[62] Rules of logic refer to entities and relations that are indeed "very strange" by comparison with trees or water molecules or laws of physics. But that is not surprising once we recognize the existence of a logical order—the realm of intentions, meaning, and truth—the order that reason introduces into thought, which is different in kind from (though not unrelated to) the natural order reason can understand but does not establish. We cannot see or touch or do an experiment to prove the rules of logic, but they are nonetheless just as objectively true (in their own way) as the laws of physics or the existence of the plant on my desk.

The same is true of values and moral norms, which are realities in the third order, the order that reason introduces into the will, and the domain

61. Mackie, *Ethics*, 38.

62. Thus, Finnis points out that Mackie's argument is performatively inconsistent, for the realm of intentions, meaning, and truth—the realm in which Mackie's argument is operating—is at least as "strange" as the realm of value and moral goodness (Finnis, *Fundamentals of Ethics*, 59).

of deliberation, choice, and action. Third-order truths are not unrelated to truths in the other orders—knowledge of metaphysics, natural science, logic, language, culture, and so on are all relevant to ethics—but they describe entities and relations inherently different from realities in the other orders, for the domain of choice and action is unique. The idea of objective moral truth is therefore only "strange" if you have an extremely narrow view of reality as limited to the first order. Yet such a vision of reality is clearly inadequate, for it cannot even account for the very activity you are engaging in when reading this book and trying to understand it. From a first-order perspective, what you are reading is just a bunch of carbon blotches on cellulose fibers we call pages (or their digital analogues). Yet in fact you recognize that—whether or not you agree with my arguments—the "carbon blotches" are words arranged in a certain logical order to convey a particular meaning. And you also recognize that reading this book is quite unlike the rising of the sun or any first-order reality, for it is an action that you are engaged in, the result of a free choice, made with a view toward some good, such as knowledge. The moral realm clearly exists, and there is truth in that realm just as there is truth in the natural, logical, and technical orders.

The standard for moral truth and the methods for arriving at it— just like the standard and methods for logical or technical truth—will nonetheless be different from the standard and methods proper to the natural sciences and other first-order disciplines. The method for arriving at moral truth is reflecting on our practical reasoning, judgment, and action, and the standard is the integral directiveness of practical reasons.[63] What that means will be explained at length in chapter 2.

---

63. However, once one has arrived at moral truth—i.e., at the principles and norms of natural law—through practical reasoning and reflection upon practical reasoning, one can then subsequently consider those principles and norms from a first-order, metaphysical perspective. For the existence of a moral order, and of the principles and norms that govern it, is itself a first-order reality that ultimately requires a metaphysical explanation. Aquinas's discussion of natural law in the *Treatise on Law* is, for the most part, a metaphysical reflection on natural law as one aspect of an ordered and intelligible universe that he believes can only be explained as the effect of a transcendent and intelligent First Cause, which Aquinas identifies with God as revealed in the Judeo-Christian tradition. Thus, Aquinas's definition of natural law as the rational creature's participation in the eternal law (i.e., the divinely ordained order of the universe) is a metaphysical definition

PUTTING IT ALL TOGETHER

Ethics is about human action, and human actions are aimed at some intelligible end or good. These ends or goods are dimensions of our flourishing as human beings. Ethics is, therefore, fundamentally a set of principles and norms that direct our actions toward human flourishing. The first principles of ethics—also called the first principles of practical reason, or the first principles of natural law—identify and direct us toward the basic categories of good. These basic goods are intrinsically valuable and irreducible to one another or to any more fundamental category of good. Each provides a basic, noninstrumental reason for action. Because they are first principles, the basic goods cannot be demonstrated or deduced from any prior principles, but instead can only be identified through reflection on our practical reasoning and judgments. Such reflection yields a set of seven basic categories of good: (1) life and health, (2) knowledge and appreciation of beauty, (3) skillful work and play, (4) friendship and sociability, (5) marriage and family, (6) integrity and authenticity, (7) and religion. The first principles of practical reason direct us toward each of these goods (and away from their opposites), for ourselves and anyone who, like us, has the basic natural capacity to recognize, act for, and benefit from them (and to cooperate with us in pursuit of them). These first principles taken individually, however, are insufficient to determine how we ought to act in any particular situation. For there are multiple goods with a potentially infinite array of particular instantiations, and there are also a multitude of people (including ourselves) who might

---

concerned with natural law's ultimate causes; see Aquinas, *Summa theologiae* I-II, q. 90, a. 2). My account here is fully compatible with Aquinas's, but, apart from my chapter 5, is limited to a consideration of natural law from an ethical (third-order) perspective. Nonetheless, as I explain in chapter 5, understanding the natural law as ultimately grounded in God's intelligent and benevolent plan for human beings (and for the universe more broadly) helps to deepen our appreciation of its obligatoriness. For instance, Grisez writes, "When we understand [the directiveness of the principles of practical reason] as guidance provided by our Creator, our sense of its dependability deepens, and with that the normative force of the moral *ought* which it generates increases"; see Grisez, "Natural Law and the Transcendent Source," 449 (emphasis original). See also Finnis, *Aquinas*, chap. 10.3–4, and Finnis, *Natural Law and Natural Rights*, chap. 13.

benefit from these goods. How, then, do we choose which good to pursue, and which person or group to benefit, particularly given our limitations of time, energy, and resources? These questions can only be answered with reference to the *integral directiveness of practical reasons*—that is, by considering all of practical reason's first principles, taken as a whole—for this is the standard of moral truth, the standard by which we can determine whether our actions are not merely intelligible, but fully practically reasonable, and therefore *morally* good. This standard, and the more specific moral norms that flow from it, will be the subject of chapter 2.

TWO

Moral Principles

In chapter 1, I argued that ethics is grounded on principles that direct our actions toward human flourishing in its various dimensions. Those principles (the first principles of practical reason) are normative and prescriptive insofar as they identify certain goods—life and health, knowledge and appreciation of beauty, performative excellence, friendship, marriage, integrity and authenticity, and religion—as intrinsically choiceworthy, as to-be-pursued, and their opposites as to-be-avoided. Yet they are not "moral" principles in the restricted modern sense of the term, for they do not directly tell us whether an action is morally right or wrong.

Imagine, for instance, that it is a Saturday afternoon. Your schedule is open. You have no pressing work that needs to be done, and no children to take care of. The weather is nice, so it occurs to you that it might be a good day to go hiking, in order to get some exercise and enjoy the beauty of nature. You don your hiking books, grab some water and snacks, and are about to head out the door when a friend calls. She is distressed, and says that there is a delicate and time-sensitive personal matter she wants to discuss with you, preferably in person. What do you do? You were really looking forward to the hike but don't want to let down your friend. You know your friend is not a fan of hiking, so inviting her along is not an option. Having just read the first chapter of this book, you decide to see if the principles outlined there can offer any guidance. You see the principles indicating that health and appreciation of beauty are to-be-pursued, and conclude that you should tell your friend you are busy and go for the hike (perhaps offering to talk another time). But then you see the principle indicating that friendship is to-be-pursued, and that your friend's peace of mind (an aspect of the good of integrity) is also to-be-pursued, and these considerations point to the opposite conclusion. Both options are intelligible, for both options aim at genuine goods, but is one more reasonable, all things considered? To answer that question, we need a set of second-level practical principles, or moral principles, that guide deliberation and choice among the competing options toward which the first-level principles direct us.

THE FIRST PRINCIPLE OF MORALITY
AND INTERMEDIATE MORAL NORMS

On the natural law view, acting morally is acting in a *fully reasonable* way. But what does this mean? Each of the basic goods (and each of their instantiations) provides a reason for action. However, not every pursuit of a basic good is *fully* reasonable, for it is possible to pursue one good in a way that fails to respect the intelligible appeal (the goodness or "to-be-pursuedness") of another good (or another person's good). Here it is important to remember that each of the basic goods provides a distinct, incommensurable reason for action. Because each of the goods contributes to our flourishing in a unique way, there is no "common denominator" or common standard of measure that would allow us to weigh or measure the value of various goods in order to determine which has the greatest overall value. This means that morally upright (i.e., fully reasonable) action cannot be a matter of *maximizing* the good, for there is no such thing as generic "goodness" that can be maximized; rather, there are distinct goods, incommensurable in their basic value.[1] There is no way, for instance, to determine whether going hiking or responding to

---

1. Though his view is at odds in some respects with new natural law theory, Chappell agrees with the theory in rejecting a maximizing approach to moral decision-making, and provides several lines of argument exposing the incoherence of such an approach (Chappell, "The Polymorphy of Practical Reason," 102–25).

your friend's request to meet will yield "more good," since the benefits promised by each option are irreducibly distinct. The notion of maximizing the good is therefore senseless.

Instead of thinking about morally right action as a matter of maximizing the good (as utilitarian moral theories do), natural law theory thinks about morality as requiring a certain attitude or posture of the will toward the basic goods, and ultimately toward all human beings, whose flourishing is constituted by participation in these goods.[2] Acting morally—acting in a *fully reasonable* way—means being responsive to *all* of practical reason's basic directives, considering those directives *integrally* or holistically, rather than individually in isolation from the others. These directives, considered integrally, tell us to preserve and promote human flourishing in all its various basic dimensions, not only for ourselves but for all human beings, both individually and in community. The integral directiveness of practical reasons thus points us toward the ideal of *integral human fulfillment*, the fulfillment of all human beings with respect to all of the basic goods, within a harmonious community.[3] Acting in a fully reasonable way—in a way that is responsive to all of practical reason's directives—therefore means acting in a way that is compatible with integral human fulfillment. This is one way of articulating natural law's master moral principle, which can be formulated as follows:

Master Moral Principle: Choose and act only in ways that are compatible with a will toward integral human fulfillment.

In other words, morally upright choices reflect and embody a certain attitude or posture of the will, a posture of openness to all human goods and to community with all persons, a posture responsive to the intelligible appeal (i.e., goodness) of all the goods for all people. Conversely, morally wrong choices close us to some fundamental aspect of human well-being or to community

2. For more on why moral norms protect the basic goods of all human beings, see notes 20 and 32 in chapter 1.

3. This principle can also be expressed as a requirement that one's actions be in line with the universal common good or the all-around flourishing of the whole human community. Morally upright action, therefore, is action compatible with membership in an ideal human community, a community in which all human beings live together in harmony and are fulfilled on all dimensions of their being. For more on this point in relation to the concept of the ultimate end of human beings, see Finnis, "Action's Most Ultimate End."

with some person or group, reflecting and embodying a will that fails to respond adequately to the goodness of at least some good for some person.

This master moral principle encompasses, at the most general level, all of morality's requirements, but in order to be a useful guide for deliberation and choice, its implications need to be spelled out more concretely through the articulation of intermediate moral norms that will, in turn, make it possible to articulate specific moral rules. One way to identify intermediate moral norms is to consider how our choices and actions could fail to be compatible with a will toward integral human fulfillment—how our choices might close us to one of the basic human goods or cut us off from community with some person or group—and to articulate norms that exclude such choices. This is what I will do in the following subsections.

Never Intentionally Damage or Destroy a Basic Human Good

Perhaps the most obvious way to close oneself to a basic good is to intentionally damage or destroy a basic good (in oneself or another), thereby setting one's will directly contrary to that good (and, if it is another person's good, cutting oneself off from community with that person). Thus we can articulate the following intermediate moral principle: *Never intentionally damage or destroy a basic human good.*

Some of the most widely acknowledged moral rules are specifications of this principle, including prohibitions on murder, torture, slavery, and rape, acts that involve intentional damage or destruction of the basic goods of life, integrity, friendship, and marriage, respectively.[4] Although some who acknowledge these rules believe that they admit of exceptions, on the new natural law view these moral prohibitions (if correctly defined) are absolute, binding in all circumstances. These absolute moral prohibitions can also be articulated (from the perspective of the beneficiary) as inalienable

---

4. All of these immoral acts damage more than one good, but for the sake of simplicity I have named only the good always necessarily intentionally damaged by, and most specific to, the act in question. For instance, torture often damages both health and integrity, but the damage to health need not be intentional and is not specific to the act of torture, whereas the damage to integrity (trying to "break" a person and undermine his agency by using his emotions against his reason and will) is, by definition, either the torturer's end or his chosen means to the end (in interrogational torture) of attaining information (Tollefsen, *Biomedical Research*, 93–100, and "Torture").

and inviolable human rights, such as the right to life (i.e., the right not to be intentionally killed), the right not to be tortured, and so on. This ability to provide a robust account of absolute moral prohibitions and of inalienable and inviolable human rights is an important feature of natural law theory. For there is something obviously wrong with any moral theory that cannot explain why actions such as genocide and rape are *always* immoral, regardless of the circumstances.

One crucial aspect of correctly defining these absolute moral prohibitions is recognizing that they apply only to *intentional* harm to basic goods, not harms accepted as side effects. To intend something is to choose it, either as an end in itself or as a means to some other end. One way to understand this is to think about choice as the adoption of a proposal for action, which includes the purpose (end) of one's action, and all (but only) the means that one takes to be necessary to achieve that purpose. For instance, let's say that I want to improve my cardiovascular health and choose to take a brisk walk for that purpose. In choosing to do so, I say "yes" to the following proposal for action: take a brisk walk to improve my cardiovascular health. If I know that the brisk walk improves my cardiovascular health by engaging my muscles, raising my heart rate, and so on, then I at least implicitly choose those states of affairs also, as means that I take to be necessary in my plan to achieve my end. But even if I know that the brisk walk will have many other effects—burning calories, inducing perspiration, dirtying my clothes, wearing out my shoes, exacerbating my knee problems, exposing me to the risk of being hit by a car—those effects, insofar as they are not part of the proposal I adopted in my choice (because they are neither my purpose nor the means chosen to achieve my purpose) are not intended in the strict sense. Instead, these unintended effects are *side effects*.

I am morally responsible for the foreseen (and reasonably foreseeable) side effects of my actions, but I am not morally responsible for side effects in the same way as I am morally responsible for what I intend. Intending damage to a basic good is always incompatible with a will toward integral human fulfillment, because it sets one's will directly contrary to that good and thus closes oneself off from it (and from community with the person whose good one intends to damage). Accepting damage to a basic good as a side effect, however, does not set one's will directly contrary to that good. For example, accepting that my walk will exacerbate my knee problems, and choosing to walk anyway, does not set my will directly contrary to the basic good of health. Going for a walk with the intent to exacerbate my knee problems (perhaps with a view toward, say, avoiding being drafted into the military), would, however, set my will contrary to the basic good of health, for damage to my health would in that case be part of the proposal for action adopted in my choice.

The distinction between intending something and accepting it as a side effect may sound like philosophical hair-splitting, but commonsense morality, and most legal systems, recognize the important moral difference between the two. The law, for instance, recognizes murder (intentional homicide) as a more severe crime than manslaughter (unintentional homicide). Further, we rely on this distinction frequently in our everyday moral judgments, saying such things as "I know you didn't mean to hurt me," or "It was just an accident," when we have reason to think that the harm someone caused was unintentional. Again, we may still hold the person responsible for being careless or negligent in some way, but we don't judge the person to be necessarily malicious in these cases. We respond very differently, however, when we think someone harmed us intentionally: "You tried to make it look like an accident, but I know that you broke my computer on purpose! You're trying to sabotage my work because you're jealous of my success." The natural law view can account for these commonsense moral judgments, because natural law recognizes that morality is ultimately about having a good will, a will properly responsive to all the basic dimensions of human flourishing and open to friendship with all persons. Nonetheless, because having a good will also requires taking due care to protect and promote human goods, harms resulting from utter indifference or reckless negligence can sometimes be just as bad as harms that are directly intended. Such harms would be violations of the moral requirement to act with fairness, in accordance with the Golden Rule.

The importance of intent in defining the nature of our actions also entails that actions can only be correctly identified by considering them from the perspective of the acting agent.[5] For the very same external behavior—spilling coffee on someone's computer—may be the embodiment of a malicious choice to sabotage someone's work, or it may just be the result of physical causes over which you have no control—someone walking by accidentally bumps into you, causing you to spill the coffee. These possibilities

5. For a more detailed articulation and defense of this point, see Tollefsen, "Is a Purely First Person Account of Human Action Defensible?"

are not exhaustive; you might also have been negligent in some way, not intending to spill the coffee, but irresponsibly failing to take due precautions despite knowing that you tend to be a klutz and are prone to such accidents.

Another example that can help to clarify the meaning and importance of intention is the case of a soldier who jumps on a live grenade to save his comrades by muffling the impact of the blast with his body. The soldier knows that this choice will almost certainly result in his death, and that he might be saved if he runs away or tries to take cover, rather than jumping on the grenade. Yet the soldier's choice is clearly not suicidal, for he does not intend his death, even though he foresees it with near certainty. This is true even though what he does intend as a means to the end of saving his comrades—the absorption of the shrapnel with his body—is causally inseparable from his death (or at least severe mutilation). Despite this causal inseparability, the soldier's death (or mutilation) is not part of the proposal for action he adopts—it is neither his end (to save his comrades) nor the means chosen to achieve his end (to muffle the impact of the blast by absorbing the shrapnel with his body). Of course, it could be the case that the soldier in question, sick of the privations of life as a soldier and unhopeful about life after the war, sees the grenade and jumps on it, thinking, "Here's my chance to put an end to my suffering and be remembered as a hero." In this version of the case, the soldier *is* intending his death, for if he survived his plan would have failed. Once again, we see that the same outward behavior can embody two very different human actions, an act of heroic self-sacrifice, on the one hand, or an act of suicide, on the other.[6]

6. The account of intention explained here is often referred to as a "strict" or "narrow" account of intention. Some have criticized this account, arguing instead that it is counterintuitive to claim that effects causally proximate to or inseparable from one's chosen end or means are not part of what one intends (see, e.g., Chappell, "The Polymorphy of Practical Reason," 102–26; McIntyre, "Doing Away with Double Effect"; Jensen, "Causal Constraints on Intention"; Long, "Fundamental Errors"; Porter, "Direct and Indirect"). Yet no critic of the view has, to my knowledge, provided an alternative account of intention that avoids the (at least) equally counterintuitive implication that a soldier jumping on a live grenade is intending his death, or that a person with knee problems who goes for a walk intends to exacerbate her knee problems. For a more in-depth defense of the strict view of intention, and a detailed response to critics, see, Tollefsen, "Is a Purely First Person Account of Human Action Defensible?"; Finnis, Grisez, and Boyle, "'Direct' and 'Indirect'"; Lee, "Distinguishing between What Is Intended"; Tollefsen, "Terminating in the Body," and Tollefsen, "Double Effect and Two Hard Cases."

Intending harm is, of course, not the only way to do something morally wrong. Acting in a way that is compatible with a will toward integral human fulfillment—alive to the rational appeal of every basic form of good (including community with every person)—requires more than just avoiding intentional harm. The mere fact that certain harms are unintended does not get us off the hook morally. We are responsible for the foreseen and foreseeable side effects of our actions. A colleague might honestly say that he did not intend to offend anyone with that sexist joke, but (at least in today's culture) most people would respond that he should have known some of his colleagues would take offense, and thus should have refrained from telling the joke out of respect for those colleagues.

What, then, are the moral norms that apply not only to what one intends but also to harms (and benefits) that one accepts as side effects?

Fairness: The Golden Rule

One moral norm governing both intended and unintended harms and benefits is the norm of fairness, often expressed and operationalized as the Golden Rule: *Do unto others as you would have others do unto you.* Or, in less archaic language: *Treat others as you would want to be treated.* The Golden Rule is relevant in any situation in which you have to decide whom to benefit. In such situations, others are always (at least) incidentally and unintentionally harmed, insofar as you might have chosen to benefit them instead. These include decisions as mundane and trivial as how to divide the apple pie you are serving for dessert, and as dramatic and serious as how to distribute ventilators to patients when there are not enough for everyone.

The Golden Rule follows from the master moral principle—*choose and act only in ways that are compatible with a will toward integral human fulfillment*—because integral human fulfillment is the fulfillment of all human beings with respect to all of the basic goods. The goods are good (i.e., to-be-pursued) not just for me and those near and dear to me, but for all human beings. It is therefore unreasonable (i.e., incompatible with a will toward integral human fulfillment) to arbitrarily prioritize the good of one person over another, for doing so unreasonably discounts the importance of a particular person's (or group's) good, and closes oneself off from community with that person (or group).

The word "arbitrarily" is crucial, however. For there may indeed be reasons to prioritize one person or group over another. And since the basic reasons governing the practical domain are basic goods, prioritization of one person's good over another ultimately can only be justified with reference to the basic goods themselves. Among the basic goods are the goods of friendship and marriage/family. The very nature of these goods requires a certain prioritization of the good of one's spouse, children, relatives, friends, and so on over others to whom one has no such relationship. This point (along with the topic of special obligations more generally) will be discussed further in chapter 3, but I mention it briefly here only to give an example of how prioritizing the good of some people over others may be reasonable and required by the basic goods themselves. There are also reasons to prioritize one's own good over the good of others to some extent, because—once one has reached maturity—one has greater knowledge of, responsibility for, and capacity to promote one's own good than that of (most) others (except perhaps one's small children).

I referred to the Golden Rule as a way to express and operationalize the norm of fairness because it serves as a heuristic device to help us determine whether or not our prioritization of one person's good (usually our own good or the good of those near and dear to us) over the good of another is reasonable. It does this by asking us to imaginatively put ourselves in the other person's place, and judge the reasonableness of our choice from that vantage point. For example, the Golden Rule would clearly be relevant to the case I outlined at the beginning of this chapter, in which you need to decide whether to respond to your friend's request for help or proceed with your hiking plan. In considering the case, ignore (for the moment) the fact that there are various goods involved. The problem of how to prioritize goods is different from the problem of how to prioritize persons—although in practice they often go together—and is dealt with in the next subsection. The Golden Rule says, Put yourself in your friend's place. If the tables were turned, would you want your friend to drop her hiking plan in order to come to your aid? The answer to that is maybe, if the situation really is urgent and important. But if the matter really isn't all that important, or if it can wait a day or two, you might not want your friend to drop her hiking plan if the tables were turned—after all, part of being a friend is that you genuinely care about the other person's well-being.

As the example indicates, the Golden Rule is a tool for moral discernment, not some kind of algorithm that automatically spits out the objectively right answer when you input the relevant facts. As such, there is an irreducible element of subjectivity to it, for its purpose is primarily to rectify the will, ensuring that there is no *willful* discounting of another's good, and thus no closing of your will to community with that person. Applying the Golden Rule correctly will require practical wisdom and experience, but simply by engaging in this imaginative exercise, sincerely trying to discern what fairness requires and following your best judgment, you ensure that your will is compatible with a will toward integral human fulfillment. This is true even if it turns out that your judgment is mistaken in the sense that you later realize you had "misread" the situation or inadvertently overlooked important facts.

Imagine, for instance, that based on what your friend tells you, you surmise that the situation is not all that urgent or important, and so you decide to tell your friend that you have plans, but would be happy to get together to talk the following day. When you do see your friend the next day, you notice her bloodshot eyes and haggard look, and discover that she has been up all night agonizing over the matter that she wants to discuss with you. You then realize that you had misjudged the situation. You apologize to your friend, telling her that if you had grasped the gravity of the situation, you would have dropped everything yesterday to meet with her. And you make a mental note to yourself that this is a friend who is not prone to exaggerate her needs or cry wolf, so that you do not make the same mistake in the future. Making such corrections—the apology and the mental note—is also a requirement of a morally upright will, for failure to make them would be an indication that you were not really attempting to sincerely apply the Golden Rule, but rather trying to rationalize an unfair and selfish choice.

Applying the Golden Rule yields many familiar and widely shared moral norms, including "Do not steal," "Do not cheat," "Wait your turn," "Do your fair share," "Keep your promises," "Don't play favorites." It is interesting to note that because these are applications of the Golden Rule, many of these norms have exceptions, unlike the norms that flow from the prohibition on intentional damage to basic human goods. For instance, "Do not steal" is an absolute norm only if stealing is defined as "taking of another's property without consent," where what counts as someone's property is not merely a legal matter but rather a moral matter that does not always track legal ownership rights. For the right to private ownership of goods in itself flows from the Golden Rule (because everyone is better off when private property is generally respected), and thus the Golden Rule also sets limits on that right.[7] When, for example, one person is in extreme and urgent need, and another person has enough to spare, the person in need has a right to take what he needs — it is, morally speaking, *his* property, even if the other person has legal title to it.[8] (This presumes that there are no other ways for the person to get what he needs without violating another person's legal property rights.) Similarly, there will be circumstances in which it is not unfair (and therefore not wrong) to break a promise, as when, for instance, you cancel a lunch meeting because you are sick. The Golden Rule is also the basis of many common legal norms, such as antidiscrimination laws or the principle that laws should protect all people equally.

The Vocation Principle:
Establishing a Reasonable Priority among Goods

Unfairness—arbitrary prioritization of one person's good over another's—is incompatible with a will toward integral human fulfillment because it fails to be responsive to the intrinsic rational appeal of every person's good. Likewise, arbitrary prioritization of one basic good (or instantiation of a good) over another fails to be responsive to the intrinsic rational appeal of every good. Just as the Golden Rule guides us to respond adequately to every *person's* good, the Vocation Principle guides us to respond adequately to every *good* by providing a basis for establishing a reasonable (nonarbitrary) priority among goods.

Prioritization among goods, like prioritization among persons, is only reasonable when that prioritization is justified by the goods themselves, for there are no reasons for choosing and acting apart from goods. Prioritization of goods is required by the goods themselves insofar as it is necessary for any deep and meaningful realization of a good. It is reasonable to prefer deeper realizations of a good (e.g., playing a Mozart sonata) to more superficial realizations (e.g., playing chopsticks). Yet any deep and meaningful contribution to human flourishing with respect to any of the basic goods requires a

7. For more on this point, see Finnis, *Natural Law and Natural Rights*, 169–73.
8. See Aquinas, *Summa theologiae* II-II, q. 66, a. 7.

considerable investment of time, energy, and other scarce resources. Getting to the point at which one can play a Mozart sonata takes years of practicing the piano (at least for those of us who are not musical prodigies), usually under the guidance of an instructor. All of that time, energy, and money could have been used for other things—learning a language, playing a sport, spending time with friends, volunteering at a soup kitchen, donating to refugees, and so on. What justifies this use of resources (if it is justified) is the deep and significant contribution to human flourishing such an investment makes possible.

Given that one can only make a meaningful contribution to human flourishing by making commitments and long-term investments of time, energy, and resources in pursuit of some particular good(s)—which means forgoing opportunities to pursue other goods—the question then becomes, How does one decide which good(s) to prioritize in one's life? Just as with the application of the Golden Rule, there is an irreducible element of subjectivity here, and the answer is likely to be morally underdetermined—there is likely to be a wide range of morally acceptable answers. What matters here is not so much getting the "right" answer (for there usually is not a single, objective right answer to this question), but rather approaching the question with moral seriousness, with a will responsive to the intelligible appeal of all dimensions of human flourishing, avoiding the arbitrary discounting of any form of good that would close one's will toward that good. What is required, in other words, is to cultivate a vocational sense of life (with "vocation" understood broadly, not in a specifically religious sense) and to order one's priorities in line with one's vocational commitments. This requirement is what I call the Vocation Principle.

As children mature to adulthood, they (with the help of parents, educators, mentors, friends) need to discern what particular aspect(s) of human flourishing they are going to (primarily) dedicate their lives and energies to. This discernment should take into account their talents, inclinations, and opportunities, and also how those talents, inclinations, and opportunities match up with the needs of their communities. The path embarked upon—choosing college versus technical school or on-the-job training; choosing an area of study; choosing whether, when, and whom to marry—involves various commitments, and those commitments (enabling one to contribute more deeply to certain aspects of human flourishing) are reasons to prioritize certain goods (those to which one is vocationally committed) over others (those that are not integral to one's vocation). The Vocation Principle requires engaging seriously in such discernment—with a sense of responsibility to make use of one's talents and opportunities to contribute meaningfully to human flourishing—and making and following through with the corresponding commitments (unless there are sufficient reasons to change course). Like the Golden Rule, this principle rectifies the will, ensuring that one remains responsive and open to all of the dimensions of human flourishing even while (as is inevitable) prioritizing some goods over others. It thus rules out unreasonable prioritization of goods—doing so merely on the basis of emotional attractions or aversions, or out of disdain for certain forms of good—but does not yield a single right answer, or require that one choose the vocational path that "maximizes" one's contribution to human flourishing (for given the incommensurable basic value of the goods, a maximizing approach is literally incoherent and senseless).

Of course, in many instances a person's vocational path is not straightforward. One starts out, for instance, preparing for a career in biological research, only to discover that one's talents and personality make one better suited to a more socially interactive career in business or teaching. Or one marries and determines that a slightly different career path will be more compatible with one's responsibilities as a spouse and parent. Persevering in a particular vocational path merely out of inertia, even if it turns out that one is not suited for it, or that it conflicts with other responsibilities, is unreasonable. Responsiveness to the intelligible appeal of human goods requires that one be open to a change of course when this promises to contribute more deeply to human flourishing for oneself and others. At the same time, the farther along one travels on a particular path—investing significant time and resources in it, developing specialized knowledge and skills, building relationships in which others come to rely on you in various ways—the less likely it is that a radical change in trajectory will be reasonable (rather than being motivated primarily by emotions unintegrated with reason, as when one seeks a radical vocational change merely because one's initial enthusiasm has faded).[9] Practical reasonableness therefore requires persevering in commitments despite obstacles or emotional ups and downs, unless there are

9. See the section on virtues for a more detailed discussion about how unintegrated emotions can fetter practical reason's integral directiveness, leading to immoral choices.

sufficient reasons (grounded in human goods) for changing course. At the same time, practical reasonableness also requires being open and responsive to such reasons, rather than maintaining commitments with blind fanaticism even in the face of reasons to revise them.[10] For choices must always be guided by the ideal of integral human fulfillment, an ideal that cannot be exhausted by any particular mode of pursuing it,[11] and that thus requires continued openness to new and better ways of promoting human flourishing.

The Unity of Life Principle: Integrating Pursuits and Commitments in View of an Ultimate End

We have seen that making and persevering (when reasonable) in commitments of various sorts is necessary for deep realizations of human goods,

---

10. What counts as "sufficient reasons" for breaking a commitment depends on the nature of the commitment. Arguably there are cases—such as a marriage or the commitment to certain religious vocations—in which the commitment is inherently permanent at least in principle.

11. This point, which we might call an antifanaticism norm, or a norm requiring a certain degree of detachment from one's particular projects and goals, dovetails nicely with MacIntyre's suggestion in *Ethics in the Conflicts of Modernity*, that "we complete and perfect our lives by allowing them to remain incomplete. A good life is one in which an agent, although continuing to rank order particular and finite goods, treats none of these goods as necessary for the completion of his or her life, so leaving her or himself open to a final good beyond all such goods" (231). Philosophically, new natural law theorists see "integral human fulfillment" as this final good. One can also recognize, even from a purely philosophical perspective, that one should take harmony with God as one's ultimate end, for if one recognizes that God is the source of the moral order and he seeks our good, then one can also recognize that pursuing the good in morally upright ways is a way of cooperating with God and following his will (see Grisez, Boyle, and Finnis, "Practical Principles," 143–45). From a purely philosophical perspective, it is not clear that the ideal of integral human fulfillment can ever become a reality. From a Christian theological perspective, however, Grisez and others have argued that we are promised this fulfillment in the Kingdom of God, which will involve fulfillment in all human goods (including harmony with God), in addition to the beatific vision (which is not, strictly speaking, a fulfillment of human nature, but which is made possible by the elevation of our nature through grace) (146–47). This promise of fulfillment in the Kingdom thus provides additional motivation for believers to lead a morally upright life, because by leading a morally upright life one's will remains open to integral human fulfillment, and thus capable of participating in and enjoying the heavenly kingdom. See chapter 5 for a fuller discussion of these points.

and thus justifies ordering our priorities in line with those commitments, giving us a reason to prioritize some goods over others. But our lives involve a wide variety of pursuits and commitments. If these are not to work at cross-purposes (which would undermine our ability to effectively promote human flourishing), they must be harmonized and integrated with one another. Seeking this integration is a moral requirement, for it is not compatible with a will toward integral human fulfillment to knowingly and willingly configure one's life in a way that makes one less effective than one could be (while acting in ways consistent with moral principles) in the realization of human goods that one has already determined one ought to pursue.[12] I call this the Unity of Life Principle, which could be seen as a corollary to the Vocation Principle. Integrating one's pursuits and commitments will require the establishment of an order or hierarchy among them. On what reasonable basis can such a hierarchy be established?

Although each of the basic goods offers a distinct, incommensurable benefit, from a moral perspective (following the integral directiveness of practical reason's first principles) certain basic priorities can be established. For example, the reflexive goods of integrity and authenticity, together consisting of harmony among feelings, judgments, choices, and actions, can only be pursued in a way that is consistent with integral human fulfillment by bringing feelings, choices, and actions into line with morally true judgments.[13] In any case that involves a choice between a morally right and a morally wrong option, therefore, one must conform one's feelings and choices to what one understands to be morally required. Thus the human good of virtue—which is synonymous with integrity and authenticity considered from the moral perspective (taking into consideration all of the principles of practical reason)—takes priority in any situation of morally significant choosing, and the pursuit of virtue can be an overarching purpose that integrates many of one's pursuits and commitments.

---

12. This reference to being effective in the realization of human goods might sound like a form of utilitarian calculus, but it is not, for the standard here is not the "greatest good," a concept that is senseless on the natural law view, given that each of the basic goods and their instantiations are incommensurable in value. Rather, the standard is a will adequately responsive to human flourishing in all of its various basic dimensions.

13. See Grisez, Boyle, and Finnis, "Practical Principles," 138.

In many instances, however, one's choices are morally underdetermined, meaning that one is choosing from a variety of options that are all morally acceptable. The choice of a career path, or of whether or not to marry, is often morally underdetermined. We will return in a moment to consider whether or not these morally underdetermined choices can be unified by an overarching purpose, but first it is worth noting that once one makes such choices—committing oneself to a particular profession, to marriage, and so on—these commitments entail obligations that order and structure one's life to a significant extent, and one must strive to harmonize them so that, say, one's professional commitments do not prevent one from fulfilling one's family commitments, or vice versa. This might mean, for instance, that someone committed to an intense and all-encompassing professional vocation that effectively requires all of her time and energy might decide that she should not marry, or that she should delay marriage until she is willing and able to devote sufficient time and energy to her family. On the other hand, someone who seeks to marry and raise a family should make professional choices in line with his family obligations, even if this at times means passing up opportunities for advancement that would be incompatible with what he owes to his wife and children.

A commitment to virtue and to a harmonized set of vocational commitments will therefore order and structure a great deal of a person's life. Even so, there may still be peripheral activities—hobbies and recreational pursuits, for example—that are not fully integrated or harmonized with one's other commitments. Is there an overarching commitment—a single, ultimate purpose—that can reasonably govern and integrate *all* of one's choices, actions, and other commitments? Yes. That overarching commitment can be found in the basic human good of religion or harmony with God. For religion is the only good that can reasonably govern, and be at stake in, every choice we make (including choices among morally acceptable options), without treating the goods we pursue in those choices as merely instrumental.[14] We can, for example, seek professional excellence for its own sake, while also

14. For more on the uniquely pervasive and architectonic role that religion can play in the moral life, see Grisez, "Natural Law, God, Religion and Human Fulfillment," and Moschella, "Beyond Equal Liberty." In later work, Grisez slightly modifies his view, arguing that the ultimate end for which every choice should be made is "integral communal fulfilment," defined as "divine good together with the well-being and flourishing of created persons in respect to all of their fundamental goods" (Grisez, "The True Ultimate

ordering this pursuit to the further end of serving God by corresponding to the gifts God has given us and enabling them to bear fruit. Likewise, we can strive to be good spouses or good parents not only because of what we owe to our spouse and children, but also because we understand these family duties as part of our God-given vocation, a concrete reflection of God's will for us in our daily lives. Discerning which career path to take, or whether and whom to marry, similarly become not simply a matter of considering one's talents and inclinations along with society's needs, but of considering all of these things precisely as signs of the particular vocation that God has in mind for us. From this perspective, even the most apparently trivial choices and actions can acquire heightened significance if done with a view toward loving God and fulfilling God's will. The Spanish mystic Saint Teresa of Avila (1515–82), for instance, told the nuns of her order, "Know that even when you are in the kitchen, our Lord is moving among the pots and pans," by which she meant that in fulfilling these mundane duties out of love for God, recognizing these tasks to be concrete ways of fulfilling God's will, they can acquire a transcendent value.[15] One might say something similar about hobbies and recreational activities undertaken with this same spirit, which requires that they be in line with one's vocational commitments, even if somewhat peripheral to them.

The person who takes harmony with God as her single ultimate end can therefore harmoniously subsume all of her morally upright pursuits and commitments under this overarching purpose, without treating them as merely instrumental, by seeing these pursuits as a way of cooperating with God, who is the source of the moral order and who wills our good.[16] It is

---

End," 57). Here I retain the term "integral human fulfilment," because the notion of "integral communal fulfilment" can misleadingly suggest that it is possible for us, on the basis of our natural human capacities, to act for nonhuman goods. Nonetheless, when we recognize that harmony with God is an aspect of integral human fulfilment, that we ought to take harmony with God as our ultimate end, and that cooperating with God in pursuit of integral human fulfilment is an implicit aspect of the ultimate end of harmony with God, there ends up being little (if any) substantive difference between the account I offer here and Grisez's updated view.

15.   Teresa of Avila, *The Book of Foundations*, chap. 5.8.

16.   For Christians, this end can be further specified as harmony with God and cooperation with him in bringing about the kingdom of heaven, recognizing that "life on earth is no mere means to the kingdom but its embryonic stage" (Grisez, Boyle, and Finnis, "Practical Principles," 146). See chapter 5 for a fuller discussion of this point.

the uniquely transcendent nature of the good of religion—along with the understanding of God as the ultimate metaphysical source of the goodness of all human goods, and the source of our capacity to know and freely pursue those goods—that makes the good of religion uniquely suitable to play this architectonic role in the moral life.[17] For those who are aware of this possibility, doing so is a moral requirement, for it is the only way to reasonably unify and harmonize all of one's pursuits and commitments.[18]

Further, in light of this understanding of God, we can come to see the ideal of integral human fulfillment—the ideal of a perfectly harmonious community in which human beings are fulfilled in all dimensions of their being—as an end toward which God is directing us (for God is the source of the directiveness of practical reasons, which, when considered integrally, point toward this ideal). Thus, even though we recognize that this ideal is never fully realizable through human efforts alone, we can nonetheless hope that if we cooperate with God by energetically pursuing the good in morally upright ways, he will somehow supply what our efforts alone cannot achieve. With this in mind, we can see how the ultimate end of harmony with God implicitly includes the end of cooperating with God in bringing about integral human fulfillment, which now becomes not merely an ideal but an end, albeit one that we know we cannot achieve alone. I will discuss these points further in chapter 5.

I have now outlined some of the intermediate moral norms that flow from natural law's master moral principle: *Choose and act only in ways that are compatible with a will toward integral human fulfillment.* These norms are the following: *Never intentionally damage or destroy a basic human good*; the Golden Rule (requiring fairness in determining whom to benefit); the Vocation Principle (requiring the establishment of a reasonable order of pri-

17.   In principle, natural reason alone can enable us to attain the relevant speculative knowledge about God (as the transcendent, noncontingent source of existence and meaning, as a personal and providential God who seeks our fulfillment and our cooperation in realizing that fulfillment) that is needed to be able to make such an overarching religious commitment. Nonetheless, in practice, moral and theoretical obstacles make this knowledge difficult to attain without the aid of divine revelation and grace. See Grisez, "Natural Law, God, Religion, Human Fulfillment."

18.   Although distinct in its emphasis, Alasdair MacIntyre's view of the moral life as a narrative unity complements the account I have offered here; see, e.g., MacIntyre, *After Virtue*, chap. 15.

ority among goods) and its corollary, the Unity of Life Principle (requiring the integration and harmonization of all of one's pursuits and commitments in view of the single ultimate end of harmony with God, which includes cooperation with God in the pursuit of integral human fulfillment). These are not the only intermediate moral norms implied by the master moral principle, but I believe that any other intermediate moral norm will fall into one of these broad categories, for these categories correspond to the basic ways in which one's will can fail to be compatible with a will toward integral human fulfillment (choosing directly contrary to a good, or choosing in a way that arbitrarily discounts some person or good).

THE DOCTRINE OF DOUBLE EFFECT

Actions often have many effects, some good and some bad, some intended and some not. Indeed, insofar as every choice is a choice to pursue one good rather than another (or to benefit one person rather than another), every choice has at least incidental bad effects when compared to the alternatives—the bad effect of failing to do some good that one could have done if one had made a different choice. In order to determine when it is morally permissible to make a choice that has foreseeable bad effects, moral theorists have proposed what is often referred to as the Doctrine of Double Effect (DDE),[19]

---

19.   Historically, the doctrine of double effect is typically traced to Aquinas's discussion of self-defense in the *Summa theologiae*. In this passage, Aquinas claims that intentional killing is always wrong (at least for private citizens), but self-defense (even by lethal means) can be morally acceptable insofar as the attacker's death is an unintended side effect of an act aimed at saving one's own life. The term "double effect" comes from Aquinas's claim that "nothing hinders one act from having two effects, one of which is intended, while the other is beside the intention." The reason why this is morally relevant, on Aquinas's view, is that "moral acts take their species according to what is intended, and not according to what is beside the intention" (Aquinas, *Summa theologiae* II-II, q. 64, a. 7). In other words, Aquinas believes that the agent's intent is crucial for determining the nature of an action in the morally relevant sense, and determining the nature (or species) of an action with precision is important because Aquinas believes that certain types of actions are intrinsically evil, and therefore always prohibited regardless of the circumstances. This does not mean that foreseen side effects are morally irrelevant, but only that the moral norms governing the acceptance of side effects are different from (and in some respects less stringent than) the moral norms governing what we intend.

which has been formulated in a variety of ways.[20] At the core of these various formulations is the claim that (1) intending certain harms, as an end or as a means, is always morally wrong, but (2) accepting such harms may be morally acceptable if there is a proportionate reason to do so. According to the principles outlined above, the harms it is never permissible to intend are harms to basic human goods. What about the second prong of the DDE, typically referred to as the "proportionality criterion"? This criterion is often interpreted as requiring that the good effects one intends "outweigh" the unintended bad side effects. It is often interpreted, in other words, as if it involved some form of utilitarian calculus.[21]

Yet proportionality cannot be determined by the application of a utilitarian calculus, because such a calculus is usually both impossible and incoherent. A utilitarian calculus would only be possible and meaningful if human goods were commensurable in value, as is the case when you are comparing more or less of the same value—the lives of five human beings versus the life of one human being, with no knowledge of the particulars that make those lives incommensurable.[22] Most real-life cases, however, are

20.   For an account of the various traditional formulations and a clarification of their meaning, see Boyle, "Toward Understanding the Principle of Double Effect." One influential formulation has four criteria, but I believe that the first three of these are all tests to ensure that the harm or evil is not intended either as an end or as a means. Thus, the principle can be more simply captured as involving (1) a prohibition on harms to basic goods that are intended as an end or as a means, and (2) a proportionality criterion, understood as explained later in this section.

21.   The hypothetical trolley problems that pervade the double-effect literature give the illusion that such a calculus is possible, because the competing goods at stake are presented in a way that makes them commensurable. If a runaway trolley is careening toward five unknown people, and you could save the five by diverting the trolley onto another track onto which there is only one unknown person, it is clear that the choice to save five people is proportionate to the unintended side effect of killing one person. Yet once more details about the people are provided, numbers alone are insufficient to make the proportionality determination. What if the one person who will be killed if you divert the trolley away from the five is your wife? And what if the five are convicted criminals?

22.   Finnis lists a number of other cases in which value comparisons are possible: "States of affairs considered in abstraction from their origins, context and consequences (for example, their relation to a choosing human will) can often be compared in value; a happy village five minutes before and five minutes after a devastating hurricane. And many other comparisons of value are possible. Moral good can be ranked higher than

not like this, for most involve distinct goods that each offer a distinct, in-commensurable benefit. The case discussed at the outset—Do you go hiking or help your distressed friend?—is one such case. It is clear in this case that the choice to go hiking need not involve any intent to harm your friend or your friendship, though you recognize that these are possible side effects of your choice. Is acceptance of these harms proportionate? No calculation or "weighing" is possible here, because the goods (your health and appreciation of beauty versus your friendship and your friend's peace of mind) offer distinct benefits that cannot be weighed or measured against each other with regard to their basic value. We therefore need to think of the proportionality criterion as requiring that there be proportionate *moral* reasons for accepting the bad side effects, and this can only be determined by considering whether one's acceptance of those side effects itself runs afoul of any moral norms. In other words, determining proportionality requires considering whether or not any other moral norms (apart from the norm forbidding intentional damage or destruction of basic human goods) are violated by one's choice.

The moral norms most relevant to the acceptance of bad side effects are the moral norms forbidding arbitrary prioritization of one person's good over another's or of one good over another. The Golden Rule, for instance, is primarily what will help you to determine whether or not it is permissible to continue with your hiking plans despite the foreseen harms to your friend. Or, to take a weightier example, determining whether it is morally permissible to bomb a munitions factory in the course of a just war, even though the civilians living near the factory are likely to be killed or injured as a side effect, would require applying the Golden Rule. One could do this by considering, for instance, whether one would be willing to accept these side effects if the civilians killed were citizens of one's own country (presuming that one

---

nonmoral, intelligible good higher than merely sensible good, basic good than instrumental, divine and human than animal, heavenly than earthly. More of the same can be compared with less of the same; a genocidal society is worse than a murderous individual; killing is worse than wounding." Thus, explains Finnis, the "incommensurability which makes proportionalism [or utilitarianism] irrational is incommensurability of goods involved in *options*"—e.g., in situations that require a genuine choice, because more than one option has intelligible appeal (Finnis, *Moral Absolutes*, 53; emphasis original).

adequately values one's own citizens' lives).[23] If not, then one's decision to proceed with the bombing is likely to be unfair and therefore immoral, reflecting an unreasonable discounting of the value of those civilians' lives.

In double-effect cases that involve competing goods—should I take this medication to alleviate my cold symptoms even though it will make me extremely drowsy, preventing me from doing any serious work?—the Vocation Principle will be the most relevant to determining proportionality. If, for instance, I have pressing commitments or obligations that I would be unable to fulfill if I took the cold medicine (but able to fulfill if I did not), then taking the medicine despite the bad side effects is probably not proportionate. If, on the other hand, I have no such commitments and am planning to spend the day resting in hopes of recovering more quickly, the drowsiness would not be a disproportionate side effect (indeed, in that case it may even be an incidental benefit).

In sum, the correct way to understand the proportionality condition of the DDE is to think of it not as a matter of weighing benefits versus harms, but rather as requiring that there be proportionate moral reasons for one's choice, which means determining that the acceptance of the bad side effect(s) does not in itself violate any moral norm. I do not pretend to offer an exhaustive list, but the moral norms that are most likely to be relevant to this determination are the Golden Rule (or fairness principle) and the Vocation Principle. Thus, I propose that the DDE be formulated as follows:

> Doctrine of Double Effect: Harms it is never permissible to intend (i.e., harms to basic human goods) may be permissible to accept as side effects, if and only if the acceptance of these side effects does not itself violate any moral norm—for example, does not unfairly prioritize one person's or group's good over another's, and does not arbitrarily prioritize one good (or instantiation of a good) over another.

This formulation may seem to lack a genuine proportionality condition, but this is not the case, for the second clause is equivalent to "if and only if there

---

23. Of course, one could go wrong in this case by simply viewing all human lives as dispensable means to the goal of winning the war; this attitude would not be unfair, but would be incompatible with a will toward integral human fulfillment because it unreasonably discounts the value of human life.

are proportionate moral reasons." I prefer the above formulation, however, because it more clearly indicates what it means for there to be "proportionate moral reasons" to act despite the foreseen harmful side effects.[24]

Formulated as a list of questions to guide deliberation, my formulation of the DDE would look like this:

1. Is the harm intended (as an end or a means)?
   If the answer to this question is yes, the action is wrong, and no further analysis is needed. If the answer to this question is no, then the analysis continues:
2. Does the acceptance of the harm as a side effect violate any moral norm?
   a. Is it unfair? (Does it violate the Golden Rule?)
   b. Does it arbitrarily prioritize one good over another? (This can only be answered in light of one's vocational commitments and obligations—or, in the case of a community, in light of that community's specific purpose or common good—which enables one to establish a reasonable order of priority among goods.)

For the action to be morally permissible, the answer to all of these questions must be no. Formulated in this way, the DDE basically summarizes all of the intermediate moral norms I have discussed.

Up to this point, I have articulated moral principles from the perspective of what the integral directiveness of practical reasons points us toward—integral human fulfillment—as the regulatory ideal for a morally upright will. This way of articulating moral principles has the advantage of highlighting the inherent connection between morality and human flourishing.

---

24. This formulation also has the advantage of making the DDE's underlying rationale—its connection to the more basic moral principles—more transparent. This is important given that many contemporary moral philosophers have criticized the DDE for lacking a coherent rationale, largely because they fail to appreciate the DDE's broader theoretical context as part of a natural law approach to ethics in which certain types of acts (defined by intent) are absolutely prohibited. See, e.g., Steinhoff, "Wild Goose Chase"; Kershnar and Kelly, "The Right-Based Criticism"; Scanlon, *Moral Dimensions*, chap. 1 ("The Illusory Appeal of Double Effect"). For a detailed response to these critiques and a more in-depth discussion of the DDE, see Moschella, "Contextualizing, Clarifying and Defending the Doctrine of Double Effect."

It also has the advantage of making it easy to see how many widely accepted moral norms and rules are rooted in these principles. However, this approach has the disadvantage of sounding strange to those who are used to thinking about morality in terms of virtues, as it was most frequently discussed by classical thinkers in the natural law tradition, including Aristotle and Aquinas. More substantively, it fails to articulate the crucial role that virtues play in the moral life — enabling us to reliably make sound moral judgments and act upon them — and says little about the importance of education in virtue or of membership in communities that provide such education.[25]

25.   The following section should help to make clear that new natural law theorists do recognize, along with Jean Porter, that in many cases one will not be able to fully specify the requirements of natural law "apart from the traditions and practices of some specific community," for these traditions and practices will necessarily play a crucial role in one's moral education and in one's vocational discernment. New natural law theory also recognizes that a full theoretical defense of moral norms "must rest on a more comprehensive philosophical, scientific or theological account which locates them in a wider context of reflection and explanation" (Porter, "Does the Natural Law Provide," 91). Porter thus misunderstands the new natural law account when she presents it as claiming that "practical norms can adequately (perhaps only) be analyzed in terms of the autonomous functioning of practical reason" (90). For new natural law theorists have never claimed that natural law is based on "'pure practical reason' in a Kantian sense," or that practical reason functions *autonomously*, without any reliance on prior speculative knowledge (80) (see also the section "Nature, Natural Law, and Practical Rationality" in my chapter 1 and corresponding notes). There is also no opposition between the new natural law account and Porter's view that no rational defense of moral norms will be "rationally *compelling* to all well-disposed persons," for new natural law theorists recognize that the theoretical presuppositions of natural law, and the specifications of natural law beyond the first principles, can be obscured by various factors, including miseducation or a corrupt culture, even though they are in principle knowable through reason alone. Whether or not the new natural law view is compatible with Porter's claim that one cannot arrive at any fully determinate, universal moral norms without the help of Christian revelation depends on exactly what she means by this (91). If she means merely (as the above quotation suggests) that such fully determinate moral norms may not be rationally compelling to all well-disposed persons regardless of education and cultural context, this is a claim that new natural law theorists can accept. If, on the other hand, she means that in principle one cannot arrive at any fully specific, universal moral norms through reason alone, then her view is at odds with new natural law theory, which holds that, at the very least, rational reflection can enable one to specify certain absolute moral prohibitions, binding always and everywhere — as Aristotle did in recognizing, for instance, that murder and adultery are always morally wrong (*Nicomachean Ethics* 1107a8–12). It is unclear, however, that Porter would deny this claim.

A complementary account is needed, therefore, to show more clearly how virtues fit into this approach. Accordingly, in the next section I will discuss virtues as the embodiment of moral principles, and look at a different way of formulating moral norms that makes this connection more transparent.

VIRTUES: THE EMBODIMENT OF MORAL PRINCIPLES

Moral virtues are, broadly speaking, qualities of mind and character that dispose us to make sound moral judgments and act on them. New natural law theorists, especially Germain Grisez, have made important but largely unappreciated contributions to virtue ethics—a problem this section hopes to help remedy. Although the theory does focus more on moral principles than on virtues, this is not because virtues are considered unimportant, but rather because, without moral principles, we cannot determine what counts as a virtue in the first place.[26] Indeed, one of the contributions that new natural law theorists have made to virtue ethics is precisely to clarify the relationship between moral principles and virtues. Risking imprisonment or violent death to make money selling illegal drugs is not, for instance, an example of genuine courage, for according to the classical definition, courage is a disposition to overcome difficulties and dangers for the sake of what is genuinely good and morally right.[27] We cannot know what counts as true courage, therefore, unless we already know what is genuinely good and morally right. Aristotle's standard for this (and thus his standard for moral truth) is the judgment of the person

26. At an even more basic level, Angela Knobel argues that, on Aquinas's view, natural habitual knowledge of the first principles of practical reason is the starting point for moral virtue, the foundation of our aptitude for virtue (Knobel, *Aquinas and the Infused Moral Virtues*, 18–24).

27. Aristotle, for instance, writes that "it is for a noble end that the brave man endures and acts as courage directs" (*Nicomachean Ethics* 1115b24). Likewise, Aquinas writes that "fortitude of soul must be that which binds the will firmly to the good of reason in face of the greatest evils" (Aquinas, *Summa theologiae* II-II, q. 123, a. 4). More generally, Aquinas states that virtue "is that which makes a man good," and "man's good is to be in accordance with reason" (II-II, q. 123, a. 1). It is, in other words, practical reasonableness that is the standard for virtue.

who is fully practically reasonable.[28] The new natural law approach is fully compatible with this—for it recognizes the importance of moral exemplars in moral education and deliberation—but goes beyond it by spelling out more concretely what practical reasonableness requires. Natural law's principles, in other words, are the standards for identifying the practically reasonable person. A character trait is virtuous if it inclines one to act in accordance with moral truth, and the standard for moral truth is practical reasonableness (i.e., the integral directiveness of practical reason's first principles, and the moral norms that flow from that integral directiveness).[29]

Practical reasonableness is therefore both a standard for moral truth and, when considered as a quality of character, a virtue. This virtue is often referred to as "prudence," but the term "prudence" can be misleading because in common speech it often connotes self-interested calculation. I therefore prefer to refer to this virtue, which is a stable disposition to make and act upon sound moral judgments, as "practical reasonableness" or "practical wisdom." All of the moral principles and norms discussed in the previous section are requirements of practical reasonableness, implicit in the moral judgments of the practically reasonable agent, although the perfectly virtuous agent will often not need to explicitly advert to these principles in order to make a sound moral judgment. Explicit application of these principles and norms when one is unsure of what one ought to do, considering the advice and example of others who are more virtuous, and reflecting on one's past actions to identify and learn from errors will help one to become

28. "Virtue, then, is a state of character concerned with choice, lying in a mean, i.e., the mean relative to us, this being determined by a rational principle, and by that principle by which the man of practical wisdom would determine it" (Aristotle, *Nicomachean Ethics* 1106b36–1107a2). Finnis notes that though this claim is not necessarily circular—just as it is not circular to say that something is sweet if it tastes sweet to a healthy person—it is nonetheless theoretically insufficient, for one needs independent criteria to determine who counts as practically reasonable (Finnis, *Aquinas*, 48–50).

29. "*Prudentia* [practical reasonableness] itself is part of the definition, content, and influence of every other moral virtue; by it one judges where a virtue ends and becomes a vice; and it enables one to do so by applying principles, ultimately the first practical principles. So principles, propositional practical truths, are more fundamental than virtues; for virtues are the various aspects of a stable and ready willingness to make good choices, and, like everything in the will, are a response to reasons, and reasons are propositional" (Finnis, *Aquinas*, 124).

more practically reasonable, enabling one over time to make sound moral judgments with greater ease and reliability.[30]

I will say a bit more later in this section about how to grow in the virtue of practical reasonableness, drawing on some original insights from Grisez, but first I want to discuss the relationship between practical reasonableness and other virtues, typically referred to as "moral virtues" in the strict sense. Practical reasonableness is sometimes categorized as an intellectual virtue rather than a moral virtue, because it is a virtue that perfects our capacity to make sound moral judgments, which is an intellectual capacity. Though the term "moral virtue" is sometimes used broadly to include practical reasonableness, it can also be used narrowly to refer to virtues that perfect our inclinations or appetites, including both subrational inclinations (emotions) and rational inclination (will). It is not possible to be practically reasonable without also being morally virtuous, for one of the main obstacles to making and following sound moral judgments is the influence of inclinations that are not fully integrated with reason. These unintegrated inclinations are internal obstacles that can fetter, obscure, or distort practical reason's guidance, leading us to act in ways that are less than fully reasonable. Aquinas states, "The presence of vices and sins in man is owing to the fact that he follows the inclination of his sensitive nature against the order of his reason."[31] Conversely, to the extent that one's inclinations are integrated with reason through the development of moral virtues, those virtuous inclinations can assist us in making and following sound moral judgments.[32]

---

30. I do not emphasize it here, but it is worth noting that there is a crucial social component to this process. For we do not typically come to learn what is right and wrong by reading books of moral philosophy, but rather from the admonitions and example of parents, relatives, teachers, clergy, friends, etc. If the advice they offer is sound, and if (more importantly) their example is good, it will be much easier for one to develop practical wisdom than if the opposite is the case. Yet as long as one's upbringing and culture provide the opportunity to experience and participate in basic human goods (even in an impoverished way), one will have at least implicit knowledge of the first principles of practical reason, from which one can reason to the moral principles outlined here. Thus, people can and do come to criticize the moral standards and practices of their family and broader culture.

31. Aquinas, *Summa theologiae* I-II. q. 71, a. 2, ad 3.

32. Knobel provides a helpful example: "When one continually and habitually feels 'in one's heart' the goodness of fidelity, one will be more alert to actions that might

The truth of this is obvious from everyday experience, or at least the experience of those of us who are not yet fully virtuous. For instance, we know we should get to work on that challenging but important project, but feel sluggish and somewhat fearful of the effort it will require, and fearful that those efforts might fail. Under the sway of these feelings, we look for another (easier) task that we "need" to do—check email, perhaps, or go grocery shopping, or organize our desk—and so we put off the project, rationalizing our procrastination by telling ourselves that once these other tasks are out of the way, we will be able to give our undivided attention to it. Or, to return to the example discussed at the beginning of the chapter, in which a distressed friend calls and asks to get together just as you are about to go hiking, your strong desire to continue with your hiking plan, and aversion to the emotionally difficult task of helping your friend deal with her problem, might lead you to downplay your friend's distress and not give due consideration to what you owe to your friend, instead telling yourself, "I deserve to do something fun. I'm sure she'll be fine without me." On the other hand, if you have integrated your emotional inclinations with reason by cultivating the virtues of justice, generosity, and compassion, your virtuous emotional inclinations can support rather than fetter your ability to deliberate soundly about what to do.

Focusing on unintegrated inclinations as the source of immoral choices and actions leads to another way of formulating the master moral principle: *Act in accordance with unfettered reason.* In other words, when inclinations conflict with reason, follow reason.[33] By reflecting on the various ways in

---

not be consistent with fidelity, and even to those apparently innocuous acts that, if indulged in now, might pose a threat to fidelity in the long run. It is in this way that an appetitive habit can nonetheless shape and direct our moral reasoning" (Knobel, *Aquinas and the Infused Moral Virtues*, 36). Grisez's account seems to place more emphasis on unintegrated emotions as obstacles to sound moral judgment than on virtuous emotional dispositions as aids to moral judgment, but the discussion below about the need to expand the scope of one's emotional motivation in order to be adequately appreciative of and dedicated to the full range of human goods indicates that his account does recognize the positive role of virtuous emotional dispositions in moral judgment.

33.   I use the term "inclinations" here, rather than the term "feelings" or "emotions" (typically used by Grisez), because, as Finnis points out, reason can be fettered not only by disordered subrational inclinations, but also by disordered inclinations of the will (Finnis,

which unintegrated inclinations can lead us to act immorally by fettering practical reason's directiveness, another set of intermediate moral principles, which Grisez calls "modes of responsibility," can be identified.[34] The modes of responsibility are embodied in virtues of character that correspond to them and are formed precisely by integrating the relevant inclinations with reason through choices in line with the modes.

"Reflections and Responses," 579; see also Aquinas, *Summa theologiae* I, q. 63, a. 2). In human beings, such disordered inclinations of the will are likely to be combined with or be the result of disordered subrational inclinations, which is perhaps why both Aquinas and Grisez focus primarily on unintegrated subrational inclinations when discussing the obstacles to morally upright choices and actions. "Now the human will is hindered in two ways from following the rectitude of reason. First, through being drawn by some object of pleasure to something other than what the rectitude of reason requires; and this obstacle is removed by the virtue of temperance. Secondly, through the will being disinclined to follow that which is in accordance with reason, on account of some difficulty that presents itself. In order to remove this obstacle fortitude of the mind is requisite" (Aquinas, *Summa theologiae* II-II, q. 123, a. 1). In *De malo*, Aquinas explains that the will itself can become disordered as a result of prior immoral choices made under the sway of emotion, leading to the formation of a bad habit that can then be the source of further immoral choices made without the direct influence of emotion. He writes that although "an emotion indeed sometimes inclines the will to the transient good"—such as pleasure—thus leading the person to act immorally, in other instances "a habit sometimes inclines the will, when customary behavior has, as it were, turned the inclination to such a good into a habit or natural disposition for the transient good, and then the will of itself is inclined to the good by its own motion apart from any emotion" (*De malo*, q. 3, a. 12). In the *Summa theologiae*, Aquinas writes that though the will by nature inclines toward the good, the will's inclinations may nonetheless be disordered by seeking a particular good (or seeking to avoid a particular evil) in a way that is contrary to the "order of reason" (i.e., to the integral directiveness of practical reason) (I-II, q. 78, a. 3).

34. The term "modes of responsibility" is synonymous with the term "intermediate moral norms," but I reserve its use to this section in order to distinguish this approach to deriving moral norms (focused on the problem of unintegrated inclinations that fetter our reasoning) from the approach taken above (focused on the problems for practical reason created by the multiplicity of intelligible goods and of persons who can be fulfilled by these goods). My account here draws on but does not directly follow Grisez's account in *Christian Moral Principles*, partially for the sake of brevity and partially because I am synthesizing that account with his later attempt at a more systematic derivation of the modes in appendix 1 of Grisez, *Difficult Moral Questions*, which offers a number of new insights and has not received the scholarly attention it merits.

The ways in which inclinations can fetter, obscure, or distort practical reason's integral directiveness can be divided into three main categories:

1. Unintegrated subrational inclinations (emotions) can lead us to act (or fail to act) for no real reason, that is, "just because I feel like it/ don't feel like it." Such acts are rationalized with reference to some illusory good, often the illusory and short-lived inner harmony achieved by gratifying unmet desire.[35] The modes of responsibility that address this first danger are embodied in the cardinal virtues of temperance (which moderates our desire for pleasure in accordance with reason) and fortitude (which moderates our emotional response to dangers and difficulties in accordance with reason).

2. Unintegrated inclinations (both rational and subrational) can lead us to act on the basis of unreasonable preference among persons or goods. The modes of responsibility corresponding to this second set of dangers are embodied in various aspects of the virtues of justice (which disposes our will to give others what is due to them) and practical wisdom.

3. The sentient nature of subrational (emotional) motivations can unreasonably narrow the range of goods that we attend to or are motivated to pursue, thus distorting our judgment. Recognizing and overcoming these limits through various imaginative exercises, and acting accordingly, is essential for the virtue of practical wisdom.

35.   In all of the instances when one acts on emotional motivation, the act can be rationalized with reference to the good of integrity or inner harmony, because acting on one's emotions will relieve the inner emotional tension and create a (short-lived) harmony between reason and emotion by subordinating reason to emotion. (Note that such rationalization is necessary if the act is to be a genuine human act, the object of a free choice, for every act aims at some good.) For example, "the vengeful person chooses, fettering reason by means of one of its own practical principles: that which directs toward the harmony of feelings with one another, and with judgments and choices" (Grisez, Boyle, and Finnis, "Practical Principles," 124). I refer to such rationalization as acting for a defective or illusory instantiation of a good (or acting for no "real" or "genuine" reason), insofar as lasting inner harmony requires governing emotion by reason, not the other way around, and because the inner harmony sought by subordinating reason to emotion is incompatible with moral truth. Further, because character traits—"which organize the various aspects of the complex human personality"—are judged on the basis of whether or not they are in line with moral truth, choices that organize one's personality in a way that subordinates reason to emotion are vicious choices that contribute to a vicious character (129).

In what follows, I will discuss each of these categories in turn, explaining the modes of responsibility that correspond to them and the virtues that embody those modes.

Acting for No Real Reason

Emotions that lead us to act for no real reason—and their corresponding modes of responsibility—can be grouped into four sets.[36] First, negative emotions such as hostility and anger can motivate one to seek to destroy one's own or others' good (rationalizing this with reference to some defective or illusory instantiation of a good). One might, for instance, seek to harm someone in order to "get even" (a defective instantiation of the good of social harmony). Such acts are clearly contrary to the integral directiveness of practical reason, and thus there is a mode of responsibility that forbids accepting or choosing harm to any intelligible human good out of hostility, anger, or other negative emotions.[37] By choosing not to act on such hostile emotions and to channel the energy of those emotions toward morally good objects, one organizes one's personality in a way that is in line with moral truth, and develops virtues such as meekness and patience.

Second, positive emotional desires—such as desires for pleasure and comfort—can lead us to act in ways that are unconnected to any genuine human good, as when one seeks a high from drugs. Such acts, even when they are not directly harmful to some basic good (such as health), are, at the very least, a waste of time and energy that would be better spent in pursuit of genuine goods, and they undermine integrity by subordinating reason to emotion, which may lead to temporary inner harmony, but will set the stage for greater disharmony in the long run.[38] Thus, there is another mode of responsibility forbidding the satisfaction of emotional desire in isolation

36. These unintegrated emotions can lead us to act (or fail to act) for no real reason apart from the intelligible good of achieving inner harmony by relieving one's inner emotional tension. See note 35, above. This clarification should be kept in mind throughout this section every time I speak of emotions leading us to act or fail to act in the absence of a reason (i.e., in isolation from a corresponding intelligible good or evil). See Grisez, *Christian Moral Principles*, 8.H.1.

37. Grisez, *Christian Moral Principles*, 8.G.

38. See Lee and George, *Body–Self Dualism*, chap. 3.

from any intelligible good.[39] Virtues such as temperance and self-control are embodiments of this mode.

Third, just as emotional desires can lead us to act for no real reason, emotional aversions such as repugnance or fear of pain can lead us to refrain or desist from acting for no real reason. For instance, someone might fail to help a person who has been injured out of repugnance at the sight of blood, or shy away from going to the dentist simply because the experience is likely to be unpleasant. The mode of responsibility corresponding to this set of unintegrated emotions forbids acting (or deliberately refraining to act) on the basis of an emotional aversion that does not correspond to a genuine intelligible evil.[40] The virtue that embodies this mode is fortitude/courage.

Fourth, languor, apathy, or sluggishness can lead one to fail to act in pursuit of human goods, despite lacking any genuine reason to refrain from acting. A person might, for example, know that it would be good to go out and get some exercise, or get started on a pending project, or return a phone call from a friend, but fail to do so merely out of sluggishness. The mode of responsibility that corresponds to this danger is this: "One should not be deterred by felt inertia from acting for intelligible goods."[41] This mode is embodied in virtues such as diligence and industriousness.

Unreasonable Preferences among Persons or Goods

The above-mentioned modes of responsibility all correspond to ways in which unintegrated subrational inclinations can motivate action (or inaction) in the absence of a corresponding intelligible good or evil (apart from relieving inner tension).[42] Yet inclinations unintegrated with practical

---

39. Grisez, *Christian Moral Principles*, 8.C.1. Grisez also articulates a related mode of responsibility that forbids "sacrificing reality to appearance" by preferring "the conscious experience of enjoying a good" to a real or deeper participation in that good, such as when "a sick man who could have treatment which would really cure his condition prefers less effective treatment which offers a feeling of quick relief" (8.F.1–3).

40. Grisez, *Christian Moral Principles*, 8.D.1.

41. Grisez, *Christian Moral Principles*, 8.A.1.

42. See notes 35 and 36, above (on acting for no "real" reason).

reason's directiveness can also lead us to act immorally in cases that do involve intelligible goods (or evils).

One such case is when our inclinations lead us to unreasonably prefer our own good and the good of those near and dear to us to the good of others. Some degree of preference for ourselves and those close to us is reasonable (as explained when discussing the Golden Rule), but these inclinations, if not integrated with reason, will lead us to act unfairly. Grisez's articulation of this mode of responsibility is this: "One should not, in response to different feelings toward different persons, willingly proceed with a preference for anyone unless the preference is required by intelligible goods themselves."[43] This formulation has the advantage of making it easy to see how the mode flows from the principles of practical reason in their integral directiveness. However, a more common formulation of this mode is the Golden Rule, which has the advantage of suggesting a concrete method for following the mode by imaginatively putting oneself in another's shoes. Further, this exercise of imaginatively identifying oneself with another is a way of educating one's inclinations, extending one's sphere of concern so that, even at the emotional level, one becomes more inclined to act fairly. Thus Grisez suggests that "regularly using the Golden Rule in moral judgments" can help one to "grow in the virtue of justice."[44]

Just as unintegrated inclinations can lead to unreasonable preferences among persons, they can also lead to unreasonable preferences among goods, subordinating one good to another by deliberately harming one instance of a good in order to achieve another. Pharmaceutical researchers might, for instance, seek to obtain knowledge by exposing people to risky drugs without fully informed consent. The mode of responsibility that forbids acting on such desires is this: "One should not be moved by a stronger desire for one instance of an intelligible good to act for it by choosing to destroy, damage or impede some other instance of an intelligible good."[45] Grisez calls the virtue corresponding to this mode "reverence"—which could

---

43. Grisez, *Christian Moral Principles*, 8.E.1. Grisez's emphasis here is primarily on how subrational inclinations lead one to act unfairly, but I believe that the word "feelings" here should be used to include inclinations of the will. See note 33, above.

44. Grisez, *Difficult Moral Questions*, A.1.

45. Grisez, *Christian Moral Principles*, 8.H.1.

be considered part of the cardinal virtue of practical wisdom—and the opposed vice "craftiness" or "amoral expediency."[46]

Although Grisez's analysis of the dangers presented by unintegrated inclinations that can lead to unreasonable preferences among goods focuses only on emotions, it is worth noting that inclinations of the will can also lead to such unreasonable preferences, as when pride or envy leads one to give priority to a project or goal merely because it is one's own.

Practical Wisdom and Emotional Motivation

Attentiveness to the limits of emotional motivation and the danger of unintegrated inclinations can provide additional practical insights regarding growth in practical wisdom. The dangers of unintegrated inclinations imply the need to seek counsel from practically wise advisers and otherwise make ourselves accountable to others in order to avoid the common temptations to self-deception and rationalization.[47] In addition, although practical wisdom is an intellectual virtue, the limitations of our emotional motivations (because of their sentient nature) can impede our judgment by leading us to be insufficiently attentive to certain goods or persons that might be affected by our actions. And even when we are aware of all the goods at stake, if that awareness lacks emotional resonance, we may lack the necessary emotional motivation to act accordingly. Thus, identifying the natural limits of our emotional motivations and considering how to transcend those limits is crucial for the development of practical wisdom. Note that in speaking of the "natural" limits of emotional motivation, I use the term "natural" to refer to the first-order, animal aspect of human nature, to which emotional motivation belongs.

Grisez identifies these natural limits by considering the ways in which emotional motivation, because it "pertains to sentient nature," is not "naturally adequate to motivate us to act for intelligible goods and to avoid intelligible bads."[48] He argues that natural emotional motivation is inadequate in

46. Grisez, *Christian Moral Principles*, 8.H.4. Traditionally, virtues have been categorized according to the anthropological (first-order) criterion of which faculties they perfect, but Grisez categorizes the virtues based on their correspondence to different moral norms, a third-order criterion with more direct practical relevance.

47. Germain Grisez, *Living a Christian Life*, 5.A.1. MacIntyre, *Dependent Rational Animals*, 96, also emphasizes this point.

48. Grisez, *Difficult Moral Questions*, A.1.

four ways. The first of these inadequacies—the lack of emotional concern for the good of others to whom we have no attachment—was already discussed, and application of the Golden Rule was suggested as a way to expand one's sphere of emotional concern, bringing it into line with the requirements of practical reason. Second, natural emotional motivation is inclined toward sensible goods (or the sensible aspect of goods), but is inadequate with respect to the realization of goods that transcend the sensible realm. Third, natural emotional motivation is limited to imaginable goals based on prior experience, and is thus inadequate given the need for creativity in order to promote the good and overcome evil. Fourth, natural emotional motivation is limited to transient goods, but the human good transcends time.[49]

Just as applying the Golden Rule by imaginatively putting oneself in another's place was suggested as a way to overcome the first inadequacy of our natural emotional motivations, other imaginative exercises can be used to help overcome the other three inadequacies. Expanding our emotional motivation to transcend the sensible is necessary if we are to adequately appreciate "intellectual, moral and cultural goods whose enjoyment presupposes various sorts of developed abilities—such as knowledge, moral virtue, and excellence in work and play." This requires expanding our feelings "to respond to goods whose enjoyment presupposes developed abilities one lacks."[50] For instance, a person who knows nothing about the rules of baseball is unlikely to enjoy watching a game or appreciate the excellence of a star pitcher. To expand our emotional motivations and be able to respond adequately to the full range of human goods, we need to look to exemplars who do have these abilities and appropriate emotional motivation, so as "to share, at least imaginatively, in their excellent acts," and "to learn to feel as they do."[51]

Overcoming the third natural limit on emotional motivation—which "inclines people to persist in pursuing familiar goals in familiar ways and to be strongly attached to the ways and means, the projects and institutions that have served in fulfilling their commitments," even when they have ceased to serve their purpose, or when new means, institutions, or projects would be more effective—requires "an imaginative exercise that will enable us to put into a larger but still concrete context the goals—and, indeed, all

---

49. Grisez, *Difficult Moral Questions*, A.1.
50. Grisez, *Difficult Moral Questions*, A.1.
51. Grisez, *Difficult Moral Questions*, A.1.

the imaginable aspects — of everything good we have done, are doing, and might yet do."[52] For nonbelievers, one way to do this is to imagine one's life from the perspective of one's deathbed or to consider how one will be judged by future generations. For Christians and others with similar beliefs regarding life after death, Grisez suggests meditating on how "their lives in this world prepare material for the heavenly kingdom," which will include "all the good fruits of their human nature and effort . . ., unmarred by evil and completed, in the fullness of the kingdom."[53]

A similar imaginative exercise can help us to overcome the fourth natural limit on emotional motivation, its focus on transient, temporal goods. Overcoming this limitation is important particularly when fidelity to moral requirements demands considerable sacrifice; motivation to act morally in such circumstances will falter unless one "considers intelligible goods lasting and solidly real." To bolster our motivation in such circumstances, it is necessary to engage in "an imaginative exercise that sets those things apart and lifts them out of the flow of time," and, once again, consideration of the afterlife is perhaps the most powerful way to do this.[54]

Growth in the virtue of practical wisdom therefore requires frequent engagement in these imaginative exercises that expand our emotional motivations beyond the limits of our animal nature (thus educating our emotions and integrating them more fully with reason), and also engagement in reflective analysis using these exercises (along with consideration of all of the modes of responsibility) when deliberating about how to act, in order to uncover unintegrated or unreasonably limited emotional motivations that might be distorting our judgment. This sort of reflective analysis may lead one to recognize that some of the options one is considering are not fully reasonable, not fully responsive to the integral directiveness of practical reason, but rather based on unintegrated or unreasonably limited emotional motivation that fetters one's reasoning.[55] Often, however, such a reflective analysis may nonetheless still

52. Grisez, *Difficult Moral Questions*, A.1.

53. Grisez, *Difficult Moral Questions*, A.1.

54. Grisez, *Difficult Moral Questions*, A.1. See also the discussion on God and moral motivation in my chapter 5.

55. For concrete examples of this, see the cases discussed by Grisez, *Living a Christian Life*, 5.G.3–5.

leave one with two or more morally acceptable options from which to choose. For the morally upright person who has an overarching commitment to living in harmony with God by living in accordance with all of the guidance God provides, making such a choice will be understood as a matter of prayerfully discerning which of these good deeds God is calling one to perform.[56]

It should be clear from the foregoing discussion that new natural law theory recognizes the importance of virtue for the moral life. New natural law theory not only articulates the connection between virtues and moral principles, but also offers a systematic consideration of how various categories of inclination can lead us to act immorally—and of the need for corresponding moral virtues to integrate inclinations with reason, thus facilitating morally sound judgment and morally upright action. By showing how unintegrated inclinations and the inadequacy of our untrained emotional motivations are the primary obstacles preventing us from recognizing and doing what is morally right, Grisez's account explains why cultivating virtue is a moral imperative. Grisez offers a systematic account of the ways in which unintegrated emotions are inadequate for the appreciation and pursuit of intelligible goods, and also presents concrete methods for overcoming this inadequacy by engaging in the sort of reflective analysis I've described above. These methods help us to overcome the fettering of reason by unintegrated emotion, and educate our emotions so that they assist rather than hinder our ability to choose and act in accordance with practical reason's integral directiveness. Our ability to do this will also depend on the counsel of others whose judgment is trustworthy, and on being part of a community of such others who can provide us with moral exemplars, help us overcome our blind spots, and hold us accountable. The lasting effect of such choices, made in accordance with unfettered reason, will be the development of a morally virtuous character, which will in turn enable us to more easily judge what is right, do it, and take delight in the good at all levels of our being.

---

56.   Grisez, *Living a Christian Life*, 5.J. Discernment involves returning to emotions, "this time seeking to determine how well possibilities otherwise judged good comport with the rest of one's individual personality" (5.J.1). It is important to note here that one should not rely on emotions to determine whether an option is morally acceptable. Rather, such discernment should only be used to choose among options that one has already judged to be morally acceptable on the basis of rational reflection.

THREE

The Social Dimension
of Human Flourishing

Around the year 1800, a boy about twelve years old was found and captured in the forest of southern France. The boy, now known as Victor of Aveyron, is thought to have spent most of his childhood in the wild, isolated from society. Concerned only with food, sleep, and survival, Victor initially behaved more like a wild animal than a human being. He was eventually taken in by a young doctor named Jean Itard, who spent years attempting to educate Victor and teach him to speak, to no avail.[1] Victor's story, like that of other tragic accounts of children raised without human social interactions, is a vivid illustration of the fact that human beings cannot flourish apart from human society.[2] We come into the world utterly vulnerable and dependent on the care of others, not only for physical survival but also (and perhaps more crucially) for our psychological, moral, and intellectual development. Indeed, the few

---

1. Yousef, "Savage or Solitary?" See also François Truffaut, dir., *The Wild Child* (1970).
2. Weston, "Wild Child." See also Perry and Szalavitz, *The Boy Who Was Raised as a Dog.*

accounts we have of human beings such as Victor who grew up in isolation from society indicate that our distinctively human rational capacities can only develop to maturity within a community of other human beings. Further, some forms of human community—friendship, marriage, and family—are not merely instrumentally important, but are basic human goods, constitutive elements of our flourishing.

But what is community? What are the different types of community, and what role does each play in our flourishing? How does recognizing the importance of community for human flourishing help us to specify our obligations toward others—our obligations of justice? These are the questions I will explore in this chapter. In doing so, I will divide communities into three broad types, each necessary for human flourishing in its own way—(1) friendship (broadly understood), (2) marriage and family, and (3) political community. However, a detailed discussion of political community (which itself can be understood as embodying a diffuse form of friendship called "civic friendship") will be reserved for chapter 4. This chapter, then, focuses on the subpolitical communities that compose the broader political community. Apart from offering an opportunity to consider more fully the social dimension of human flourishing and in particular the nature of the basic goods of friendship and marriage/family, this chapter will also set the stage for a proper understanding of political community as a community composed not of atomistic individuals but rather of prepolitical communities with their own proper sphere of authority and competence, which the political community has an obligation to respect. This will be crucial for understanding the *subsidiary* nature of the political community as a community that exists to assist the subpolitical communities that compose it, without obliterating them or usurping their proper sphere of competence.

THE NATURE OF COMMUNITY

Community is a type of interpersonal *unity*. But in what way are community members united?[3] It may be helpful here to return to the concept of the

---

3. The account I provide here is highly indebted to the analysis of community in Finnis, *Natural Law and Natural Rights*, chap. 6.

four orders I explained in chapter 1: (1) the natural order (which reason knows but does not establish), (2) the logical order (which reason introduces into its own operations), (3) the moral/existential order (which reason introduces into the will), and (4) the technical order (which reason introduces into external things). Like truth, "unity" is an analogical term with a slightly different meaning in each of the orders. For example, the paradigmatic form of unity in the natural order is the unity of a substance, such as the unity of the various parts of my body to form a single organism.[4] In the logical order, various propositions can be related to each other in a certain way to form a unified argument. In the technical order, various materials can be joined together and arranged to serve a particular purpose, as when pieces of wood are joined together to make a table. The unity of a community of persons does involve or presuppose some unity in these orders: for example, the first-order genetic unity of family members or, more diffusely, of the whole human race; the second-order unity of speaking, listening, and understanding that is involved in communication; the fourth-order unity of common language and customs. However, a community is primarily a third-order reality that consists in a unity of wills through common action for a common good, a unity that can vary in breadth and depth depending on the nature of the community.

Because community requires common action for a common good, the existence of communities presupposes the existence of genuine common goods. What makes a good *common* in the most robust sense is that many people can participate in it, and that this participation is noncompetitive, meaning that the good can be shared without being diminished. For example, Sam and Sally can work together on an experiment aimed at acquiring a better understanding of biology. The knowledge they obtain benefits each of them, and does so noncompetitively, for Sam's understanding of the subject matter does not take away from Sally's; on the contrary, it might actually help to contribute to Sally's understanding, and vice versa. Cooperating in the pursuit of knowledge — a genuinely common good — is therefore different from, say, cooperating in the pursuit of money, for the money that Sam gets from the venture is money that Sally does not get, and vice versa. The foundation for the existence of common goods — and thus for

4. See Moschella, "Integrated but Not Whole?"

the possibility of community—is that, as I argued in chapter 1, there is a set of basic human goods that are constitutive aspects of the flourishing of all human beings. Each of these goods can be shared without being diminished. Practical reason directs us to pursue basic goods not just for ourselves but for all who can benefit from them and potentially cooperate with us in pursuit of them (i.e., all human beings). Further, friendship, which is constituted in part by willing another's good, is itself a basic good. Anytime we pursue the good of another, therefore, we are also benefiting ourselves at least with respect to the basic good of friendship. The account of basic goods offered in chapter 1 therefore provides a foundation for the possibility of genuine community.

Note that when we are talking about community, we are talking, broadly speaking, about the basic human good of friendship. Not every form of community, however, is a friendship in the full-fledged sense. In his discussion of friendship, Aristotle divides friendships into what he calls "friendships of utility," "friendships of pleasure" and "friendships of virtue," presenting friendship of virtue as the fullest form of friendship.[5] Building on Aristotle's discussion, Finnis argues for dividing friendships into business friendships, play friendships, and friendships in the unqualified sense.[6]

To illustrate this division, consider the following examples:

1. Gertrude, Gus, and Gary are joint owners of a pizzeria, which they manage and run themselves, dividing up the various tasks required. Gertrude is in charge of accounting, advertising, building management, purchasing supplies, and employee relations. Gus and Gary work alternate shifts making the pizzas and managing the day-to-day operations of the pizzeria. Gertrude, Gus, and Gary have united their wills toward the common good of running a profitable pizzeria, which in turn enables them to sustain themselves and their families, and they have coordinated their activities for the sake of that common good. This form of community is an example of what we might call a business community.

5. Aristotle, *Nicomachean Ethics*, bk. 8.
6. Finnis, *Natural Law and Natural Rights*, 6.3–4.

2. Molly and Megan meet every Saturday morning to play tennis. They unite their wills and coordinate their schedules and activities in view of the common good of playing tennis. As distinct from the business community formed by Gertrude, Gus, and Gary, the play community formed by Molly and Megan is one in which the common activity—playing tennis together—is itself the common good that unites them, rather than being merely instrumental to a common good (like earning a profit) that is extrinsic to the common activity.

3. Andy and Arnold are close friends. They do a variety of things together: meet to talk about life and common interests over a beer or a shared meal, go running together, and offer each other advice and support when needed. Each cares about the other's well-being, seeking in a variety of ways to foster it, and each knows that this is the case. The point of Andy and Arnold's coordination and shared activity, by contrast with the previous two scenarios, is their relationship itself, and the overall flourishing of both parties. And though all three of the communities discussed can be considered forms of friendship, Andy and Arnold's relationship is a friendship (and a community) in the fullest and most robust sense, for their union of wills is both broader (extending to the overall flourishing of both parties) and deeper (sought for its own sake, not merely for instrumental purposes) than in the other two examples.

In all three of these cases—which are oversimplified for the sake of illustrating certain distinctions, and do not exhaust the options for human community—we find that community consists in two or more people uniting their wills in pursuit of some common good, and coordinating their activity for the sake of that good. Thus, the two key elements of community (and friendship) are *common action* toward a *common good*, freely chosen as such. Human beings are capable of genuine community in a way that nonhuman animals are not. Wolves may hunt in packs and bees may all contribute to the maintenance of the hive, but these behaviors are (as far as we know) purely instinctive; wolves and bees cannot choose to behave other than they do, for they cannot choose at all. Strictly speaking, therefore, community, understood primarily as a unity of wills, is only possible for human beings.

As the three examples of friendship illustrate, this unity of wills can vary in breadth and depth. The unity of wills among Gertrude, Gus, and Gary (presuming it does not extend beyond what was described above) is quite narrow and shallow. Its object is a very limited common good—making a profit by selling pizza—and it is common only in the thin sense that it is a coinciding of private objectives (the desire of each to earn money), which they can only achieve through cooperation. Similarly, their activity is common only in the thin sense that it is coordinated, and the common activity is not sought for its own sake (as it would be if they were seeking to excel at the craft of pizza-making), but merely for instrumental and extrinsic purposes. This, then, is an extremely thin form of community, involving a narrow and shallow unity of wills, aimed at the merely instrumental purpose of earning money, and not essentially requiring any willing of the good of the other parties for their own sake. Note that here I am constructing an extreme example to illustrate a concept, not claiming that all or even most business relationships are like this or should be like this—indeed, I will argue that the opposite is true.

The play community formed by Molly and Megan is likewise quite narrow—focused specifically on the common good of playing tennis—but involves a somewhat deeper unity than that of the previous friendship, insofar as the good they seek (a well-played game of tennis) is genuinely common to both rather than involving a mere coincidence of private objectives. This good is also intrinsically valuable—an instantiation of the basic human good of performative excellence—rather than merely instrumental. Thus, their common action—playing tennis—is not merely instrumental, but is itself the good that they are jointly seeking. However, like the business community, this form of community does not require a direct concern of the parties for each other's overall well-being, but only a much more limited and instrumental concern for the other's well-being insofar as it affects her capacity to play the game.

Although the first two sets of relationships are both forms of community that can be called friendships in a broad sense, the relationship between Andy and Arnold is a friendship in the fullest, paradigmatic sense of the term. It is also the broadest and deepest of the three types of communities being discussed. For in this case the common good is the friendship itself, and the friends' common activities are sought as contributing to and constitutive of the friendship. Further, the common good of the friendship is essentially constituted by the friends' mutual willing of each other's all-around flourishing. Thus, in this paradigmatic case of friendship, the good of one's friend becomes one's own good, and vice versa.[7]

The three types of community discussed here — business community, play community and friendship in the full sense — are presented as ideal types for the sake of illustrating how communities can vary in breadth and depth with respect to the common activity and common good that unify their members. In real life, however, the categories blur. Indeed, although there is nothing inherently wrong with the thinner forms of community discussed in the first two cases, such forms of community would be morally suspect if they did not at least involve the basic level of willing the overall flourishing of the others required by the integral directiveness of practical reasons — directing us toward the fulfillment of all human beings with respect to all of the basic goods. MacIntyre notes — using the example of a purely business relationship one has with the local butcher — that if the butcher suffers a heart attack while you are in the shop, you cannot just walk out of the shop indifferent to his fate, but at the very least should call an ambulance on his behalf, attempt to inform his family, and follow up afterward to see how he is doing.[8]

Further, in real life the communities we call businesses can, and arguably should (to the extent feasible), contribute more deeply to the members' flourishing in a variety of ways. For instance, rather than aiming merely at earning a profit — a purely instrumental and not truly common end — Gertrude and company could aim to make excellent pizza and provide a service to the broader community (and also to earn a profit thereby). This would make the good at which they aim — performative excellence — intrinsically and not just instrumentally valuable, and also truly common

---

7. Recognizing friendship as a basic human good shows the fundamental flaw in thinking of morality as in competition with "rational self-interest," or in terms of altruism versus egoism; see, e.g., Bloomfield, ed., *Morality and Self-Interest*. For insofar as others are friends or potential friends, in acting for them, I am also acting for my own good (Finnis, *Natural Law and Natural Rights*, 134, 141–43).

8. He notes that, even as a "purely" economic or business relationship, the relationship will surely be damaged if one fails to respond to the butcher's medical emergency with due concern for his well-being (MacIntyre, *Dependent Rational Animals*, 117).

(for they will excel as a team) rather than a mere coinciding of private objectives. It would also connect the common good of their business community to the common good of the larger political society, both instrumentally (by providing a service to other members of the community) and intrinsically (for, as I argue in chapter 4, the common good of political society is constituted in part by the flourishing of the community's members).[9] Their community would thus be deeper and more enriching for all of the members.

In addition, Gertrude and company might broaden and deepen their community by valuing, for their own sake, the interpersonal interactions that their joint enterprise makes possible, and caring about the overall well-being of the others. They may not develop deep or intimate friendships with one another, but they can foster an atmosphere of friendly camaraderie, asking about each other's families, chatting about hobbies or matters of common interest, offering a sympathetic ear or a word of advice when one of them is going through a difficult time, and so on.

It is obvious that this broader and richer form of business community contributes much more to the members' flourishing than the emaciated version described at the outset. Given that most adult human beings spend a significant portion of their waking hours working — typically together with others in some form of cooperative enterprise, be it a grocery store, law firm, bank, factory, farm, hospital, school, construction company — organizing such enterprises in a way that (to the extent possible) facilitates and instantiates such broader and richer forms of community seems to be a requirement of practical reasonableness.

THE ROLE OF COMMUNITY IN
HUMAN FLOURISHING: THE LIFE OF SUSIE

One way to consider the role that various types of community play in human flourishing is to think about the needs of a human being through-

9. Such a connection is, I will argue in chapter 4, a requirement of practical reason implied by the master moral principle, which (in requiring us to act in ways compatible with a will toward integral human fulfillment), implicitly directs us to favor and foster the common good of our communities.

out the entire lifespan. All too often philosophers tend to think only or primarily about mature, healthy adults when they consider what is required for human flourishing. Yet we are temporal beings whose development into mature and healthy adults is highly precarious and dependent on being provided with proper care by others during the early years of our lives. Even throughout adulthood, and especially as we approach the end of our life's journey, we are likely to go through periods of illness, injury, or other situations of significant dependence on others. Our dependence on others is not only or even primarily physical, however, as the stories of children such as Victor of Aveyron suggest. Rather, our moral and intellectual development are dependent upon the education we receive and the communities we belong to, especially during childhood, but also (in a less intense way) throughout our lives. So let us take a journey through the hypothetical life of Susie, considering as we do what sorts of communities Susie will need in order to flourish.

The Family

Susie begins to exist when her father's sperm fuses with her mother's egg, commencing an entirely new and unique trajectory of development that is Susie's biological life.[10] Although at this stage Susie's presence is still unknown and she has not yet been given a name, Susie is, on the biological level, already united in a very particular way to the two people who are (through their egg and sperm and their act of sexual intercourse) the biological cause of her existence and identity. This link is a permanent one, for though many aspects of Susie's personal identity may shift over time (her size, physical appearance, self-understanding, goals, beliefs, character, profession, religion, and so on), what fundamentally makes Susie who she is, and makes her remain essentially the same person

10. This is the case for all human beings except for identical twins, who result from the division of an early embryo (a form of asexual reproduction possible at only the earliest stages of human life). For a detailed biological and philosophical defense of the claim that the life of a human being begins at sperm–egg fusion, see Condic and Condic, *Human Embryos, Human Beings*; for a briefer defense of this claim, see Lee and Moschella, "Embryology and Science Denial."

despite the many changes she undergoes, is her biological identity as a particular human organism.[11]

Susie is, of course, not merely a particular kind of animal organism, but a *rational* animal organism whose rational capacities—capacities for conceptual thought and free choice—will, unless impeded by illness, untimely death, or lack of human social interaction, gradually manifest themselves over time. These rational capacities will begin to manifest themselves in early childhood and come to full maturity in adulthood. I will say more in a moment about what sort of community Susie needs to be a part of in order to facilitate this development of her rational capacities, but first I would like to highlight a need that stems from Susie's identity as a particular rational animal, as someone whose identity has a biological foundation, but who can later come to understand herself and her identity at a conceptual and ethical level. That need is the need to, as it were, bring to completion her biological relationship with her parents by extending it into a uniquely human and therefore rational and free relationship—a community in the fullest sense of the term. To state this as a "need" might sound too strong, for certainly there are many people who, for a variety of reasons, never know or develop a full-fledged interpersonal relationship with their biological parents, and who nonetheless lead flourishing lives. Yet when I say that Susie has a "need" to be in full-fledged community with her biological parents, what I mean is that this is an objective, important, and in some respects irreplaceable good for Susie, and that its lack therefore constitutes an objective harm that detracts (though not insurmountably) from her ability to flourish.

What, precisely, does this harm consist in? Or, to put the question positively, what are the unique benefits to Susie of being in full-fledged community with her biological parents? We can divide these benefits into two categories, but in practice the two are interconnected: identity-formation benefits and relational benefits. As Susie matures, she will need to develop

11. For a detailed explication and defense of this view of personal identity against rival views that see identity as rooted primarily in psychology, and thus deny that the body (except perhaps the higher brain) is essential and intrinsic to personal identity, see Lee and George, *Body-Self Dualism*. Note that this view does not reduce identity to biological identity, for it is fully compatible with the claim that there are aspects of the human person, i.e., the capacities for conceptual thought and free choice—that transcend our biological identity.

an integrated understanding of her overall personal identity, which includes an understanding of her identity at the bodily level, and of how this fits in with her identity at the social and ethical level. Developing such a coherent self-understanding is part of the basic human good of integrity, which we discussed in chapter 1. Being in full-fledged community with her biological parents — ideally, being raised jointly by them in an intact biological family — provides a unique set of benefits in this respect. We learn much about our bodily identity and about how that bodily identity might be integrated into an overall personal identity through the example of our biological parents (and, more diffusely, the broader kinship network to which we typically have access through our biological parents). For our parents are, jointly, the source of our biological identity, and from them (both individually and in their relationship to each other) we can get a sense of the potentialities and pitfalls of our particular biological constitution, learn how to be at peace with our physical appearance, and be reassured that others with similar "raw materials" have managed to navigate the complex task of personal identity formation.[12]

The experience of many children conceived through assisted reproductive technologies with sperm from anonymous "donors" helps to corroborate this claim about the important identity-formation benefits of being raised jointly by one's biological parents, and about the difficulties children face when one or both biological parents are absent. (I put "donors" in quotation marks because most are paid for their "donation.") A 2010 study of donor-conceived young adults found that many felt robbed of important insights into their identity. For instance, Olivia Pratten, a Canadian journalist and donor-conceived person, is quoted by the study's authors: "I think of myself as a puzzle. The only picture I have ever known is half complete." Similar sentiments are expressed by Lindsay Greenawalt from Ohio: "I feel my right to know who I am and where I come from has been taken away from me." The study indicated that such feelings were common among donor-conceived persons, with two-thirds of those surveyed agreeing with the statement, "My sperm donor is half of who I am."[13] Likewise, another study published in 2011 found that 82 percent of those who knew they were donor-conceived hoped to "be in

---

12. Velleman, "Persons in Prospect," 258.
13. Marquardt, Glenn, and Clark, *My Daddy's Name Is Donor*, 21.

contact some day with their donor."[14] Such findings are not surprising given similar research about the special identity-formation challenges faced by adopted children (discussed later in this section).

The identity-formation benefits of being raised by one's biological parents can at least partially be replaced by enabling children to have some level of contact with the biological parent(s) who are not raising them, as is often made possible by open adoption arrangements.[15] This is not true, however, for the second set of benefits that our hypothetical child Susie receives from being raised in an intact biological family. I label this second set of benefits *relational benefits*, the most important of which is being loved (and knowing herself to be loved) by her biological parents. Because Susie's biological parents are the biological cause of her existence and identity, she is permanently and intimately linked to them, and their love (or its absence) reasonably matters to Susie in a way that the love of a stranger or casual acquaintance does not. We reasonably expect greater love (understood not primarily as a feeling but as a commitment to another's well-being) from those with whom we have an intimate relationship than from strangers. Common experience testifies to this: the degree of love that I expect from my husband is much higher than the degree of love I expect from a stranger, and a relatively minor slight from my husband may hurt me more than outright rudeness from a stranger.

Let me explain this point about relational benefits further by returning to the consideration of what sort of community would ideally facilitate Susie's flourishing. Once Susie is old enough to get a sense (even vaguely) of how people come into being, she will begin to wonder about her biological origins. If she is being raised by her biological parents in an intact biological family, and feels secure in her parents' love for her (and each other), her biological origin story will be continuous and harmonious with her current family situation. Yet if (for whatever reason) she is not being raised by (both of) her biological parents, there will be a discontinuity that gives rise to difficult

14. Beeson, Jennings, and Kramer, "Offspring Searching for Their Sperm Donors," 2419.

15. For a discussion of the benefits (and risks) of open adoption for children, see Siegel, "Growing Up in Open Adoption," and Smith et al., "Review of Benefits and Risks for Children in Open Adoption."

questions. Not only will Susie wonder about who her biological parents are, what they are like, what characteristics she shares with them, and so on (aspects of the identity-formation issues I just discussed), but she will also wonder why her biological parents are not raising her. Did they not want her? Was she not good enough? Did they not care about her? Psychologists tell us that it is common for adopted children and others not raised by their biological parents to pose these sorts of questions (often only to themselves), and to suffer from feelings of rejection or abandonment (at least if they are not able to receive satisfactory answers, answers that enable them to understand their biological parents' choice not to raise them as a choice made out of love, for their benefit, rather than as a choice that reflects indifference or rejection).[16] Thus the unique and important relational benefit that Susie receives by being in full-fledged community with her biological parents—by being raised by them in an intact biological family—is (if they are good parents) a secure and unproblematic knowledge of being loved by those who brought her into being, and of having a unity between her biological relationships and her social/family relationships. Given that our sense of identity has a strong relational component—with family relationships typically playing an especially significant role—this latter relationship benefit is also an important benefit facilitating the development of a coherent sense of identity.[17]

16. Psychologist James Garbarino states: "Children who are rejected by one or both of their parents are likely to attribute the rejection to something lacking in themselves. 'What's wrong with me that my parents don't want me?' is their inevitable, often silent question. Adults who were adopted as young children often cannot even ask this question without the aid of counseling" (Garbarino, *Lost Boys*, 44); see also Child Welfare Information Gateway, *The Impact of Adoption*. Perhaps one of the benefits of open adoption is that in some cases it may enable adopted children to learn that their biological parents did and do love them, and that their adoption plan was an expression of that love in the midst of nonideal circumstances.

17. MacIntyre says (approvingly summarizing the position of Edith Stein): "My self-knowledge derives in part from others and from what they know of me from their external standpoints. And the knowledge of myself that I arrive at, whether through disciplined attention to my own mental acts, the knowledge of the 'I' as 'I,' or through what I learn about myself from others to whom I am other, the knowledge of the 'I' as 'other,' is the knowledge of a self bodily situated within a nexus of social and natural relationships" (MacIntyre, *Edith Stein*, 136). Similarly, in *Dependent Rational Animals*, MacIntyre argues

Recognizing these advantages of being raised within an intact biological family—and the corresponding challenges of being raised apart from one or both biological parents—in no way denigrates the practice of adoption, which in some circumstances (when the biological parents are unable to raise their child themselves) is the best way to love and provide for a child's needs in the midst of a nonideal situation. Indeed, my husband and I are in the process of adopting a child, and all of the preadoption education we have received acknowledges these challenges by counseling adoptive parents to be open with their children about their origins and to support children as they navigate the challenges of their dual identity and process feelings of grief, rejection, or abandonment that may arise.[18] Adoptee Elena Hall, who is now a social worker and has published a collection of memoirs from adoptees, reflects on the unanswered questions and identity challenges that adoptees face: "Adoptees have gray areas in their lives that shouldn't be gray, because in a perfect world a family unit would be strong and stay together."[19]

Given these important identity-formation and relational benefits, therefore, the ideal scenario for Susie's flourishing is to be raised jointly by her biological parents within an intact family unit.[20] And this is most likely to happen if, when Susie is conceived, her parents are already committed to an

---

that confirmation of our presumed continuity of identity by the objective, criteria-based judgments of others is key for our confidence in the reliability of our self-ascriptions. He concludes that "I can be said truly to know who and what I am, only because there are others who can be said truly to know who and what I am" (95).

18. See, e.g., Eldrige, *Twenty Things*; Verrier, *The Primal Wound*.

19. Hall, *Through Adopted Eyes*, 2.

20. This point is supported by extensive social science research. For example, a Child Trends Research Brief concludes the following: "Research clearly demonstrates that family structure matters for children, and the family structure that helps children the most is a family headed by two biological parents in a low-conflict marriage. Children in single-parent families, children born to unmarried mothers, and children in stepfamilies or cohabiting relationships face higher risks of poor outcomes." The brief emphasizes that "it is not simply the presence of two parents, . . . but the presence of two biological parents that seems to support children's development" (Moore et al., "Marriage from a Child's Perspective," 1–2, 6). The brief does indicate, however, that the research it summarizes does not include any data on same-sex parents or adoptive parents. Nonetheless, more recent research including such data appears to corroborate these findings; see, e.g., Sullins, "Emotional Problems among Children," and Sullins, "The Case for Mom and Dad." It is

exclusive, lifelong union of the sort that is inherently oriented toward procreation and family life—if her parents are already married.[21] For if they are not, Susie is likely to end up in a situation in which one of her biological parents (usually the father) is largely absent from her life, or a situation in which she must spend her childhood going back and forth between households, with all of the complexities, confusion, and strife that this often entails.[22] Susie's parents might, of course, end up marrying after she is conceived, but if the marriage is precipitated largely by the pregnancy, rather than being the result of serious mutual discernment regarding the suitability of the other person as a spouse, this has its own dangers for Susie, namely, the danger that her parents are unsuited to each other and will end up separated or divorced, or in a high-conflict relationship, none of which is an ideal scenario for Susie. This is

---

worth emphasizing that none of these studies denies that nonbiological parents (same-sex or opposite-sex) can be loving and committed parents; nor do they deny that in some circumstances being raised by such parents might be the best option for a child. Rather, this research simply claims to show the special benefit to children of conjoined biological parenthood, and thus of marriage as I have defined it—a point I defend on philosophical grounds both here and elsewhere; see, e.g., Moschella, *To Whom Do Children Belong?*

21. Note that I do not mean legal marriage here, but rather marriage in the moral sense, which entails a comprehensive commitment—a permanent commitment that encompasses a broad sharing of the whole of life of the sort that would be suitable for raising children together, and that is exclusive with respect to sexual intercourse, which is the act that seals and actualizes the marriage as a uniquely comprehensive union (the only sort of union that unites two people on all dimensions of their being, mind, heart, *and* body). For it is only through sexual intercourse that two human beings can join to form one organic unit, coordinating jointly toward the single biological end of reproduction. Given the existence of unilateral no-fault divorce and other current features of legal marriage, at least in the United States, entering into a legal marriage does not necessarily involve such a commitment.

22. Apart from the loss of a paternal relationship with her biological father, in this scenario Susie is also in a much more economically precarious situation than if raised in a two-parent household. Ron Haskins of the Brookings Institution, for example, cites data showing the disproportionately high poverty rates of children raised by single mothers: "In 2009, the poverty rate for children in married-couple families was 11.0 percent. By contrast, the poverty rate for children in female-headed families was 44.3 percent" (Haskins, "Combating Poverty"). He also cites a Brookings analysis showing that "if we had the marriage rate we had in 1970, the poverty rate would fall by more than 25 percent." See also Kearney, *The Two-Parent Privilege.*

not to say that "shotgun" marriages are always a bad idea; when the parents are sufficiently compatible, one might even argue that they are morally obligated to marry as a matter of justice to the child. My point here is simply that sexual attraction is clearly not sufficient for marital compatibility, and that there is therefore good reason to think that, all else being equal, "shotgun" marriages will tend to be less stable and harmonious than marriages entered into without such external pressure. What all of this means is that the natural law prohibition on premarital and extramarital sexual intercourse flows not only from respect for the basic good of marriage, but also from what we owe, in justice, to the future children whom our sexual acts might bring into being—that we bring them into the world, insofar as it is within our control, within an intact family in which they will receive the stable, united love and care of their married biological parents.[23]

The family, based on marriage as I defined it in chapter 1, is a unique form of human community, different in kind from friendship, and not just different in the degree of unity of wills, which is what differentiated friendship in the fullest sense from business and play communities. What makes the family unique is that the marital community, which is at the foundation of the family, is the only community in which two distinct human beings literally unite at the bodily level, becoming one organic unit in the act of sexual intercourse, which unites the two halves of the human reproductive system to form one complete reproductive system. This unique bodily unity is ethically significant not only because it makes possible the most all-encompassing form of human relationship—a unity that includes all basic dimensions of the person: mind, heart, and body—but also because the spouses unite bodily through an act that is biologically ordered to the procreation of new human beings. And the biological connection between those new human beings and their parents is also uniquely strong, for the parents' actions and biological material are the direct biological cause of the child's existence and identity. The bodies of mother and child work together

---

23. Aquinas's argument for why extramarital sex is a grave moral wrong also proceeds along these lines, focusing on the needs of the child who might be conceived (*Summa theologiae* II-II, q. 154, a. 2). For a more detailed account of the natural law prohibition on nonmarital sex as contrary to the good of marriage, see, e.g., Lee and George, *Conjugal Union*, and Lee and George, *Body-Self Dualism*, chap. 6; Finnis, "Marriage"; and Moschella, "Sexual Ethics, Human Nature."

symbiotically during gestation, and important psychological bonds are formed during this time. These bonds are further strengthened after birth through breastfeeding, in which the bodies of mother and child once again work together in a symbiotic relationship.[24] Then there are the biological connections between siblings, who share a high proportion of their genetic makeup with each other, and are linked to one another through their common progenitors. Conceiving children within the context of marriage is also the scenario in which siblings are most likely to be raised together within the same family, which is another important benefit. The sibling relationship, parent–child relationship, and spousal relationship involve different types of biological connections, but the family as a whole has a biological unity that has special ethical significance in large part because of the needs of children.

It might be objected that Susie can receive all of the same benefits if her biological parents are not married but are cohabiting. If we are thinking primarily about the ideal scenario for children, why should the marriage-based family be normative? Why does marriage matter? It matters because only marriage entails a lifelong and exclusive commitment, and thus only marriage provides the foundation for a secure and stable family life. Cohabiting couples generally do not have the same level of commitment to each other and to the relationship that married couples have. Often, couples who cohabit are not sure if they should get married, and think that cohabiting will help them to figure out whether or not they are a good match.[25] It is therefore not surprising that cohabiting couples—even cohabiting couples with children—break up at higher rates than married couples. Summarizing decades of research, Sara McLanahan and Isabel Sawhill have pointed out that "cohabiting unions are very unstable. . . . About half of couples who are cohabiting at their child's birth will split by the time the child is five. Many of these young parents will go on to form new relationships and to have additional children with new partners. The consequences of this instability for children are not good," negatively affecting "children's cognitive and

24. The benefits of breastfeeding for children are well known, but recent research has also emphasized its benefits for the mother; see, e.g., Moberg, *The Oxytocin Factor*, and Ellison, *The Mommy Brain*.

25. Rhoades, "How Moving In Together Makes It Harder to Know If He's the One."

emotional development in ways that constrain their life chances."[26] Wendy Manning also notes that "children born to cohabiting parents experience nearly three times as many family transitions (entering into or dissolving a marital or cohabiting union) as those born to married parents (1.4 versus 0.5)."[27] This means that if Susie is born to cohabiting parents, she is much more likely to suffer from family instability and to end up being raised by a single parent—with all of the attendant risks to her well-being, including a higher risk of living in poverty, and a higher likelihood of delinquency, violent behavior, mental health problems, poor performance in school, and attempted suicide.[28] The empirical research therefore clearly supports my claims that marriage matters for children's well-being and that, all else being equal, being raised by one's married biological parents gives one the best chances of leading a flourishing life.[29]

The marriage-based family, therefore, is the most basic community that Susie needs (ideally) for her flourishing, especially during her childhood. Good parents will provide Susie not only with what she needs for her physical survival and development, but also with the psychological security that comes with knowing she is unconditionally loved by them, and the moral and intellectual education that she needs to develop her rational capacities.[30] Parents may, of course, provide this education in part by seeking out the help of others in the broader community, enrolling Susie in a suitable school, and so on.

26. McLanahan and Sawhill, "Marriage and Child Wellbeing Revisited"; and Gunnar, "Children's Experience of Family Disruption."

27. Manning, "Cohabitation and Child Well-Being," 54.

28. Haskins, "Combating Poverty"; and Amato, "The Impact of Family Formation," 86.

29. For a helpful summary of this research, see Kearney, *The Two-Parent Privilege*, and Kaczor and Kaczor, *The Seven Big Myths about Marriage*, esp. chap. 4.

30. Drawing on studies carried out by D. W. Winnicott, MacIntyre argues that the first condition necessary for the child to develop these capacities is a sense of security and unqualified trust in the caregiver (earned by the caregiver's loving recognition of the child and responsiveness to the child's needs). A secure environment enables the infant to relax, opening the conditions for creative experimentation with the environment or play. The sense of self that children acquire through playful interaction with their surroundings is a necessary basis for acquiring practical reasoning capacities, because without such a sense of self one would lack the necessary independence for making ethical decisions (MacIntyre, *Dependent Rational Animals*, 91).

Focusing now on what Susie needs for her moral development, the basic task of parents is to enable her to overcome the tyranny of subrational desire in order to be capable of recognizing and acting for intelligible goods, even in the face of conflicting emotions.[31] This will require a variety of things. Susie will, for instance, need to be exposed to examples of the full range of basic human goods, so that she acquires the experiences and inchoate speculative knowledge that can then be the basis for her eventual practical insight into the intrinsic and intelligible choiceworthiness of those goods. Further, Susie will need to learn language by hearing it spoken by her parents and others, for language will be necessary for Susie to eventually have a conceptual grasp of intelligible goods as distinct from what she happens to desire. Language will also be necessary for Susie to learn to give an account of her actions to herself and others, and to understand such accounts when provided by others, thus developing the capacity to reflect on and evaluate her own and others' reasons for action.

Susie's parents and other educators will also need to discipline her desires, preparing the ground for the development of full-fledged virtues by channeling her emotional motivations (which are the only motivations that she has until reaching the age of reason) toward objects that are genuinely good, pursued in a morally upright way. Parents will thus make the practical judgments about what Susie should do that Susie herself is not yet capable of making, and appeal to various emotional motivations to get her to behave accordingly. They might, for instance, appeal to Susie's desire to please them ("Do it for mommy"), her desire for a particular reward ("If you eat your broccoli, you can have some ice cream for dessert"), or her fear of punishment ("If you don't pick up your toys, I will put them away for the rest of the day and you won't be able to play with them until tomorrow"). And because small children learn primarily by imitation, it will be crucial for her parents to model morally upright behavior—for their example will have a much greater influence on Susie's moral development than their explicit moral exhortations. All of this will help to educate Susie's desires in line with her genuine good, helping her to develop the habits that—once

31. MacIntyre explains that for us to develop our practical reasoning capacities, we need relationships that foster "the ability to evaluate, modify, or reject our practical judgments," "the ability to imagine realistically alternative possible futures," and "the ability to stand back from our desires" (MacIntyre, *Dependent Rational Animals*, 83).

she is capable of rational motivation and practical judgment—can then slowly mature into full-fledged moral virtues, which will in turn facilitate her growth in practical wisdom, thus facilitating further growth in moral virtue, and so on in a virtuous circle. The deep interconnection between the psychological security that unconditionally loving parents provide, the related desire to please and imitate parents that this love engenders in children, and the crucial role that these desires play in facilitating children's moral education reinforces the deeply personal nature of this educational task, and the unique, irreplaceable role of parents as primary educators.[32]

Intermediate Associations

The family is crucial for Susie's flourishing at all levels, particularly for the development of her rational capacities, including her capacity for practical reasoning and morally upright choice and action. Yet the family is not self-sufficient to meet all of Susie's needs.[33] The family is, of course, almost certainly dependent at least to some extent on a larger economy to meet its needs, and on the larger political community for the basic peace, order, and security without which our flourishing is dramatically imperiled, and for a variety of goods and services (utilities, roads, etc.). (I will leave further discussion of political community to chapter 4, focusing here on intermediate associations—associations between the family, which is the basic unit of society, and the political community as a whole—sometimes also called the realm of "civil society.") The family is also, on its own, unable to expose Susie to the full range of human goods. Perhaps, for instance, mom and dad have musical talent, but no athletic skill, or are quite knowledgeable about history, but not about the natural sciences, and so on. Susie's parents will likely also find their efforts at moral education frustrated if those efforts are not reinforced by broader social networks (such as the families with whom they regularly inter-

32. For more on the implications of this for understanding the grounds of parental rights in education, see Moschella, *To Whom Do Children Belong?*

33. The importance of a child's broader social environment for her flourishing is supported by research indicating that being raised in a neighborhood with a high percentage of families headed by married parents is a strong predictor of upward social mobility even for children raised by single parents (Chetty et al., "The Opportunity Atlas").

act and/or with whose children Susie becomes friends) and institutions (such as churches and schools).[34] Further, as Susie grows and begins to seriously consider her future vocation in life, her parents will necessarily offer her quite limited models. They of course can only directly model married life, not other paths that do not involve marriage, and can only directly model the careers that they themselves are pursuing. Perhaps, however, Susie's vocation and talents lie elsewhere. And if Susie does decide to marry, she will need a spouse, and that person will have to be someone outside of her family.

There is, therefore, a need for a variety of intermediate institutions that can support the family in its task of facilitating Susie's flourishing and preparing her to discern her vocation and reasonably govern her own life as she reaches adulthood.[35] Susie's parents may, for instance, work together with other parents to organize a school in order to provide their children with a

34. An interesting example of this is the growing awareness of the negative effects of too much "screen time" and social media use on children and adolescents, coupled with the difficulty parents have attempting to address this problem in isolation. For if, say, all of a child's peers communicate with each other solely via social media, the child will be socially isolated without it. Likewise, if schools or sports teams set up communication systems that rely on social media apps, this can sometimes effectively force parents to give their children a smartphone before they think it is appropriate for the child to have one. Thus, it is important to recognize the need for broader community and institutional efforts to support parents in limiting their children's use of these technologies. For instance, I recently learned about a group of parents in my own neighborhood who took a pledge not to give their children smartphones and to limit their family's use of social media, instead fostering a variety of in-person interactions and activities that they believe are more conducive to their children's healthy development and growth in virtue (Myers, "Taking the Postman Pledge"). Similarly, a boarding school in Massachusetts recently tried banning smartphones for all students and faculty in order to foster a restoration of genuine community and remove barriers to learning, with significant positive results (Jargon, "This School Took Away Smartphones"). For more on the dangers of the new "phone-based childhood," and on the need for collective action to solve the problem, see Haidt, *The Anxious Generation*.

35. There is an abundance of recent literature documenting the crucial importance of civil society institutions, and especially religious congregations, for the thriving of individuals, families, and society as a whole. Such institutions, and the strong social networks that they create and sustain, tend both to encourage the formation and maintenance of intact families and to buffer the effects of family breakdown for all involved. See, e.g., Putnam, *Our Kids*; Dunkelman, *The Vanishing Neighbor*; Levin, *The Fractured Republic*, and Levin, *A Time to Build*; Kaplan, *Fragile Neighborhoods*; Murray, *Coming Apart*; Carney, *Alienated America*; Bellah et al., *Habits of the Heart*.

suitable education and opportunities to socialize. The broader political community may also facilitate parents' educational task by setting up schools, but this should always be done in a way that respects parents' primary authority in this sphere.[36] Organizations such as hospitals and medical associations can help to provide care for Susie when she faces more serious illnesses. Religious congregations can help with Susie's religious education, provide opportunities for communal worship and other religious practices, and also facilitate a host of other resources to support families both within and beyond their congregation.[37] For example, in many religious congregations, such as my own local parish, families organize themselves in such a way as to provide mutual support for each other—sharing goods and advice, stepping in to help when one family is dealing with difficult circumstances, organizing meal trains for families after the birth of a child, hosting events that allow adults to socialize while the children play in a safe space, and so on.[38] Athletic, cultural, musical, professional, or artistic groups of

36. See, e.g., Moschella, *To Whom Do Children Belong?*, and Moschella, "Defending the Fundamental Rights of Parents."

37. From a Catholic theological perspective, the Church is not a mere intermediate association, but is one of the three basic societies necessary for human flourishing (along with the family and the political community); see Hittinger, "The Three Necessary Societies." Here, however, I am exploring what can be known from a purely philosophical perspective. And though the architectonic role of the good of religion (discussed in chapter 2) would suggest that communities dedicated to this good have special importance for human flourishing, more than that cannot be concluded on the basis of rational reflection alone. It is noteworthy, however, that there is abundant empirical research supporting the indispensable and special role of religious communities for the flourishing of individuals and society as a whole (see note 38, below).

38. Of course, neighbors could organize such a network independent of a religious congregation, but in practice membership in religious congregations facilitates the development of such networks, which then (as is the case with my own parish network) often extend to include others in the local community who are not part of the congregation. Timothy Carney, for instance, talks about how his own parish community fills these needs for local families, and notes that this is "immensely valuable for promoting family formation and strengthening marriage. The nuclear family isn't meant to be self-contained, and so much of what makes modern family life difficult is the isolation of parents" (Carney, *Alienated America*, 296). Carney recognizes that nonreligious institutions can, in principle, fulfill these functions, but claims that in practice religious congregations are "the fundamental institution of American civil society," and that "in many middle-class or working-class towns, the strongest institutions are built upon churches" (287, 298). Part

various sorts can offer opportunities for Susie to explore and experience a broader range of human goods than her family alone can expose her to, perhaps revealing talents that may contribute to her vocational discernment, or provide ongoing avenues for enrichment and community involvement into adulthood. Businesses and other organizations will be needed to provide a range of goods and services, and also to provide opportunities for employment both for Susie's parents, so that they can support the family, and eventually for Susie herself. Charitable associations will assist the needy and vulnerable in the community, and also provide important opportunities for Susie to learn the virtues of solidarity, mercy, generosity, and justice, and perhaps to awaken in her a desire to pursue a vocational path that directly addresses some of the needs she is thereby exposed to.

Unlike the family, which is an essential human community (itself instantiating a basic human good and serving an irreplaceable function), and which arguably has an ideal form for the reasons mentioned above, there are a potentially infinite variety of types and forms of intermediate associations, for human goods are inherently open-ended, potentially infinite in their instantiations, and capable of being pursued in an inexhaustible variety of ways. This means that it is impossible to fully specify the forms of subpolitical association necessary to ideally facilitate Susie's flourishing.[39] What can be said, however, is that in virtually any developed society, flourishing will require, at minimum, economic, religious, and educational forms of association to supplement and support the family, and that ideally there would be a sufficient variety of intermediate associations to cover the full range of human goods, and meet the full range of basic human needs.

---

of this may be simply a historical accident, but there is also a strong affinity between the religious and moral values these congregations preach and the practical social functions that they fulfill (298). Robert Putnam's research also shows the crucial importance of religious congregations for overcoming individualism and building the social capital that is so important for individual and societal flourishing (Putnam, *American Grace*). Alexis de Tocqueville likewise highlighted the special role religious communities play in counteracting the individualistic tendencies of democratic societies, arguing that there is no religion "that does not impose on each some duties toward the human species or in common with it, and that does not thus draw him, from time to time, away from contemplation of himself. . . . Religious peoples are therefore naturally strong in precisely the spot where democratic peoples are weak" (Tocqueville, *Democracy in America*, 419).

39. On the crucial importance of religious associations, see notes 37 and 38, above.

Once Susie reaches adulthood and has settled upon a particular vocational path, perhaps including marriage and a family of her own, the communities that she needs to flourish will largely be of the same types as what she has needed up to this point. For she will rely on these same communities and institutions to help her (and her spouse) in their task of raising their own children, supporting themselves, forming and maintaining a variety of friendships, serving the broader community, and continuing to develop and exercise their talents through professional work and/or involvement in volunteer organizations dedicated to a wide variety of ends (cultural, educational, athletic, charitable, religious, etc.). Susie's reliance on her parents will diminish in this phase of life, but their advice and assistance as she tries to raise her own children will be extremely valuable, and the ability for the children to know their grandparents and broader kinship network will also be an important benefit to them. The time will likely come when Susie will be called upon to help provide (or otherwise ensure that they receive) the care that her parents need in their old age. This will be facilitated if there are reliable, high-quality, and reasonably affordable institutions, such as assisted-living communities, nursing homes, hospitals, associations of in-home caregivers, and so on, along with religious communities to assist with spiritual preparation for death—institutions Susie herself may need to rely upon to help provide for her own needs later in life. Such institutions, together with the love and care of a supportive community of family and friends, can help Susie to flourish in her final years (as well as her health allows), and to approach death with peace.[40]

As we have briefly considered the forms of community necessary for the flourishing of a human being throughout the lifespan, we have built a fairly complex picture of society, with families at the foundation, and a wide variety of intermediate associations that facilitate particular aspects of human well-being, complementing the family and making up for its insufficiencies. This complexity, however, raises new problems, including the problem of

40. Her ability to do so will, in part, depend on the extent to which she has acquired what MacIntyre calls the "virtues of acknowledged dependence," enabling her to acknowledge her need for others' assistance as her health declines, and to accept that assistance with grace and gratitude, rather than resenting it and pining for the relative independence of her youth (MacIntyre, *Dependent Rational Animals*, chap. 10). Conversely, those caring for her will need to develop and exercise the virtue that MacIntyre calls "just generosity," which requires "acting from attentive and affectionate regard" for others (122).

how to justly and efficiently coordinate the activities of these families and associations so that they can live in harmony. These, and other problems that families and intermediate associations are incapable of resolving well without some overarching coordinating authority, point to the need for an overarching, political community, which I will discuss in chapter 4. Before doing so, however, I would like to build on what has been said so far about the various forms of human community and their importance for human flourishing to consider how this helps us to concretize the demands of justice by specifying the obligations that we have to others and by justifying a certain degree of partiality toward fellow members of these communities.

JUSTICE AND SPECIAL OBLIGATIONS

The virtue of justice is classically defined as the habitual disposition to render to each person what is his or her due. When we speak about the requirements of justice, we mean the aspects of morality that deal with our obligations to other people. Thus, *other-directedness* is one of the essential characteristics of justice.[41] Another essential characteristic is that justice aims at giving someone what is owed or due, and thus the concept of justice is inseparable from the concept of obligation or *duty*. Finally, the third essential element in the concept of justice is that one determines what is owed to another with reference to the maintenance or establishment of a certain *equality* between the parties. The equality aimed at might be direct equivalence, as when one barters with another person and expects that the good or service exchanged will be equal to the value of the good or service received, thus maintaining equality between the parties, with neither left worse off by comparison with the other as a result of the exchange. Or the relevant equality aimed at might be proportionality, as when portions of food are distributed in accordance with people's age, size, and nutritional needs. Which sort of equality it is appropriate to aim at or which criteria are relevant to determining what is proportionate will vary based on the nature of the relationship, interaction, exchange, and/or good being distributed. To take an example from Aristotle, flutes should arguably be distributed in

41. My analysis here draws on Finnis, *Natural Law and Natural Rights*, 8.1.

accordance with the recipients' ability to play them, or honors in accordance with merit, whereas things such as food should likely be distributed primarily according to need.[42]

Very few of the requirements of justice are fully and universally specified by the natural law. These requirements are the absolute moral prohibitions that flow from the moral norm forbidding intentional damage or destruction of basic human goods. Considered from the perspective of the beneficiary, these absolute moral prohibitions are absolute and inviolable claim rights. These rights, such as the right not to be murdered, tortured, raped, or enslaved, belong to every human being, and impose a strict duty on every human being to refrain from actions that violate these rights.[43] Such negative rights—rights not to be harmed in certain ways—are absolute, universally binding, and fully specified, but the same is not true of positive rights, rights to receive a particular benefit. Although all people might be said to have basic positive rights to receive what they need to flourish at least up to a certain basic threshold, determining precisely what is owed to any particular person also involves prudential judgment in light of a variety of factors: (1) need (relative to the basic requirements of human flourishing, up to a certain basic threshold), (2) function (need not relative to the basic requirements of human flourishing, but relative to a person's function or role in the community), (3) capacity to make good use of the resources/goods provided (e.g., flutes to flute-players), and (4) desert (both positive and negative).[44]

---

42. Aristotle, *Politics*, 1282b.

43. Thus, these rights are fully specified claim rights in the Hohfeldian sense, for each aspect of the three-term relation that constitutes a right—the beneficiary, duty-holder, and duty—are all clear (Finnis, *Natural Law and Natural Rights*, 8.2).

44. Finnis, *Natural Law and Natural Rights*, 174–75. Finnis adds a fifth that cannot be easily summarized by a short label, but he describes it as follows: "In the distribution of the costs and losses of communal enterprise fairness will often turn on whether some parties have created or at least foreseen and accepted avoidable risks while others have neither created them nor had opportunity of foreseeing or of avoiding or insuring against them" (175). I have omitted this for the sake of simplicity and also because I believe it can be captured under the umbrella of "desert" as long as this is understood not only positively (as meriting rewards through one's contributions to the common good) but also negatively (as deserving punishment for actions seriously contrary to the common good, or as deserving to suffer the negative effects of risks freely accepted).

There is also the problem of determining who (be it an individual or a community) has the primary responsibility to give what is owed. For justice should not be thought of primarily as a quality of a particular state of affairs, but rather as a quality of a human action or of the character of a human person (formed through repeated actions).[45] We therefore need to consider what justice requires from the perspective of an agent deliberating about how to act in a practically reasonable (morally upright) way, trying to determine what his specific obligations are to others, and how to reasonably prioritize different people's needs, given limited time, energy and resources.[46]

This problem of specifying our obligations to others is what I will focus on in the remainder of this section, for my aim here is not to provide a comprehensive overview of justice, but primarily to consider how the forms of community we have with others are relevant to determining what we owe to them. What I seek to address, in other words, is what is often referred to as the "problem of partiality"—of how to justify prioritizing the good of one person or group over another.[47] This is a "problem" because, given the basic equality of all human beings, and the natural law account's claim that practical reason directs us to respect and promote the good (in its various basic forms) of all human beings, there has to be some reason to justify partiality. This issue was considered briefly in chapter 2's discussion of fairness and the Golden Rule, which suggested that partiality could be justified insofar as various basic goods, especially friendship and marriage, require it.[48] Here I will expand on that discussion in light of what I have said in this

45. Finnis, *Natural Law and Natural Rights*, 175.

46. For simplicity I refer here to individual agents, but the same considerations apply to group agents.

47. For a sense of the contemporary debate, see Keller, *Partiality*.

48. Partiality to oneself is also related to the goods of integrity and authenticity, for one can only participate in these goods (which, from a moral perspective, require the development of a virtuous character) through one's own free choices and actions. Others can facilitate your growth in virtue through education, advice, good example, etc., but no one (other than yourself) can make you virtuous. The same is also true of the other reflexive goods—friendship, marriage, and religion—which can only be instantiated through one's own free choices and actions. Here, however, I am focused on the justification of partiality to others.

chapter about the various forms of community and their importance—both intrinsic and instrumental—for human flourishing.[49]

Let us first consider friendship in its various forms. It is obvious that friendship in the fullest sense—involving mutual commitment to the other's flourishing and shared activity sought for the sake of the friendship itself—inherently requires partiality. For friendship by definition involves a special commitment to the well-being of one's friend, above and beyond the general respect and concern for everyone's well-being that natural law requires. If someone called herself my friend but devoted no more time, energy, or resources to me than to a stranger, I would quickly conclude that she was not my friend after all. Even thinner forms of friendship, such as the business and play communities we have discussed, require some prioritization of the other community members at least with regard to the specific purpose of the community; for example, in giving business advice and help, one should generally prioritize one's own business partners over others. All of the intermediate associations we discussed earlier would also fall into one of these broad categories of friendship. Achieving the goods proper to any of these forms of community inherently requires some degree of partiality toward the community's members. A world without partiality would therefore be a world without any forms of friendship, a world in which our lives would be greatly impoverished.

The justification of partiality toward family members (especially nuclear-family members) is even stronger. For the uniquely comprehensive union and commitment that define marriage entail direct, lifelong, and

---

49. Finnis provides a helpful summary of the various considerations at play, which I take my analysis (which focuses primarily on relationships and interdependence, but does not claim to be exhaustive) to be consonant with: "What is thus required of particular persons depends essentially on what responsibilities they respectively have, whether by virtue of voluntary commitments (e.g. assumption of rulership) or by virtue of past or present receipt of benefits from another (e.g. as children, in relation to their respective parents), or by virtue of the dependence of others upon them (e.g. as parents, in relation to their own children), or by virtue of a network of relationships of actual and potential interdependencies (such as exist strongly, for one set of reasons, amongst members of a family living unit, and strongly, for another set of reasons, amongst members of a sound political community, and to a lesser but increasing extent between the communities that together make up the whole community of mankind)" (Finnis, *Natural Law and Natural Rights*, 175).

all-encompassing special responsibility for the well-being of one's spouse. Even full-fledged friendships do not usually involve anything even approaching this level of all-around responsibility for another person, nor are they inherently permanent, for friends may grow apart as interests diverge, or as careers, families, or other commitments take up more of one's time or require moving to a distant location, making frequent shared activity impossible. There is nothing inherently wrong with this, for there is no inherent obligation to prioritize the maintenance of a friendship over other competing goods and obligations. Such an obligation does exist in marriage, however, because of its inherent permanence. Such permanence is required in part because of the needs of the children that might result from one's marital union—in particular, the children's need (ideally) to be part of an intact family, united in community with their parents and siblings. This need is particularly strong during childhood and adolescence as children are developing their sense of personal identity, but it continues throughout life. The rupture in family unity caused by divorce has negative practical and psychological consequences even for adult children, for the rupture of their parents' relationship is, in some sense, a rupture within themselves, because they literally embody their parents' union.[50]

The special responsibilities of parents toward their children are likewise all-encompassing and to some extent lifelong, but they are most intense when the children are small. As children grow and slowly begin to direct their own lives—first in very small ways and then in larger matters as they mature—primary responsibility for their well-being begins to shift from their parents to themselves. The case of parents and small children is perhaps the only case in which a person's responsibility for another's well-being is at least equal to or perhaps even greater than that person's responsibility for his own well-being. For small children are completely unable to exercise

---

50. A recent study summarizes the effects of divorce on adult children: "Adult offspring have a hard time emotionally adjusting to the new family structure, their relationship with their parents suffers, and they are relied on for emotional and financial support by their parents. Additionally, adult offspring question their own ability to negotiate intimate relationships and the value of marriage" (Shanholtz, Irgens, and Beck, "Are the Adults Alright?" 4).

agency, unable to direct themselves toward their own good. They are thus entirely reliant on their parents (and other caregivers) to do this for them. Because of the uniquely intimate and permanent personal relationship that biological parents have with their children—as the joint biological cause of the children's very existence and identity—they have a natural obligation to provide for their children's needs, which in the early stages of life are comprehensive. Only when there are strong child-centered reasons (such as incompetence) for doing so is it morally acceptable for parents to leave those natural obligations unfulfilled and seek out others, such as adoptive parents, to take on their role. Because of the deep personal bonds between parents and children (initially biological, but then also psychological and volitional), and because of children's utter dependency, what parents (either biological or adoptive) owe to their children is a high-priority commitment to their well-being.[51] For what children need to flourish is their parents' *love*, and love in the relevant sense just is a high-priority commitment to another's well-being, which necessarily entails partiality.[52]

What we have seen is that justice not only allows but requires partiality toward those with whom we are in community, and that the degree and

51. This commitment is not incompatible with a high-priority commitment to one's spouse, for maintaining a strong and loving marital relationship is itself crucial for the well-being of children. Likewise, this commitment is not incompatible with taking due care of one's own well-being, for one will not be able to be a good parent (which includes modeling a life of virtue and an appreciation of all the basic forms of good) if one neglects any fundamental dimension of one's own well-being.

52. S. Matthew Liao argues persuasively that children have a right to be loved, because "being loved is a fundamental condition for children to pursue a good life" (Liao, *The Right to be Loved*, 99). Here I speak of love primarily as a disposition of the will, but I believe Liao is correct to claim that the love children have a right to includes an emotional component. In response to the objection that the emotional aspect of love cannot be commanded, Liao points out that we can "bring about particular emotions" by, for instance, calling to mind the reasons to have those emotions, or by placing ourselves in situations likely to give rise to those emotions (104). According to Liao, parents who do not spontaneously feel affection for their child can and should use such methods to cultivate that affection (chap. 4). Liao also presents an argument, complementary to the one I provided above, for why biological parents are the ones with the primary duty to love their children, but he argues that all others have associate duties toward children that can be discharged by, for instance, supporting workplace or government policies that help parents fulfill their responsibilities (chap. 5).

scope of this partiality depends on the nature of the community.[53] Thus the degree and scope of the partiality one owes to one's friends (broadly construed) will vary depending on the depth and breadth of the friendship. Because of the inherently intimate and all-encompassing nature of the marital relationship and the parent–child relationship, however, such relationships (at least until children reach maturity) require the highest degree of partiality. Once children become adults, they will, in turn, have special obligations for their parents' well-being in part because of the great debt that they owe them, but their highest priority obligations will be to their own spouse and children or, if they do not marry, to the fulfillment of their particular vocational commitments more generally.

None of the above implies that justice requires or even allows us to give absolute priority to the well-being of friends and family over the well-being of strangers. For the type and degree of another's need, and our particular ability to meet that need are—even apart from any special relationship we may have with that person—also important factors in determining what we owe to others. The dire and urgent need of a stranger will thus generally take priority over less serious needs of friends and family members—as when you stop to help an elderly man who appears to have passed out on his daily walk, leading you to miss your daughter's soccer game. Yet most questions about how to prioritize our time, energy, and resources do not have such clear answers. Should I volunteer at the soup kitchen on Saturday afternoons, even if this means spending less time with my children? Should I take my family on an expensive vacation to the beach, or forgo the vacation and donate that money to help those in dire need (perhaps victims of war, natural disaster, or famine)? As with all questions about how to prioritize one person or group's good over another's, the Golden Rule needs to be applied in such cases, and there is likely to be a range of acceptable answers. Perhaps my children already get plenty of time with me, and Saturday afternoons can be a special time for the children to spend with their father. Or perhaps I can find a volunteer opportunity in which the children can take part. Perhaps we can donate to those in dire need while still taking a family vacation if we, say, rent a campsite, or stay at a less expensive hotel, or go somewhere within driving distance rather than traveling by plane.

53. This will also apply to the political community, which I will discuss in chapter 4.

The function of the Golden Rule is not so much to get the "right" answer—for in such matters there is usually a range of morally acceptable answers—but to rectify the will, ensuring that the well-being of others is given due consideration in our deliberations. And the main goal of this section has been to explain why—given the crucial importance of community for human flourishing—the degree of consideration owed to any particular person or group will reasonably vary depending on the nature of one's relationship with that person. Finnis summarizes the relevant factors nicely: "Of each and all of us it is true that, because of one's promises, and/or one's parenthood, and/or one's debts of gratitude, and/or one's relations of interdependence with or assumption of authority in relation to ascertained persons or communities, one cannot reasonably give equal 'weight,' or equal concern, to the interests of every person anywhere whose interests one could ascertain and affect."[54] Justice, in other words, does not merely allow but requires that we give greater consideration to the good of some than others. Nonetheless, as even the examples mentioned above imply, following the Golden Rule in attempting to specify our positive obligations of justice toward others—and to distinguish between reasonable partiality and the rationalization of selfishness—can be quite demanding, and requires a great deal of practical wisdom and moral virtue.

54. Finnis, *Natural Law and Natural Rights*, 177.

FOUR

The Political Dimension
of Human Flourishing

What is political community and what role does political community play in human flourishing? Most of us simply take it for granted that all who live in our geographic region form part of a political community, organized according to a particular system of government, which has the authority to establish and coercively enforce rules (usually in the form of laws) that guide our conduct. But why do we (or should we) organize ourselves into political communities at all? Why do we (or should we) generally accept the authority of our government and the laws it enacts? And what, if any, are the limits on the government's authority?

In chapter 3, I discussed the importance of community for human flourishing, not only for physical survival but even more importantly for the development of our intellectual and moral capacities. The chapter highlighted the crucial role of the family for human flourishing, and the need for a variety of intermediate associations — religious, economic, cultural — to support and complement the family in order to meet the diverse needs of human beings and to provide opportunities for participation in the full range of human goods. For although the common good of the family includes the overall flourishing of its members, the family is insufficient on its own to achieve this end. At the same time, intermediate associations can partly overcome the insufficiencies of the family in facilitating human flourishing, but new problems are also created as society grows large and complex enough to meet the full range of human needs, including the problem of how to coordinate the activities of families and associations in a just and reliable manner, enabling all of these communities to live together in peace. Further, there are a number of society-wide needs — such as public utilities and security from internal and external threats — that neither families nor intermediate associations can justly and reliably supply on their own. Therefore, although families and intermediate associations have the responsibility and authority to direct their own internal affairs in the service of their own goods, they cannot justly, efficiently, and reliably achieve these goods unless they unite to form a political community with overarching political authority.

Since natural law directs us to act in ways that respect and promote human flourishing, and since political community is necessary for human flourishing, natural law directs us to form political communities. But what, precisely, is political community, and how does it differ from families and other forms of subpolitical community? Because communities are defined by the common good for which they exist, fully answering this question will require offering an account of the common good of the political community. The nature of political community and of the political common good will, therefore, be the subject of the first two sections of this chapter. Having clarified the nature of the political common good, in the following sections I will then consider the nature, purpose, and limits of political authority, which is (ideally) exercised for the sake of the political common good. Understanding the limits of political authority will also require understanding the relationship between natural law and positive law, and explaining why political authority should generally be exercised through the rule of law.

I have devoted separate sections to the concepts of political community, the political common good, and political authority and its limits, but it is important to emphasize at the outset that these concepts are inherently interconnected. The nature and purpose of political community cannot be explained without reference to the political common good, and the political common good cannot be explained without reference to the need for an overarching political authority to coordinate the various individuals and subpolitical communities that make up the political community in order to justly and reliably secure the conditions needed for their pursuit of flourishing (conditions that constitute the political common good). Further, the limits of political authority can only be fully understood in relation to the limits of the political common good, which political authority exists to serve. The content of each of these sections, therefore, can only be fully understood in light of what is said in the others.

My goal in this chapter is to offer an account of political community from the perspective of the natural law theory outlined in the previous chapters.[1] In doing so, I seek to highlight how this account differs from both Aristotelian and liberal accounts of politics in a way that arguably captures the best of both. On the one hand, the account I offer here (as with the broader natural law account presented in this book) is essentially Aristotelian insofar as it sees both ethics and politics as fundamentally about respecting and promoting human flourishing. On the other hand, my account views the government's role in promoting human flourishing as more limited and indirect than the traditional Aristotelian account, which is typically interpreted as holding that government and law should aim directly at the full moral perfection of the community's members.[2] In this respect, the natural law account I offer is similar to liberal accounts, since it defends many of the civil liberties (freedom of speech, association, religion, etc.) and other aspects of limited government typically associated with liberalism. I will explain toward the end of the chapter, however, that the natural law defense of limited government is fundamentally different from the liberal one, for it is grounded not on the liberal claim that government ought to be neutral about the good, but rather on the claim that—because of the nature of government and the nature of human flourishing—the government's role in promoting human flourishing is indirect and subsidiary to the role

---

1. Thus, the account provided here is heavily indebted to the work of other new natural law theorists, especially John Finnis, Robert George, and Christopher Tollefsen.

2. Aristotle, *Nicomachean Ethics* 1099b30, and *Politics* 1281a1. For contemporary examples of this view, see Schindler, *The Politics of the Real*, and Pakaluk, "Is the Common Good of Political Society Limited?"

of individuals, families, and other subpolitical communities.[3] Indeed, contrary to common misconceptions, Aquinas himself arguably held a similarly limited view of the scope of government authority.[4] The account of political community offered here, which flows from the claims about human flourishing and morality made in the previous chapters, is therefore largely Aristotelian in its premises — grounding political community on a substantive account of human flourishing and a recognition that we form political communities not merely to survive but to thrive — but draws on those non-liberal premises to reach practical conclusions in defense of limited government that overlap with the conclusions of liberal thinkers.

Before I proceed, it may be helpful to clarify the meaning of some key terms that could give rise to confusion. When I refer to "political community" without further qualification, I mean the large society of individuals and subpolitical communities that are governed by an overarching political authority (and that typically, though not necessarily, live together in a particular region). But when I refer to "political community as such," I am referring to the specifically political aspect of the political community — its possession and exercise of coercive political authority. This distinction between "political community" and "political community as such" corresponds to the distinction between the "all-inclusive common good" (or just "common good"), which is the common good of the political community, and the "specifically political common good" (or just "political common good"), which is that aspect of the all-inclusive common good for which political authority is responsible (and which sets the scope and limits of that

---

3. Liberalism is, of course, notoriously difficult to define, and the views of thinkers typically classified as liberal — perhaps most famously John Locke, John Stuart Mill, and John Rawls — differ on many points. Nonetheless, an aspiration to government neutrality on controversial questions about the good life is typically considered one of the defining features of the liberal project. See, e.g., Dworkin, *A Matter of Principle*, 191; and Rawls, *Political Liberalism*, 9–10. For a helpful overview of liberalism's core commitments, see Smith, "Christians and/as Liberals?," 1500–1503.

4. Finnis, *Aquinas*, chap. 7, argues for this interpretation of Aquinas's political theory. Porter, though disagreeing with some aspects of Finnis's interpretation of Aquinas's moral theory, believes that Finnis is persuasive in his claims about Aquinas's support of limited government (Porter, "Reason, Nature and the End of Human Life," 483–84).

authority).[5] The importance of these distinctions and the justification for making them should become clear in the course of the argument, but for now I will simply signal that they are crucial to my attempt to "square the circle" by both acknowledging (along with Aristotle) that political community aims at the all-around flourishing of its members and also arguing (along with liberalism) that coercive political authority has a limited and indirect role in contributing to this aim.

THE POLITICAL COMMUNITY AS A COMMUNITY OF COMMUNITIES

What is the purpose of political community? In other words, what is the good or set of goods that individuals and subpolitical communities seek to obtain by forming and being members of a political community? We can begin thinking about this by considering political community in relation to subpolitical communities, especially families.

In a broad sense, the political community aims at the overall flourishing of its members. For the political community's purpose is much more all-encompassing than, say, the purpose of a baseball team or a medical association. In this sense, the political community is similar to the family, which also seeks to promote the overall flourishing of its members. However, there are important differences between the two. One of those differences is that the family directly instantiates the basic human good of marriage, which includes within it the goods of procreation and family relationships. Therefore, though marriage has many instrumental benefits, and the family community of which it is the foundation aims to promote the overall flourishing of its members, the basic point or common good of marriage is marriage itself—that uniquely all-encompassing form of interpersonal communion, inherently oriented to procreation and family life, made possible by the sexual complementarity of man and woman. Further,

5. I take these distinctions from Finnis, *Aquinas*, chap. 7, but I employ them here (along with other insights from the book) because I believe that they capture important truths, independently of whether they are in fact present in Aquinas's political thought.

the unique interpersonal unions among family members — parent–child relationships, sibling relationships, grandparent–grandchild relationships, and so on — are also aspects of this basic good.

By contrast, the political community's value is mostly instrumental, rather than intrinsic, for the instrumental benefits of political community — the necessary assistance it provides to the more basic communities that compose it — are what make it so crucial for human flourishing, and what make the formation of political community a requirement of practical reason. I will explain these benefits in greater detail in the next section on the specifically political common good.

Although political community is not itself a distinct basic good, it does instantiate a form of the basic good of friendship.[6] It does this most specifically (but not only) through its special role in restorative justice (i.e., punishing criminals to restore the balance of justice upset by their wrongdoing, and ensuring that victims of injustice are compensated for their losses).[7] There is also ideally a broad civic friendship constituted by cooperation for the all-inclusive common good of the political community, which consists in the overall flourishing of the community's members. Yet as there are many deeper and fuller forms of friendship that one can pursue, the common good that is primarily the reason for entering into political commu-

6. Thus, on my view, the political common good has both instrumental and intrinsic elements. George Duke notes, in commenting on Mark Murphy's division of conceptions of the political common good into instrumentalist, distinctive (intrinsic), and aggregative, that "it is unnecessary for the natural law theorist to hold one conception of the common good to the exclusion of the others. Murphy's three conceptions can in fact be understood as representing different dimensions of the common good, rather than irreconcilable alternatives" (Duke, "Distinctive Common Good"; Murphy, "The Common Good").

7. The administration of justice by impartial judges in accordance with the rule of law is a distinctive function of political authority. "To punish pertains to none but the framer of the law, by whose authority the pain is inflicted" (Aquinas, *Summa theologiae* I-II, q. 92, a. 2, ad 3; see also q. 90, a. 3, ad 2). Finnis explains that the reason why only political authorities have the power to "rightly threaten or impose penalties that are fully coercive" is that "none of us can rightly be simultaneously prosecutor, judge, and witness." As a result, "private persons and bodies are not equipped for *judgment*, especially judgment according to publicly established *law*, and so cannot rightly impose the irreparable measures which may be needed to restore justice and peace" (Finnis, *Aquinas*, 248–49; see also 210–15; and see Finnis, *Natural Law and Natural Rights*, 10.1).

nity does not seem to be political or civic friendship in itself.[8] The shared ideals and goals, common action, and mutual affection and benevolence constitutive of friendship are ideally present to some extent in civic friendship, but typically in a much less intense manner than in other forms of friendship. Thus, the primary reason for entering into political community seems to be its instrumental value rather than its intrinsic value.

Perhaps one might argue that political community, like marriage, is a unique basic good that is different in kind from other forms of friendship. Yet marriage is a basic good distinct from friendship because it is the only sort of interpersonal union that literally unites two human beings at the bodily level by forming one complete reproductive system in sexual intercourse, and is also a union inherently oriented to procreation and family life. Thus, the marital community includes a dimension of our being—the bodily dimension—that friendship lacks. By contrast, the distinctive features of political community—which are its nature as an overarching community with overarching coercive authority, large enough to contain within it all that is needed for its members' flourishing—do not seem to make available to us a basic good that is different in kind from the forms of friendship instantiated in many smaller and more limited communities. I should clarify here that I am not denying all differences in kind between political community and other forms of friendship, for the government's overarching coercive authority and the nonvoluntary nature of participation in the political community are indeed differences in kind. Rather, I am only denying the existence of in-kind differences that would make political community a distinct basic good—a distinct type of intrinsic reason for action—for these unique features of political community have value only because they make possible the crucial instrumental purposes of political community. Further, the political community is larger, more expansive in its aims, and more self-sufficient than, say, a baseball team or a medical association, but these are likewise differences that are only instrumentally important. And the greater expansiveness of the political community also means that the friendship it embodies is thinner and more diffuse than that found in subpolitical communities. It thus seems that political community is neither a basic good distinct in kind from friendship, nor a form of friendship that—precisely as friendship—cannot be found more richly in other forms of

8. See Finnis, *Aquinas*, 245.

community. Allow me to emphasize here that my point is not to deny that civic friendship can be sought for its own sake—it can—but simply to explain why I believe that civic friendship by itself is not the primary reason why human beings do or should form political communities.

Further, the political community differs from the family in that it is composed not primarily of individuals, but of families and other subpolitical communities, each of which have their own proper good. The picture of political society being presented here is therefore a layered one, involving, as it were, multiple circles of community, some of which are concentric, some of which are relatively independent, and some of which have partially overlapping memberships, common goods, and spheres of authority. The basic unit of society is the family. A group of families or of individuals from several different families may form part of other communities, such as churches, neighborhoods, workplaces, schools, cultural associations, and the like. The particular goods that these larger communities exist to promote will overlap in certain respects with the overall flourishing that the family exists to promote for its members. For example, the common good for which an elementary school exists is the education of children, and this overlaps with one aspect of the common good of the family, with the school playing a subsidiary role in helping parents to fulfill their educational responsibilities.

The political community is the outer layer of these circles of community, an overarching community with overarching coercive authority to coordinate and regulate the activities of the individuals, families, and other communities within its jurisdiction for the sake of the political common good. It is a level of community that is theoretically complete insofar as it is supposed to contain within itself all that is needed for the all-around human flourishing of its members.[9] The specific form that political community will take can vary significantly depending on historical and cultural contingencies, but I believe this broad characterization captures the key distinguishing features of political community: (1) it is an overarching community composed of families and other subpolitical communities; (2) it has overarching, coercive authority in matters within its jurisdiction (determined by the specifically political common good); and (3) it is relatively complete or self-sufficient for the needs of its members.

9. Aristotle, *Politics*, bk. 1; Aquinas, *Summa theologiae* I-II, q. 90, a. 2.

I should clarify here that when I characterize the political community as an overarching community with overarching coordinating authority, this does not mean that all of the communities within the political community are fully encompassed by it or under the jurisdiction of political authority in every respect. Some communities, albeit subpolitical and subject to political authority in some respects, are outside the bounds of political authority in other respects. Consider, for instance, a typical Catholic parish. In some respects, the parish is a subpolitical community, under the relevant political authorities in matters that are within their jurisdiction (i.e., matters related to the specifically political common good). For example, if the parish wants to organize a procession through the neighborhood streets, it will need to obtain a permit from the local government. Or if the pastor fraudulently funnels parish funds into his private bank account, he will be subject to criminal punishment. In other respects—such as matters related to doctrine, liturgy, or other things specific to its religious identity and mission—the parish is not subject to political authorities (for such matters are outside their jurisdiction), but rather subject to the relevant religious authorities (the bishop, the pope, Canon Law, etc.).

The claim that the political community is an overarching community with overarching coercive authority therefore needs to be qualified: *The political community has overarching coercive authority only in matters that are within its sphere of competence*—only in matters related to the specifically political common good.[10] In other words, political authority's scope is limited

---

10. Schindler argues that limited accounts of the political common good (like the account I present here) are inherently problematic because they "[entail] an inversion of the relationship between the whole and its parts" (Schindler, *The Politics of the Real*, 92). What he seems to mean by this is that the "whole"—what he calls "integral good" or what I would call all-around flourishing—ends up becoming subordinate to the "part," the more limited and largely instrumental aspects of the human good for which the political community as such is responsible. This subordination of the whole to the part occurs, on Schindler's view, insofar as the political community is the "overarching context" within which the "the integral good has its reality to the extent that it becomes actual" (92). What this argument fails to recognize, however, is precisely the point that I am making here, namely, that the political community as such is overarching in some respects (only in matters related to its specific common good), but not in others (those matters that are outside the scope of its specific common good). Schindler might respond that if the political community as such did recognize that it is "responsible *only* for a good that it took to be nothing more than part of a greater whole, then it would have to recognize the

by its specific purpose and justification, which is the political common good. And even in those matters that do relate to the political common good, political authorities have an obligation to respect the more direct authority that subpolitical communities, especially families, have over their internal affairs. This point will be discussed further later when considering the principle of subsidiary in the section "The Limits of Political Authority."

THE COMMON GOOD OF POLITICAL COMMUNITY: ALL-INCLUSIVE COMMON GOOD VERSUS SPECIFICALLY POLITICAL COMMON GOOD

Recognizing the layered and complex nature of society is important for understanding the limits of the specifically political common good. In particular, it helps us to understand why the responsibility of political authority is to facilitate the political community's members' pursuit of their own good, not to directly secure their all-around flourishing or moral perfection. Thus, the political community as such is *subsidiary* to the subpolitical communities that compose it, existing to assist them, but not to substitute for their own exercise of agency in pursuit of their flourishing.[11] This is in large

---

authority of the body responsible for the integral good as such" (94). In other words, claims Schindler, the political community would have to "recognize the authority of the Church specifically with respect to the integral human good" (94). He asks the rhetorical question: "Is it possible to admit that one does not have competence in a particular area without opening oneself to the authority of one who does?" (95). Yet it is not difficult to see how the answer to this question could be "no," if one recognizes that the political community as such has no special competence to reliably identify the community that does have competence and authority with respect to the integral human good. Schindler's argument also fails to distinguish between the all-inclusive common good of the political community, responsibility for which is distributed throughout society, and the specifically political common good for which coercive political authority is responsible.

11. Yves Simon helpfully distinguishes between political authority, which aims not at the *proper* good of individuals or subpolitical communities but at the *common* good of society as a whole, and paternalistic authority, which aims at an individual's or group's proper good and substitutes for that individual's or group's own judgment and agency. He argues that, unlike paternalistic authority, political authority is needed not to make up for some deficiency in the capacity of individuals and subpolitical communities to direct themselves to their proper goods, but rather to resolve coordination problems (broadly construed) for the common good; see Simon, *Philosophy of Democratic Government*, 7–9.

part because the political community's members are, most directly, adults or subpolitical communities (especially families) headed by adults. And adults (those with relatively mature capacities for rational deliberation and choice) are the ones most directly responsible for the pursuit of their own flourishing, because they are the only ones fully capable of doing so, for at least three reasons.

First, many human goods, such as friendship, integrity, and religion, can only be achieved by freely choosing them. These goods are reflexive, meaning that participation in them is constituted by a certain type of choice. Coerced attendance at religious services, for instance, is simply not religious worship at all, but rather a set of external behaviors that outwardly mimic religious worship. Similarly, inviting someone for a drink is not an act of friendship unless that act stems from genuine good will. This means that, even though political authority's directives can and should facilitate individuals' pursuit of these goods, attempting to coerce pursuit of these goods is futile and even counterproductive insofar as it creates incentives for people to act in ways that are actually contrary to genuine participations in these goods by, for instance, faking religious devotion for political purposes. Robert George explains why political coercion would damage rather than facilitate participation in the good of religion: "Coercion deflects people from really choosing that human good, for it seeks to dominate their deliberations with the prospect of a quite different good—of freedom from imminent pain, loss, or other harms, or of some other non-religious advantage."[12] The same could be said with regard to other reflexive goods.

Second, the Vocation Principle (discussed in chapter 2) indicates that one must establish and follow a reasonable order of priorities among goods, and that this can only be done on the basis of one's overall vocation and corresponding obligations. The government is not competent to judge how individuals ought to prioritize competing goods in their lives, for it is extremely unlikely that the government will have a more accurate grasp of people's vocational obligations than those people themselves. Nor is the government competent to determine which vocational path one ought to pursue in the first place, for vocational discernment includes both objective and subjective factors, and requires intimate knowledge of a person's capacities, inclinations, and circumstances.

12. George, *Making Men Moral*, 221–22.

One might argue that these first two arguments depend in part on empirical judgments about the likely effects of government attempts to, for instance, coerce religious practice, or about the government's lack of the relevant knowledge to direct people toward suitable vocational commitments and actions in line with those commitments. I believe that the lessons of history and common experience support such empirical judgments, but there is a third, deeper reason why the government's role in facilitating human flourishing must necessarily be indirect. This reason is based on the very nature of human flourishing. Our flourishing as human beings consists not primarily in the mere possession of certain goods—even if these goods, including knowledge or health, are genuine goods that have intrinsic value—but rather in choices and activities by which we constitute ourselves as persons whose wills are fully open to and appreciative of the human good in all of its dimensions. Even in the highly unlikely hypothetical scenario in which the government could consistently make better judgments about what I ought to do than I could, the government can never deliberate, choose, and act for me. Government can never, in other words, replace my own exercise of agency, my own acts of will through which I constitute myself as a certain sort of person.

This is, I believe, one of the lessons of Robert Nozick's famous "experience machine" argument: "Suppose there were an experience machine that would give you any experience that you desired. Super-duper neuropsychologists could stimulate your brain so that you would think and feel you were writing a great novel, or making a friend, or reading an interesting book. All the time you would be floating in a tank, with electrodes attached to your brain."[13] Nozick believes that, if given the option to plug into this machine for life, preprogramming the machine in accordance with your preferences, most people would refuse. Although the machine would give you the illusion of your ideal life—and although, once in the machine, you would not know it was merely an illusion—plugging into the machine means giving up the ability to exercise agency, to develop yourself into a certain sort of person. Even if some people would choose to plug into the experience machine, the natural law view presented in this book implies that such a choice would be morally wrong, for such a choice would render

13. Nozick, *Anarchy, State, and Utopia*, 42.

them incapable of pursuing any genuine goods. It would be the moral equivalent of suicide.

The exercise of agency in freely pursuing goods and in organizing one's life in line with one's vocation and obligations is, for all of these reasons, part and parcel of human flourishing. Further, the exercise of agency in pursuit of goods and in the fulfillment of one's vocational obligations is not simply an individual matter, but has an irreducibly social dimension. I argued in chapter 3 that being in community with others gives rise to special obligations for their well-being and for the well-being of the community as a whole. In many cases, fulfilling those special obligations requires exercising authority over those within one's care. For example, the fulfillment of parental obligations—which is a central element of many people's vocational obligations—requires exercising authority over one's children, making decisions about what is in their best interests, because they are not yet mature enough to make those decisions on their own. For the government to usurp that authority would be to prevent parents from fulfilling their vocational obligations, and would therefore be contrary to their flourishing, and to the flourishing of the family community as a whole.[14] Similarly, the ability to form and contribute to the governance of a variety of intermediate associations is also a crucial arena for the exercise of agency in the pursuit of human goods and in the fulfillment of one's obligations.

Families and intermediate associations are the primary sites of human flourishing, both because they instantiate basic goods in deeper and more direct ways than the political community and because it is usually within these subpolitical communities that people can most directly promote individual and common goods. Precisely in order to best facilitate the flourishing of the political community's members, therefore, the government needs to refrain from attempting to micromanage their lives, and allow people freely to pursue their good (and the good of their communities), only interfering when the specifically political common good requires it.

The above argument implies that, although the political community's purpose is the overall flourishing of its members—the *all-inclusive common good*—political authority can in principle only achieve this good indirectly,

14. See Moschella, *To Whom Do Children Belong?*, and Moschella, "Defending the Fundamental Rights of Parents."

in a way that respects the primary and more direct responsibility of the community's members to pursue their own flourishing (and the flourishing of their communities) in accord with their own particular vocations and obligations.[15] What this means, in other words, is that responsibility for the all-inclusive common good does not fall entirely on the political community (and its corresponding authority) just as such, but is rather distributed among the various layers of society in accordance with their proper spheres of competence.[16] Remember that when I refer to the "political community as such," I am referring to the specifically political aspect of the political community, particularly the exercise of coercive political authority through government and law, by contrast with those parts of the political community—including families and civic associations—that are not specifically political.

For example, one crucial aspect of the all-inclusive common good of society is the procreation and education of children, which is a basic requirement for any society to be able to sustain itself over time. Yet responsibility for this aspect of the common good lies primarily with the family, not with the political community as such. The role of the political community as such in this area should therefore usually be indirect and subsidiary, assisting parents in their educational task without usurping parents' authority, and fostering a culture in which children are likely to be conceived and raised within an intact family, which, I argued in chapter 3, is the ideal setting for their flourishing.

Similar things could be said about helping people to grow in moral virtue. According to the natural law view I outlined in chapters 1 and 2, virtue is central to human flourishing and is therefore part of the all-inclusive common good. In this sense, Aristotle was correct to claim that the political community (in the broad sense) should seek to promote the moral virtue of its members. The problem with the Aristotelian view, however, is that it tends to

---

15. Finnis, *Aquinas*, 236.

16. Finnis argues that, on Aquinas's view, "the reasonable pursuit of the 'all-inclusive' common good is stratified, into three distinct specializations of responsibility," or species of practical reasonableness: "individual practical reasonableness . . ., domestic practical reasonableness, and political practical reasonableness" (Finnis, *Aquinas*, 236). He clarifies that the latter "neither absorbs the other two nor even includes, directly, the whole of their content," for political jurisdiction only regards "promotion of the *public good*," or specifically political common good (237).

translate this general claim about the political community broadly speaking into a more specific claim about the government's direct responsibility and authority for achieving this purpose. Yet the political community is more than the government (the organs of political authority), and responsibility for the all-inclusive common good of the political community does not belong to the government alone. Rather, responsibility for different aspects of the all-inclusive common good is distributed among the various layers of society, in accordance with their proper spheres of competence.[17]

Because moral virtue requires not only performing morally upright actions but also having the correct internal dispositions, government is ill-suited to the task of promoting the whole of virtue.[18] Government can and should require or forbid certain external actions in order to promote peace and justice in society, but government is simply not competent to promote the whole of virtue. Aquinas notes that human law is limited to directing external acts because the lawgiver "is competent to judge only of outward acts."[19] Human law is also too coarse and impersonal an instrument to effectively shape inner dispositions. Shaping and judging inner dispositions

17. Pakaluk believes that it is problematic to deny the Aristotelian claim that the government is directly responsible for the all-inclusive common good, even if one recognizes that political society in some sense does aim at the all-inclusive common good, because "this comprehensive good is not sought corporately; if it is sought at all, it is sought only privately, within households" (Pakaluk, "Is the Common Good of Political Society Limited?," 60–61). Yet why does seeking the all-inclusive common good corporately have to mean seeking that good directly through government action? On the view I am defending here, for example, citizens may (and indeed should) vote with the all-inclusive common good in mind, form associations of various sorts to foster the all-inclusive common good, and seek to promote virtue within their families and other subpolitical communities with a view not only to their private good but also to the common good. Even legislators, who, on my view, should not legislate with a view toward promoting the moral virtue of individuals just as such (but only insofar as this is related to the political common good of justice and peace), should nonetheless have the all-inclusive common good in mind, so as to ensure that laws facilitate or at least do not hinder society's members from pursuing their all-around flourishing. Thus, the view defended here is quite far from the Rawlsian view that citizens and public officials, when acting in their public capacity, should refrain from acting on the basis of their comprehensive vision of the good.

18. I am indebted to Patrick Lee for this point; see Lee, "The Specific Common Good of the Political Community," presentation at the University of Buffalo, March 19, 2022.

19. Aquinas, *Summa theologiae* I-II, q. 100, a. 9.

of virtue require the sort of ongoing personal relationship that is found most intensely in families, friendships, and in a lesser degree in religious communities and other groups, and thus the task of fostering moral virtue belongs most directly to these subpolitical communities (and, particularly in adulthood, to individuals themselves), rather than to the political community as such. Further, the arguments made above about flourishing as self-constitution through the exercise of one's own agency also apply here—ultimately, no one can make anyone else virtuous, for one can only become virtuous by deliberating, choosing, and acting in the right way, for the right reasons. Friends, family members, and others with whom one has an intimate relationship can help one to grow in virtue, but ultimately such growth will only occur as a result of one's own free choices. However, this does not mean that government should be neutral about the good, nor does it deny the government's legitimate role in fostering public morality.[20]

With the foregoing considerations in mind, it is now possible to give a more precise description of the specific purpose of political community—of that aspect of the all-inclusive common good for which the political community (and its coercive authority) as such is directly responsible. Because the political community's members (subpolitical communities, especially families, and individuals) have primary and direct responsibility for their own flourishing, the political community exists to facilitate its members' pursuit of flourishing by providing what those individuals and subpolitical communities need but are unable to justly and reliably obtain on their own. In other words, the *specifically political common good*—the specific point of political community (and its corresponding coercive authority)—consists in *the conditions that enable the community's members to pursue their own flourishing.*[21]

20. For extended arguments on this point, see George, "The Concept of Public Morality," and George, "Making Children Moral."

21. Finnis refers to the specifically political common good as the "public good," taking this term from Aquinas (Finnis, *Aquinas*, 222–31). See, e.g. Aquinas, *De regno* 1.16. This section of *De regno* is often misread to imply that Aquinas, following Aristotle, believed that the purpose of government and law are to lead people to their full moral perfection. Finnis argues, however, that a careful analysis of Aquinas's argument shows that even in these passages he has a more limited view about the scope of political authority (Finnis, *Aquinas*, 228–31). This limitation of political authority is even clearer in the *Summa theologiae*, a

This definition of the political common good may seem rather general and abstract, lacking in concrete content. What are these "conditions" enabling people to pursue their own flourishing? Or, to put it slightly differently, how precisely is the political community supposed to facilitate the pursuit of flourishing by its members? What is the good or set of goods that individuals and subpolitical communities will be unable to justly, efficiently, and reliably obtain without forming a political community? To answer this question, it can be helpful to consider in greater detail the ways in which individuals and subpolitical communities will be hampered in the pursuit of their flourishing if they fail to organize themselves into an overarching political community with overarching coercive authority. The example of failed states—places where government has largely ceased to function—offers poignant lessons in this regard. Here I offer just one example by way of illustration.

Discussing the situation of Somalia in 2009, journalist Jeffrey Gettleman describes the capital city of Mogadishu as "one of the world's most stunning monuments to conflict: block after block, mile after mile, of scorched, gutted-out buildings."[22] Gettleman explains that "Somalia has been ripped apart by violence since the central government imploded in 1991," resulting in a country that has devolved into "a lawless, ungoverned space on the map between its neighbors and the sea."[23] In the absence of effective government, the people have suffered not only from near-constant violence and physical insecurity, but also starvation, lack of basic health care and sanitation, lack of access to education, and a host of other ills. The situation in Somalia has become slightly more stable since the installation of a new internationally backed government in 2012, but the country is still racked by starvation and violent political divisions.[24]

---

more mature work. There, Aquinas argues that, by contrast with divine law, human law (the law and government of the political community) aims at "the temporal tranquility of the state," by "directing external actions, as regards those evils which might disturb the peaceful condition of the state" (*Summa theologiae* I-II, q. 98, a. 1). Thus although my aim here is not to defend any particular interpretation of Aquinas, I believe that the view of political community presented here is compatible with Aquinas's account.

22. Gettleman, "The Most Dangerous Place," 62.

23. Gettleman, "The Most Dangerous Place," 62, 64.

24. Felbab-Brown, "Somalia's Challenges in 2023"; BBC News, "Somalia Country Profile."

These miserable living conditions are, in a sense, the opposite of the conditions that would facilitate the flourishing of the country's inhabitants. In other words, they are the opposite of the conditions that constitute the political common good. Of course, this is just one example, but I believe it can help to illustrate what can be concluded more generally by reflecting on the insufficiencies of subpolitical communities with regard to the flourishing of their members. Whereas the lack of a genuinely unified political authority can lead to violent strife among various subpolitical communities (such as rival clans in the case of Somalia), an overarching political authority can help to coordinate these various communities so that they can coexist harmoniously. Effective political authority can facilitate harmonious coexistence by, for instance, establishing and enforcing clear rules about such things as property ownership and contracts, and also by providing an independent and impartial forum—a judicial system—that makes it possible to resolve disputes and redress injustices without recourse to violence. The absence of effective political authority also leaves communities vulnerable to the threat of external attack. Further, whereas ineffective government often results in the lack of the most basic necessities, just and effective political authority can coordinate society's members—through, for instance, systems of taxation to pool resources—so as to ensure the provision and fair distribution of goods, such as clean water, electricity, bridges, roads, and parks. The need to ensure that people have access to basic necessities is especially acute for the most vulnerable members of the population, such as children, the sick, and the disabled; these are the individuals likely to suffer most in the absence of an effective government. Although primary responsibility for taking care of dependents lies with their families, tragedy or irresponsibility can leave some dependents with no one to care for them, and the burden of caregiving can sometimes surpass what families can provide on their own. Therefore, the political community has a role in ensuring that dependents receive adequate care, and in distributing the burdens of caregiving in a fair way.[25]

Thus, I believe that we can identify five broad sets of needs that subpolitical communities cannot justly and reliably attain on their own in the absence of an overarching political authority: (1) Public Order: facilitating social harmony by establishing rules and regulations for communal life;

25. For more on this point, see Tollefsen, "Disability and Social Justice."

(2) Restorative Justice and Dispute Resolution: impartially adjudicating disputes among members of the community and redressing offenses; (3) Security (army/police): defending against external and internal threats; (4) Public Goods: ensuring the provision and fair distribution of public goods, such as utilities and infrastructure; and (5) Social Welfare: assuring that the needy and dependent (children, the sick, the disabled, victims of disasters) are fairly and adequately cared for.[26] The first three needs correspond roughly to the legislative, judicial, and executive functions of government, respectively. The next two are further specifications of areas in which the legislative function of government is needed to overcome coordination problems for the common good.[27] By justly and reliably enabling these needs to be met, the government supplies the conditions that facilitate the flourishing of the community's members. These conditions of flourishing constitute the political common good, the specific common good for which the political community as such exists. Because these conditions are all elements of, or preconditions for, peaceful and just social relations, one can also refer to the political common good more generally as consisting in peace and justice.[28]

Note that the claim here is not that subpolitical communities will be entirely incapable of meeting these needs or supplying these conditions in the absence of an overarching political authority. Rather, the claim is that political authority is required in order to meet these needs both justly and reliably. The discussion of political authority in the next section will help to show why this is the case.

POLITICAL AUTHORITY

How does the political community supply the conditions necessary for the flourishing of subpolitical communities? It does so by exercising authority

---

26. This list is adapted, with some minor modifications, from the one offered by Tollefsen, "Pure Perfectionism," 208. On the distinctive role of political authority in punishment and restorative justice, see note 7, above.

27. I am grateful to Marshall Bierson for pointing out this correspondence between the insufficiencies of subpolitical communities and the three main functions of government.

28. Finnis, *Aquinas*, 226–28.

over subpolitical communities and their members through the establishment of organs of governance.[29] Political authority, exercised through some form of government, is necessary most fundamentally because none of the elements of the political common good described above can be achieved without coordination among the various individuals and subpolitical communities that make up political society. And effective coordination, especially among large groups of people, cannot effectively or reliably be achieved without authority. Further, *coercive* authority will be needed to *justly* secure these elements of the political common good. For in a society of imperfectly virtuous individuals, many will be inclined to enjoy the benefits of others' cooperative efforts without contributing their fair share, and coercion will be needed to prevent this from happening and punish offenders when it does happen.

To see why effective coordination cannot be reliably or justly achieved without authority, consider a somewhat simple example: a set of thirty families would like to build a playground in the neighborhood for their children. In order to do so, a number of decisions need to be made: Where will the playground be located? What sorts of features should the playground include? Who is going to build it? How will funds be collected to pay for the project? There are a wide variety of reasonable answers to these and similar questions, but unless the families agree on a single plan, the project will never move forward. Agreement can be obtained in only one of two ways: through unanimity or through authority, which could include an authoritative decision-making procedure, such as majority vote.

Given the existence of so many reasonable options, unanimity is highly unlikely, even if (as is rarely the case in real life) all involved are deliberating in a fully reasonable way, are in full possession of all the relevant facts, and are genuinely concerned not only with their own welfare but with the good of all. Indeed, the more intelligent, knowledgeable, and public-minded everyone is, the more ideas are likely to be generated in the deliberation process. Some form of authority will therefore be needed in order to settle on

29. A political community's organs of governance are sometimes referred to as "the state." Since the term "state" can, however, also be used as a synonym for the political community as a whole, I will instead use the term "government."

and execute a unified plan for the project.[30] The families might, for instance, elect a small committee to formulate a plan and agree to abide by their decision, or they might agree to abide by the outcome of a vote among several options proposed by the committee. Without some such designation of a particular person, group, and/or procedure as authoritative, however, the unity necessary for common action will be extremely difficult if not impossible to achieve.[31] Further, in the more realistic scenario where the families are selfishly looking out only for their own interests or the deliberations are marred by disinformation, bias, and the like, authority backed by some form of coercive force is likely to be needed in order to bring the recalcitrant into line (making sure, for instance, that all families pay their fair share to support the project).

Although in real-life societies the fact that most individuals are imperfectly virtuous (and some are outright malicious) means that political authority will need to be able to enforce its directives through coercion when necessary, and although the right to secure compliance through coercion is distinctive of political authority, the essence of authority is not that it is coercive.[32] Indeed, society would not function unless most people followed the directives of authority without needing to be coerced, and reducing political authority to its coercive element would leave us unable to distinguish government from a criminal gang. Rather, the essence of authority is that it gives us a new reason for action of a special type. More specifically, the essence of

30. Simon notes that even in a community whose members are perfectly virtuous, "if unity of action is guaranteed by no other principle than that of unanimous agreement, it becomes an entirely casual affair, the result being either stalemate or divided and destructive action" (Simon, *A General Theory of Authority*, 40).

31. Marshall Bierson pointed out to me that the problem goes even deeper than this. For the families also need a procedure to decide on the person, group, or procedure that will have authority, and this decision will also have to be either unanimous or decided by authority. In relatively small groups, such unanimity may sometimes be possible, but at the scale of a political community it will probably be impossible. It is therefore not surprising that, as a historical matter, political authority initially tends to be imposed by force.

32. The claim that the right to secure compliance through coercion is distinctive of political authority relates to claims made above about the administration of justice being a distinctive function of political authority. See note 7, above.

authority is that its directives are not just one reason among many for which we might act, but instead function as a special kind of reason that operates on a different plane relatively isolated from the general flow of our practical deliberations. The directives of authority, in other words, are second-level reasons for action that preempt or exclude other reasons that we might have acted upon if the authority had not directed us to act otherwise.[33]

In the playground example, for instance, you might have had first-level reasons to prefer a padded rubber playground surface to artificial grass, or you might have been indifferent between the options because you do not understand the reasons why one might favor one over the other. Once, however, the relevant authority—the decision of an elected committee or the outcome of a vote—makes a final decision that artificial grass will be used, that determination gives you a second-level reason not to act on your reasons for preferring padded rubber in defiance of the vote, and instead to act on the plan to use artificial grass. Or, to take an example from daily life, the fact that the traffic light is red (expressing an authoritative directive indicating that I should stop the car until the light turns green) gives me a reason to stop, even when I have no independent reason to stop (e.g., when there are no other cars or pedestrians in sight and the intersection is clear). Further, the red light gives me a reason to exclude deliberation about whether or not to stop (except in such special circumstances as medical emergencies, when I reasonably judge that the authoritative directive is not meant to apply).

The challenges of coordinating a set of families to build a playground are nothing in comparison to the challenges of coordinating an entire political community to achieve the complex and multifaceted political common good. And as the example of failed states highlights, one cannot overstate the importance for human flourishing of establishing an effective government that can overcome coordination problems through authority (backed by coercive force when needed to bring the uncooperative or malicious into line). For it is only through effective government that subpolitical communities can justly and

---

33. "The fact that an authority requires performance of an action is a reason for its performance which is not to be added to all other relevant reasons when assessing what to do, but should exclude and take the place of some of them" (Raz, *The Morality of Freedom*, 46). See also Finnis, *Natural Law and Natural Rights*, 233–34, and Raz, *Practical Reason and Norms*, 191.

reliably unite to achieve the conditions (public order, restorative justice, public goods, security, and social welfare) that will enable them to flourish. I should clarify that "effective" here means effective at promoting the political common good, not merely effective in the brute sense of being able to secure people's obedience. Because the political common good includes justice, for government to be effective in this sense it also has to be at least relatively just.

It is reasonable to treat the stipulations of government as authoritative—as giving us a reason to act that is protected from the normal flow of practical deliberation and that preempts countervailing reasons we might have to act otherwise—precisely because and insofar as doing so is necessary for achieving the unity of action required for the common good. This point has important implications for understanding the foundations of our obligation to obey the directives of political authority (i.e., laws). Contrary to the claims of influential social contract theorists such as Thomas Hobbes and John Locke in the early modern period, or John Rawls in the contemporary period, on the natural law view what makes government legitimate and gives us an obligation to obey the laws is not the actual or hypothetical consent of the political community's members. Rather, on the natural law view the source of government's legitimacy and of our obligation to obey the laws is that it can and does (albeit imperfectly) justly and efficiently resolve coordination problems for the common good.[34] We should consent to such a government, but that consent is not in itself the foundation of the government's legitimacy.

To understand this point more clearly, it is helpful to remember that the fundamental moral requirement of natural law is to choose and act in a way that is compatible with the ideal of integral human fulfillment. This ideal of integral human fulfillment is synonymous with the concept of the universal common good, or the all-around flourishing of the whole human community. Another implication of the master moral principle articulated in chapter 2, therefore, is the moral norm requiring us to favor and foster the common good.[35] Chapter 3's analysis of subpolitical communities and

---

34. Raz, *Practical Reason*, 250.

35. Long, "Fundamental Errors," 117–20, who criticizes new natural law theory for supposedly denying the priority of the common good, seems to miss this basic point, and the crucial distinction between the all-inclusive common good and the political common good.

the special obligations to which they give rise indicates that often the most reasonable way to promote the universal common good is to promote the common good of the particular communities to which one belongs, beginning with one's family, friends, church, workplace, neighborhood, and extending to the political community necessary for these subpolitical communities to survive and thrive (all in a way that respects and is alive to the requirements of the universal common good). The obligation to obey the directives of political authority is therefore an implication of the more basic moral norm requiring us to favor and foster the common good, combined with a recognition that the common good of subpolitical communities cannot be achieved without the political common good, which in turn cannot be achieved without political authority.

THE LIMITS OF POLITICAL AUTHORITY

The previous section argued that political authority is justified because it is necessary in order to justly and reliably achieve the political common good, which in turn is crucial for the overall flourishing of society's members. Yet political authority is not without limits. The limits on political authority—just like its justification—ultimately stem from considerations about the nature of human flourishing and the conditions that best promote human flourishing.

We can divide the limits on political authority into substantive limits and procedural ones. The substantive limits can in turn be subdivided into (1) limits that flow directly from the moral requirements of the natural law, and (2) limits that flow from the restricted scope of the political common good. The procedural limits on political authority are best captured by the requirements of the rule of law.

Substantive Limits on Government

With regard to the first category of substantive limits on government, political authority must be exercised in accord with the principles of natural law. The previous section argued that the authority of laws (and other government directives) is derived ultimately from their connection to the common good, which natural law requires us to promote. Therefore, as Aquinas argues, all positive laws (laws made by government) ultimately have their moral force from the natural law. The connection between positive laws and natural law is sometimes relatively direct, as when laws enforce the natural law prohibitions on rape and murder. Yet most laws relate more indirectly to natural law by way of what Aquinas calls the *determinatio* ("determination" or "specification") of the legislator.[36] The legislator's role here is an exercise of specifically political prudence, analogous to the exercise of individual prudence in making personal decisions about matters for which there are a range of practically reasonable options. For example, natural law indicates that one should drive with due regard for the preservation of life and health, but there is no single right answer in principle to questions such as how fast one should drive, when one should stop at an intersection, or which side of the road one should drive on. By establishing traffic laws, legislators specify (for those within their jurisdiction) the more general obligation to drive safely. Similar things could be said about the general moral obligation to contribute one's fair share for the provision of public goods and services, which legislators specify through tax laws.

The fact that all positive laws derive their moral force from the natural law also means that laws contrary to natural law are beyond the scope of legitimate political authority, for no such law can actually promote the common good. Any law, policy, or government action that, for instance, commands or promotes intentional killing of innocent human beings—such as the genocidal laws in Nazi Germany—would violate the moral norm prohibiting intentional destruction of basic human goods. And because the political common good is to facilitate the pursuit of flourishing by the community's members, any law that directly attacks a basic element of human flourishing is clearly contrary to the common good. Similarly, patently unfair laws that violate the Golden Rule—such as the racial segregation laws famously criticized by Martin Luther King Jr. in his "Letter from a Birmingham Jail"—are contrary to natural law and therefore illegitimate.

This point can also be expressed with reference to human rights. All genuine human rights express the requirements of justice from the perspective of the beneficiary. Absolute human rights—such as the right not to be murdered, raped, or tortured—are the flip side of the absolute moral

---

36. Aquinas, *Summa theologiae* I-II, q. 95, a. 2.

prohibition on damage to basic human goods. Any treatment of another person or group that violates the Golden Rule—such as unjustly taking a person's property, or unjust discrimination against a particular class of people—can also be understood as a violation of human rights. Any law that violates a genuine human right is, by definition, necessarily unjust, and therefore contrary to the common good and outside the scope of legitimate political authority.

The second set of substantive limits on government flows from the restricted scope of the specifically political common good, which consists in the conditions that facilitate the pursuit of flourishing by society's members. I summarized those conditions above and grouped them into the following five categories: Public Order; Restorative Justice and Dispute Resolution; Security; Public Goods; and Social Welfare. The restricted scope of the political common good implies that governments should not seek to enforce all of the requirements or prohibitions of the natural law—not use their coercive authority to lead people to the fullness of moral perfection—but instead should limit themselves to prohibiting or requiring only external, other-regarding actions that are sufficiently public to have a significant bearing on the political common good. Further, full moral perfection requires having the right inner dispositions, not only performing the right external actions. And government is poorly suited to the task of shaping inner dispositions, which requires intimate knowledge of a person. In addition, government should usually exercise its authority through laws, one feature of which is their generality. Yet general laws are too crude and broad to perform the delicate and individualized task of shaping internal virtuous dispositions, which require attentiveness to and knowledge of all the relevant individual circumstances. Purely paternalistic legislation—legislation aimed solely to promote the moral perfection of individuals—is therefore beyond the government's sphere of competence.[37]

---

37. Tollefsen, "Pure Perfectionism," 217. George has argued that purely paternalistic legislation—albeit often imprudent—is not unjust in principle. Nonetheless, his primary concern in making this argument seems to be to defend the legitimacy of laws aimed at establishing and maintaining *public* morality, and thus there is likely to be little (if any) difference between his view and my own at least in their practical implications (George, *Making Men Moral*, chap. 1).

For instance, even though natural law prohibits lying, it would be beyond the scope of government to prohibit lying in a private context, such as lying to one's friends about the reason one is declining their invitation to a party. Such lies do harm the good of friendship and the integrity of the one who tells them, thus indirectly damaging the common good, but they are insufficiently public to fall within the purview of government. Further, enforcement of a legal prohibition on private lying would require intrusive government surveillance of private conversations and relationships, taking away the intimacy and privacy that are necessary conditions for the development of genuine friendship, and this would harm the common good much more directly than private lying would. On the other hand, it does fall within the scope of government to prohibit lies that are public or have direct public effect, such as fraud or libel, and the public nature of these lies makes it possible to enforce a prohibition against them without undermining the privacy necessary for the cultivation of friendship and other goods.

This argument against purely paternalistic laws does not imply, however, that government should be neutral about the good or indifferent to morality. Government neutrality about the good is both impossible and undesirable, for every law at least implicitly and indirectly aims at protecting, promoting, or facilitating the pursuit of some aspect of human flourishing, and this connection to human flourishing is what justifies government and law in the first place. Further, even seemingly private immorality can have a significant negative effect on a community's moral ecology, making it difficult for others to lead virtuous lives and undermining the efforts of parents to instill moral virtue in their children. George argues: "Whatever authority parents have over their own children, they lack the authority to deprive other people in the community, or other people's children, of the legal liberty to perform immoral acts; only public officials possess authority of that kind. If, however, public authorities fail to combat certain vices, the impact of widespread immorality on the community's moral environment is likely to make the task of parents who rightly forbid their own children from, say, indulging in pornography, extremely difficult."[38] The promotion and preservation of public morality requires the sort of overarching coordination

38. George, *Making Men Moral*, 27; see also George, "The Concept of Public Morality."

that only political authority can effectively provide; it is therefore an aspect of the common good that falls within the government's sphere of concern.

Because the purpose of government is limited to the specifically political common good, the use of political authority for primarily spiritual ends (e.g., eternal salvation) is also out of bounds. This does not mean that political authority should ignore the basic human good of religion or be indifferent to its members' fulfillment with respect to that good, but only that the government's role in this regard is an indirect one, consisting largely in securing the conditions (peace, religious freedom) within which individuals and subpolitical communities can seek the truth about God and order their lives in accordance with their religious beliefs.[39] The Second Vatican Council's Declaration on Religious Liberty (*Dignitatis humanae*) explains: "The religious acts whereby men, in private and in public and out of a sense of personal conviction, direct their lives to God transcend by their very nature the order of terrestrial and temporal affairs. Government therefore ought indeed to take account of the religious life of the citizenry and show it favor, since the function of government is to make provision for the common welfare. However, it would clearly transgress the limits set to its power, were it to presume to command or inhibit acts that are religious."[40] In other words, because religious acts transcend the political common good, they also transcend the scope of government. The natural law argument for the juridical separation of church and state rests on this claim, together with the claims made above about the inability to coerce genuine religious acts, and also prudential claims, borne out by history, regarding the dangers—including dangers to the good of religion itself—of mixing political and religious authority.

Government is also limited because its purpose is to secure the conditions by which people can pursue their good, and freedom is a prerequisite for the pursuit of many goods. In order to fulfill its function, therefore, government must respect and protect civil liberties, including freedom of speech,

39. See Moschella, "Beyond Equal Liberty," and Finnis, "Religion and State."

40. Second Vatican Council, *Dignitatis humanae*, 3. Finnis argues that this position reflects Aquinas's view of the essential distinction between temporal (political) and spiritual (ecclesial) authority, with the former existing for the purpose of promoting earthly peace and justice within its territory, and the latter existing for the purpose of helping all human persons achieve eternal beatitude (Finnis, "Religion and State," 120). See also Finnis, *Aquinas*, 222–45; Aquinas, *Summa theologiae* I-II q. 96, a. 3; q. 98, a. 1; q. 100, a. 2.

association, and religion, plus economic freedom and private property. Freedom of speech makes possible the free exchange of ideas necessary for the attainment of knowledge, and the communication necessary for cooperation. Cooperation with others is, in turn, crucial for the pursuit of a wide range of goods, and is also intrinsically valuable insofar as it instantiates the basic human good of friendship. However, the value of free speech is instrumental; speech is only valuable insofar as it contributes to human goods. Further, some speech (even if it is valuable) may harm human goods. There can, therefore, be good reasons for government to place restrictions on speech, even valuable speech. To take a noncontroversial example, governments can forbid loud speech in a residential neighborhood in the middle of the night. Nonetheless, given the importance of free speech for the pursuit of human goods, and the danger that government officials will abuse their regulatory power to, for instance, disfavor speech that they disagree with or that is contrary to their personal interests, limits on speech require a high bar of justification, especially limits that are based on the speech's content.[41]

Similar things can be said about other civil liberties. Freedom of association respects the basic good of friendship, and recognizes that—as a communion of wills—genuine human communities can only be formed freely, and require a certain degree of privacy to facilitate the sharing of personal information and the building up of trust. Religious freedom can also be defended with reference to the special, architectonic role that the good of religion plays in the lives of those who are fully aware of its demands, together with the recognition that—like friendship—this good can only be

41. For a fuller discussion of the scope and limits of freedom of speech, see George, *Making Men Moral*, 192–208. For instance, George argues that content-based restrictions on speech can be justified only in very rare cases, cases in which "(1) the speech to be restricted is not the sort of speech that makes for true communication and cooperation, but rather, is something else, such as gratuitous abuse (as when neo-Nazis march through a neighborhood populated by Holocaust survivors shouting 'send Jews to the ovens') or sheer manipulation (as when unscrupulous advertisers attempt to induce anxious elderly people to invest in sham life-insurance policies); or (2) the cooperation made possible by the speech in question is for manifestly evil ends (as in typical cases of criminal conspiracy); or (3) the speech in question is likely to result in serious harms or injustices or prevent the realization of important goods (as in cases of speech that reveals national security secrets or the whereabouts of persons in government witness programs)" (George, *Making Men Moral*, 198–99).

participated in freely, for coerced religious acts do not instantiate the good of religion at all, but are actually contrary to human flourishing with respect to both religion and authenticity.[42]

Government should generally respect (and protect) private property because it is instrumentally necessary not only for the efficient use and care of material resources, but also for the self-constitution of individuals, for their exercise of agency, and thus for what Finnis refers to as the "good of personal autonomy in community."[43] Just imagine if the government or some private individual could, at any time and without warning, take away your house, car, clothing, food, or other property that you use for your daily life and work. The mere prospect of this would be extremely unsettling and detrimental to the pursuit of almost any human good. However, property rights are not absolute, for the earth's resources are fundamentally for the good of all.[44] This means that when our property exceeds what we need to support ourselves and our families and to facilitate the fulfillment of our professional or other vocational obligations, we have an obligation to use that excess property for the common good.[45] Although this can be done in many ways—philanthropy, investment, job-creation—because this excess property is something that we effectively hold in trust for the common good, it is not in principle unjust for the government to require us to use some of our excess wealth not only to help pay for public goods that we ourselves benefit from, but also to fund social welfare programs that provide assistance to members of society who are in need.[46] The natural law view is

42. These arguments have been developed at length elsewhere. See, e.g., Moschella, "Beyond Equal Liberty"; George, *Making Men Moral*, 219–28.

43. Finnis, *Natural Law and Natural Rights*, 169; George, *Making Men Moral*, 170; Aquinas, *Summa theologiae* II-II, q. 66, a. 2.

44. Finnis, *Natural Law and Natural Rights*, 172.

45. Finnis summarizes the argument for private ownership and its inherent limits as follows: "The point, in justice, of private property is to give owners first use and enjoyment of their thing and its fruits (including rents and profits), for it is this availability that enhances their reasonable autonomy and stimulates their productivity and care. But beyond a reasonable measure and degree of such use for them and their dependents' or co-owners' needs, they each hold the remainder of their property and its fruits as part (in justice if not in law) of the common stock. . . . At this point, owners have, in justice, duties not altogether unlike those of a trustee in English law" (Finnis, *Natural Law and Natural Rights*, 173).

46. Finnis, *Natural Law and Natural Rights*, 173.

therefore fundamentally at odds with the extreme libertarian view that sees redistributive taxation as akin to theft or forced labor, not only because the natural law account views the right to private property as instrumental and inherently limited, but also because the natural law account has a more expansive view of the political common good than the libertarian account.[47]

Another substantive limit on government that flows from the restricted scope of the political common good relates back to the nature of political community as a community composed of subpolitical communities. This limit is sometimes referred to as the "principle of subsidiarity," which indicates that larger, overarching communities, such as the political community, exist to assist the smaller, more basic communities, such as the family, that compose them, and that in providing this assistance the overarching community has an obligation to respect the self-governance of these more basic communities.[48] This principle flows not only from the very nature and purpose of political authority, but also from respect for individuals' capacity for self-constitution, and thus for the basic goods of integrity and authenticity, in addition to the basic goods of friendship and marriage.[49] The principle protects these goods by assuring that subpolitical communities (and individuals) are not swallowed up by the political community, but rather that their proper spheres of competence and authority are protected. It should be noted, however, that the principle of subsidiarity is not a one-way street regarding government's relationship to subpolitical communities, but should instead be understood as a principle of mutual assistance in which each type of community fulfills its proper role in relation to the all-inclusive common good.[50]

In other words, the principle of subsidiarity can be understood as an implication of the fact that individuals, families, and other subpolitical associations have their own particular responsibilities vis-à-vis the all-inclusive

47. Nozick, *Anarchy, State, and Utopia*, 169.

48. This principle has been consistently articulated in the social teaching of the Catholic Church. See, e.g., John Paul II, *Centesimus annus*, no. 48: "A community of a higher order should not interfere in the internal life of a community of a lower order, depriving the latter of its functions, but rather should support it in case of need and help to coordinate its activity with the activities of the rest of society, always with a view to the common good."

49. Finnis, *Natural Law and Natural Rights*, 168–69.

50. Hittinger, "The Three Necessary Societies."

common good, responsibilities that correspond to their particular competencies, and that in some instances go beyond the scope of the political common good. The special intimacy that parents have with their children gives them a unique competency (and responsibility) for their children's moral education, and more generally for making decisions about what is in their children's best interests. The government lacks this competency, and so its role in this area is normally a subsidiary one—to assist parents in fulfilling their educational and child-rearing obligations. Similarly, though the all-inclusive common good includes the all-around flourishing of every member of the political community, there are aspects of this flourishing only the individual is competent to pursue. The government is not competent, for example, to tell me how I ought to prioritize competing goods in my life, because (as the Vocation Principle indicates) such decisions can only be reasonably made from the vantage point of one's own vocational commitments and obligations. The Vocation Principle therefore implies that individuals and groups need a certain sphere of freedom from government intrusion within which they can direct their own affairs.

Procedural Limits on Government: The Rule of Law

Governing in a way that is conducive to human flourishing not only means respecting certain substantive limits on political authority, but also exercising that authority in accordance with certain procedures and forms—in accordance with the rule of law.

Before considering why exercising authority through rule of law is an important condition for the flourishing of a political community's members—and thus a requirement of natural law—it is necessary to explain what the rule of law is. Perhaps the most fully developed statement of the formal characteristics of the rule of law can be found in Lon Fuller's *The Morality of Law*. In chapter 2, Fuller outlines eight characteristics of the rule of law, which I summarize here:[51]

1. Laws are general rules that provide a consistent standard of action, as opposed to judgments made on a case-by-case basis.

51. Fuller, *The Morality of Law*, chap. 2.

2. Laws must be promulgated—they must be published and made known publicly.
3. Laws must be prospective, not retroactive; they must govern future conduct, not declare past conduct illegal.
4. Laws must have clarity and avoid vague or incoherent formulas.
5. Laws should not have contradictory or incompatible provisions.
6. Laws should not demand the impossible.
7. Laws should be relatively stable over time, and changes should not be too frequent or sudden.
8. Official action should be congruent with what the law states.

The concept of the rule of law applies not only to particular laws and their administration but to the system of government as a whole. It implies, in other words, that government itself be established and governed by a set of laws, a constitution. The U.S. Constitution, for example, sets forth the scope and limits of the power of the federal government and of each of its branches (executive, legislative, and judicial). It also outlines the requisite procedures to enact a law. Each U.S. state also has its own constitution, which serves the same purposes.

Governing in accordance with the rule of law is no guarantee of justice, for laws duly enacted and possessing all the formal characteristics outlined by Fuller may still be seriously unjust, contrary to the flourishing of society's members. Nonetheless, the formal and procedural requirements of the rule of law do in and of themselves facilitate justice and the common good in a number of ways.

First, the rule of law introduces clarity, stability, and predictability into human affairs. This is important because all the pursuits—professional, social, religious, intellectual, cultural, and so on—that contribute to our flourishing as individuals and communities are carried out over time and require a certain degree of clarity and stability in the rules and regulations that affect them. The stability and predictability of laws create the conditions within which we can exercise our agency in pursuit of various goods.[52]

Second, and relatedly, the requirements of the rule of law impose self-discipline on those in authority by limiting the processes by which laws

---

52. Finnis, *Natural Law and Natural Rights*, 272.

can be enacted and executed. This self-discipline engenders reciprocity, fairness, and respect between ruler and ruled, insofar as legal norms and procedures bind rulers to "their end of the bargain." Finnis explains that there is intrinsic value to the rule of law because it "is based on the notion that a certain quality of interaction between ruler and ruled, involving reciprocity and procedural fairness, is very valuable for its own sake; it is not merely a means to other social ends, and may not lightly be sacrificed for such other ends."[53] Thus, one might argue that the rule of law in itself represents a form of civic friendship.

The respect between ruler and ruled that the rule of law embodies is required by the dignity of human beings as rational agents. To see why this is the case, consider the way in which farmers govern their livestock by contrast with the way in which political authorities (should) govern those under their rule.[54] Farmers use various methods to, literally or figuratively, poke and prod the animals to behave as they want them to. If the methods are not cruel, this way of treating livestock seems morally acceptable. Indeed, it would be silly for a farmer to explain to his cows or chickens why they ought to behave in certain ways, for animals are incapable of understanding and acting for reasons. However, humans have the capacity to understand and act based on reasons, and we recognize certain things—such as health, knowledge, friendship, and religion—as genuinely good and part of our fulfillment as human beings. We can make free choices in pursuit of such goods, both individually and collectively. We can, in other words, deliberate and choose, and this makes us rational agents who are morally responsible for our actions. As rational agents, we ought not to be governed through poking and prodding, as farmers rule livestock. Instead, we ought to be governed in ways that respect our dignity as rational agents, and this generally requires those in authority to abide by the principles of the rule of law.

To fully understand how the rule of law embodies respect for the rational agency of those under its authority, it is also worth noting another characteristic of law: the inherent connection between law and reason. Aquinas provides the classic definition of law as an "ordinance of reason for the common good, made by him who has care of the community, and promul-

53. Finnis, *Natural Law and Natural Rights*, 274.
54. George, "Reason, Freedom and the Rule of Law," 254.

gated."[55] This means that laws are not the arbitrary or self-interested dictates of a ruler's will, but instead that the moral force of law comes from its reasonableness and its connection to the common good. Given that practical reason directs us to promote the common good of our communities, following laws that are genuine ordinances of reason for the common good respects our dignity as rational agents because we can understand the reasons behind such laws and adopt them as our own. Ideally, therefore, law governs not primarily through force, manipulation, or the threat of punishment, but by providing genuine reasons for abiding by the laws.[56]

Since law's purpose is to serve the common good, there may be exceptional circumstances in which the needs of the common good justify departures from the rule of law. Indeed, most constitutions include clauses that allow executive officials to rule by decree in cases of emergency, bypassing the usual procedures for making laws. However, departures from the rule of law inflict real costs on the common good. Besides making it difficult or impossible for individuals and groups to make and carry out plans in almost any area of life, the costs include deeper, less obvious harms. Such rule by decree can undermine the sense of reciprocity and respect between ruler and ruled, leading significant segments of society to feel they are being poked and prodded into conformity like livestock, rather than being respected as rational agents whose judgments and concerns merit consideration, even if they differ from those of ruling elites. The recent experience of living under extended emergency rule during the COVID-19 pandemic is a vivid illustration of both these points. Therefore, though emergency powers are sometimes justified, departures from the rule of law and from standard legislative procedures should be rare and of relatively short duration. The deliberations and delays of enacting legislation may tempt government officials to extend emergency powers or push the limits of executive authority in other ways, but this temptation needs to be resisted (sometimes forcefully through judicial action when necessary). For the "inefficiency" of legislative processes and constitutional checks and balances needs to be understood as a positive feature of the rule of law, promoting the legal stability

55. Aquinas, *Summa theologiae* I-II, q. 90.

56. Nonetheless, it is a distinct function of political authority to punish in accordance with the rule of law for the sake of restoring justice. See note 7, above.

and predictability essential for human flourishing and ensuring (at least in principle) that the legitimate competing interests and judgments of diverse groups be considered. Respecting these constitutional limits not only makes it more likely that laws will promote a just distribution of the benefits and burdens of common life, but also fosters and embodies the mutual respect among citizens and between ruler and ruled that is crucial for the common good.

NATURAL LAW AND LIBERALISM

The natural law account of politics I have offered here overlaps in many of its conclusions with liberal accounts, for both support limited government, the rule of law, respect for civil liberties, separation of church and state, and respect for a private sphere of freedom from government intrusion. Nonetheless, the natural law account's justification of these limits on government power are quite different from those typically offered by liberal thinkers. Many of liberalism's presuppositions—about human nature, the human good, morality, and the justification of political authority—are clearly at odds with the natural law account I have presented.[57]

For example, liberalism encompasses a variety of perspectives, but liberal justifications of individual freedom and related arguments against purely paternalistic laws are often based on claims that the state should not govern with a view toward any particular substantive account of the human good.[58] John Rawls, for instance, argues for the priority of the right over the good, that is, for an account of justice independent of comprehensive conceptions of the good.[59] By contrast with most liberal accounts, the natural law account does

---

57. See, e.g., George, *Making Men Moral*, and Moschella, "Social Contract Theory."

58. This is not to say that liberal accounts are in fact neutral about the good, for they arguably rely implicitly on substantive views about the good life even while aspiring to neutrality. James Bohman and Henry Richardson, for instance, have argued persuasively that Rawls's political liberalism, though it claims to be independent of any comprehensive conception of the good, actually ends up importing a comprehensive liberal view into the notion of what counts as a "public reason" that can provide legitimate grounds for political coercion (Bohman and Richardson, "Liberalism").

59. Rawls, *Political Liberalism*, and Rawls, "The Priority of Right"; see also Dworkin, *Taking Rights Seriously*. Raz, *The Morality of Freedom*, however, argues for a perfectionist liberal account of politics.

not believe that government and law should be neutral about the good or take no interest in the moral virtue of citizens.[60] Indeed, on the natural law view it is not possible to determine what justice requires independent of a substantive account of the human good, for acting justly is ultimately a matter of respecting the good of others in its various basic dimensions. And though I have argued that the government is not competent to inculcate the fullness of moral virtue in citizens, it is within the scope of government authority to command external acts of virtue (or forbid external acts of vice) insofar as these are related to the political common good of justice and peace, which includes the fostering and maintenance of public morality.[61]

Further, the natural law account holds that the state should not facilitate activities or forms of life that are worthless or immoral, such as hedonistic drug use or prostitution, simply because some people want to engage in them. Although liberty is an important instrumental good, on the natural law view there is no value in unreasonable choices just as such. There might be reasons to legally tolerate such bad choices to avoid greater harm, but there is no reason to promote or facilitate such choices. The account I offer above defends liberty and limited government not on the grounds of relativism or neutrality about the good, but rather on the grounds that they are instrumentally important for human flourishing and respectful of citizens as self-governing agents with authority to direct themselves (and the communities in their care) toward their own good.

Further, the natural law account I have offered here presents political community as largely instrumental, but it nonetheless recognizes that there are some noninstrumental aspects of political community and the specifically political common good, and this is also a feature that differentiates it from liberalism. For there are aspects of political society that instantiate the basic human good of friendship, and are therefore noninstrumental. The cooperation of political society's members in the pursuit of the overarching common good of the political community (not just the more limited political common good, but the all-around good of the community's members) is a form of civic friendship. "In a really well-ordered society, the

---

60. Finnis explicitly criticizes Rawls on this point, arguing that the Rawlsian view unreasonably treats favoring genuine goods as bias (Finnis, *Natural Law and Natural Rights*, 109, 130, 453). See also Tollefsen, "Pure Perfectionism," 210.

61. Finnis, *Aquinas*, 232–34.

shared final end of each is the well-being of all," writes Finnis.[62] In addition, the administration of justice (which can be understood as in some sense restoring the social harmony that has been damaged by unjust behavior) is also an instantiation of the good of friendship.[63] These aspects of political community are intrinsic goods worthy of pursuit for their own sake.

In addition, the natural law account differs from the liberal account in that it justifies political authority as natural — as a requirement of practical reason — because of its instrumental necessity for the resolution of coordination problems in view of the common good. The natural law account recognizes, along with Aristotle, that human beings are political by nature, meaning that the formation of political communities is natural to human beings because it is necessary for human flourishing. Liberal justifications of political authority, on the other hand, tend to view political community and political authority as in some sense artificial (absent from the "state of nature"), and therefore argue that it can only be justified with reference to actual or hypothetical consent.[64] On the natural law view, consent is not necessary for the justification of political authority, but a practically reasonable person should consent to political authority insofar as it justly and efficiently resolves coordination problems for the common good.[65] Unlike the liberal account, therefore, the natural law view sees the formation of political community and the establishment of political authority as natural — as

62. Finnis, *Natural Law and Natural Rights*, 157. Finnis makes this remark in the context of criticizing the Rawlsian liberal view.

63. Finnis, "Reflections and Reponses," 514 and 518–20.

64. See, e.g., Locke, *Second Treatise*; Rawls, *Political Liberalism*. The natural law account does recognize that — where authoritative rules for the location of authority do not yet exist — the notion of consent may provide a helpful "rule of thumb" indicating that "someone's stipulation has authority when practically reasonable subjects, with the common good in view, would think they ought to consent to it" (Finnis, *Natural Law and Natural Rights*, 251).

65. Finnis, *Natural Law and Natural Rights*, 250. It should be recalled here that the common good requires that authority generally be exercised through law. This means that once the initial coordination problem of establishing political authority over a set of sub-political communities has been resolved, authoritative rules indicating how authority is to be located and transmitted should be enacted — i.e., a constitutional order should be established — so that this most basic coordination problem can itself be resolved in the future through the rule of law.

requirements of practical reason—and therefore does not need to rely upon a voluntarist, consent-based account of political legitimacy.

Finally, the natural law account differs from the liberal account in viewing the family, rather than the autonomous individual, as the fundamental unit of society. The individualism of the liberal view is exemplified in the way Rawls sets up his hypothetical social contract, the parties to which are autonomous adults in the "Original Position," shorn of all family and community ties, and of any substantive account of the human good.[66] But where do Rawls's autonomous adults come from? I emphasized in chapter 3 that the natural law view recognizes human beings as deeply relational and interdependent—beings who only reach the relative independence of adulthood after years of almost complete dependence on parents and other caregivers and who are profoundly shaped by nonchosen ties to family, nation, and other communities in which we find ourselves. We come into this world as part of what MacIntyre calls a "network of givers and receivers," a web of relationships, interdependencies, and mutual obligations.[67] Similarly, Michael Sandel argues we are not the "unencumbered selves" that liberalism portrays us to be, but instead are "encumbered" by community bonds and nonchosen obligations that flow from those bonds.[68] And these "encumbrances" are not a bad thing, but give stability, depth, and meaning to our lives and identities. To be a person entirely free of these encumbrances is not—as the liberal view would have it—to be "an ideally free and rational agent," but is instead to be "a person wholly without character, without moral depth."[69] The nonchosen community bonds that MacIntyre and Sandel are referring to extend beyond the family, but they have the

---

66. Rawls, *Political Liberalism*, 22–25. Rawls argues that the Original Position is merely a "device of representation" and is not meant "to presuppose a particular metaphysical conception of the person" (27). Nonetheless, his view does indeed presuppose the controversial premise that it is possible to engage in practical deliberation without knowledge of the basic human goods. On the natural law view, however, all practical deliberation begins with a grasp of the basic human goods that provide us with basic reasons for action. Without at least an implicit grasp of basic goods, therefore, genuine practical deliberation is impossible. For more on this point, see Moschella, "Social Contract Theory."

67. MacIntyre, *Dependent Rational Animals*.

68. Sandel, "The Procedural Republic."

69. Sandel, "The Procedural Republic," 90.

family at their core (as I argued in chapter 3). Acknowledging that the family, rather than the autonomous individual, is the basic unit of society, has far-reaching political implications on issues ranging from parental rights to employment and welfare policies. This is, therefore, a crucial difference between liberalism and the natural law account of political community.

WHAT ABOUT PATRIOTISM?

Even with the clarifications made in the previous section, it might be objected that the largely instrumental account of the specifically political common good leaves us with a view of the political community as barely more than a glorified utility company. Some might worry that a political community conceived in this way can hardly inspire patriotic dedication to the common good, particularly when—as in times of war—such dedication requires considerable self-sacrifice. To borrow from MacIntyre, asking people to be willing to die for their country seems, in this context, like asking them to die for the telephone company.[70] This line of objection, however, fails for several reasons.

First, the object of patriotism is not the political community as such, considered in its specific and limited function of securing the political common good through government and law. Rather, the object of patriotism is what we might call the "nation" or the "homeland." Grisez makes an important distinction between the nation, which is the primary object of patriotism, and that nation's political organization and government.[71] To illustrate this distinction, consider Poland, which for a significant portion of its history was under the rule of various foreign powers. Even during those periods of history when Poland ceased to exist as a political society with its own government, it continued to exist as a nation and as an object of patriotic loyalty for the Polish people.

Various factors bind a group of people together into a nation, such as living in relative geographic proximity; sharing a common language, history, and culture; developing social ties through work, play, trade, intermarriage, and so

---

70. MacIntyre, "A Partial Response," 303.
71. Grisez, *Living a Christian Life*, 11.A.

on.[72] A sense of national identity and corresponding patriotic loyalty also stems from attachment to the region's particular natural features, geography, and climate. Just consider the lyrics of typical American patriotic songs. For instance, the first verse of *America, the Beautiful* invites us to sing: "O beautiful for spacious skies, for amber waves of grain, for purple mountain majesties above the fruited plain." Similarly, *God Bless America* admires "the mountains," "the prairies," and "the oceans white with foam," and *My Country 'Tis of Thee* proclaims, "I love thy rocks and rills, thy woods and templed hills." Such songs also praise national ideals, such as liberty, or aspects of national history, including periods of that history, such as the experience of the Pilgrims, which predate the nation's existence as an independent political community. There are, therefore, many factors that tie one to one's nation even considered apart from its specifically political organization and government.

Further, in a way that is analogous to one's family, one's nation with its unique culture, history, and geography shapes one's identity in important and lasting ways. And just as one owes a certain debt of gratitude and reverence to one's parents, who are the source of one's biological life and identity, so too, analogously, is one indebted to one's nation.[73] Viewing the nation's specifically political organization and government as having the limited (though still formidable and extremely important) purpose of promoting the political common good does not detract from this in any way.

Finally, the account of the political common good given above, though more limited than many Aristotelians would like it to be, goes well beyond the provision of utilities. Crucially, the political common good includes the restoration of justice through criminal punishment (and sometimes civil compensation) when the balance of justice in society has been upset by wrongdoing. To have a justice system that is impartial, that operates in accordance with law, that respects the rights of the accused to a fair trial, among other things, is no small accomplishment, and is a crucial element of the flourishing of human beings in society.[74] The existence of such a system, even acknowledging that it is not always perfectly administered or entirely free of bias and corruption, is itself a reason for patriotism. Further, all of the

---

72. Grisez, *Living a Christian Life*, 11.A.1.a
73. Aquinas, *Summa theologiae* II-II, q. 101, a. 1.
74. See note 7, above.

elements of the political common good aim at justice in certain respects— and ultimately, by means of justice, at creating the conditions within which society's members can flourish. Government does not aim merely to create order and harmony among the community's members, but to do so in a way that is just, that involves a fair distribution of the benefits and burdens of community membership. Even the provision of public utilities or the government's role in ensuring that the needy and dependent receive adequate care includes the goal of just distribution of those benefits and a just sharing of the costs. Further, that all of these functions of government should be carried out through the rule of law is, in itself, an important aspect of justice and civic friendship. The account of political community offered here, therefore, is fully compatible with a healthy patriotism.

It is also important to highlight that, on this account, fulfilling one's patriotic duty will mean not only seeking to promote just laws and policies in the political sphere, but also working to promote the all-inclusive common good in ways that go beyond the competence of government. For example, the inculcation of full moral virtue is beyond the competence of the government, but is a crucial element of the all-inclusive common good that also facilitates the political common good. By diligently fulfilling their educational responsibilities and forming their children's moral character, parents not only benefit their children and their family community, but also contribute to the broader common good of the political community. Similar things could be said with regard to religious education. In addition to contributing to the all-inclusive common good through the fulfillment of parental and broader familial responsibilities, one can seek to promote the full truth about human flourishing in one's workplace, neighborhood, and throughout civil society, through example, friendship, and respectful dialogue. One can also help to create or join organizations of various sorts that aim to promote different aspects of human flourishing, contributing through such common activities to the development of solidarity and civic friendship.[75]

---

75. The points in the previous two paragraphs show how the largely instrumental definition of the political common good presented in this chapter is compatible with an appreciation for the ways in which political community does instantiate the basic good of friendship. For a more in-depth discussion related to this point, see Lewis, "Is the Common Good an Ensemble of Conditions?"

At the same time, the natural law account I have offered here recognizes the limits of patriotism and the need to promote the good of one's country in a way that always remains open to and respectful of the universal common good, the integral flourishing of the whole human community. Thus, genuine patriotism is opposed to seeking the good of one's nation in ways that are unjust toward other nations or indifferent to their needs. The discussion in chapter 3 of how community bonds justify and require some degree of partiality to the community's members implies that national ties and the special responsibilities that a nation's government has to its people justify some prioritization of the good of one's own nation over others. Yet as also indicated in chapter 3, such prioritization has limits. Natural law forbids intentional harm to basic human goods regardless of whether the people harmed are members of one's political community or not, and regardless of the supposed benefit that one's nation stands to gain from such harm. We can think here, for example, of natural law's exceptionless prohibition on torture, or the prohibition on targeting civilians even in a just war in which one is defending one's nation from unjust aggression.[76] Beyond such absolute prohibitions (which protect inviolable human rights), any prioritization of the good of "one's own" over others must satisfy the Golden Rule. For instance, presuming that one has the resources to help and can do so effectively, doing nothing when another nation faces a devastating natural disaster or other humanitarian crisis seems akin to walking by indifferently after spotting a child drowning in a fountain. Clearly, in such situations one would reasonably want and expect the other person or nation to come to one's aid if the tables were turned. Most situations are, of course, more complex than these. There is no formula for determining precisely how much of one's own nation's resources should be used to help other nations in need, and the issue is further complicated by uncertainties about whether aid will actually be beneficial, rather than creating dependencies or propping up corrupt or ineffective governments. My point here is not to provide anything close to an answer to these difficult questions of international justice, but simply to highlight how the natural law account I have offered both supports patriotism but also moderates it by requiring that we always be attentive to the good of the whole human community.

76. For a natural law argument against torture, see Tollefsen, *Biomedical Research*, 93–100, and Tollefsen, "Torture."

CONCLUSION

In this chapter, I have built on the arguments in the previous chapters to offer an account of political community and its contribution to human flourishing. I have emphasized that although political community as a whole exists for the sake of the all-inclusive common good—the all-around flourishing of its members—the specific role of coercive political authority with respect to this common good is limited and indirect. The specific role of political authority is to secure the conditions needed to facilitate the pursuit of flourishing by society's members, remedying subpolitical communities' lack of self-sufficiency with respect to public order, restorative justice and dispute resolution, security, public goods, and social welfare. This limited view of political authority's scope may sound "liberal" in terms of practical implications, but it does not rest on a liberal commitment to keeping comprehensive views of the good life out of politics. On the contrary, it is defended precisely by considering the ways in which genuine human flourishing requires that we freely exercise our agency in pursuit of the good for ourselves and the communities under our care, and by attending to the inherent limits of the government's capacity to lead people to the fullness of virtue. Such considerations help us to see that the limits on government relate to its subsidiary nature—that it exists to assist individuals and subpolitical communities to direct themselves toward their own good—and to the related recognition that responsibility for the all-inclusive common good is distributed among the various layers of society in accordance with their spheres of competence. Thus, the natural law account I have presented here acknowledges (in line with the Aristotelian tradition) that the purpose of political community is the all-around flourishing of its members, but it also acknowledges (in line with the liberal tradition) that the role of *government* in achieving this purpose is limited to securing the conditions that facilitate flourishing, which can be summarized as justice and peace. In this way, I believe that this account captures the best insights of both traditions, placing the defense of limited government on a more solid and satisfying foundation precisely by grounding it on the objective requirements of human flourishing.

FIVE

Human Flourishing,
Morality, and God

It is July 1941 at the Auschwitz concentration camp. Prisoners are ordered to line up, and ten will be selected to starve to death in retaliation for a prisoner who appears to have escaped. When the Nazi commander selects Franciszek Gajowniczek, the prisoner cries out in dismay: "My wife! My children!" Then, to everyone's amazement, another prisoner steps forward and volunteers to take Gajowniczek's place. The guard is taken aback, and the prisoner has to repeat his request: "I am a Catholic priest from Poland; I would like to take his place because he has a wife and children." The guard accepts the offer, and Gajowniczek gratefully returns to his place among the other prisoners. The Catholic priest who voluntarily took Gajowniczek's place was Maximilian Kolbe. In 1982, Kolbe was canonized a saint by the Catholic Church, and Gajowniczek was present to honor the heroism of the man who saved his life.[1]

---

1. Pettinger, "Biography of Maximilian Kolbe."

What could motivate someone to accept death—and not just any death, but a slow, painful death by starvation—to save the life of a stranger? What could enable someone to endure such a death calmly and even cheerfully, to the point that the Nazi guards themselves expressed amazement at Kolbe's courage?[2] Of course, what Kolbe did went beyond the requirements of natural law—he had no moral obligation to sacrifice his life for his fellow prisoner. But it is nonetheless interesting to consider what could provide someone with sufficient rational motivation to make such a choice, especially since it was far from guaranteed that he would succeed in saving Gajowniczek's life or enable him to reunite with his wife and children. After all, the Nazi guard could have scoffed at Kolbe's offer and punished his boldness by taking him in addition to the other ten prisoners. And even if the offer to take Kolbe's place was accepted, Gajowniczek's chances of survival were still slim. Further, Gajowniczek's wife and children were also likely to die before the end of the war, if they had not died already. In fact, his wife survived and he was reunited with her after the war, but his two sons were killed in a bombardment.[3]

These sorts of uncertainties about whether our choices and actions will in fact give rise to the good outcomes that motivated them are not limited to such dramatic cases as this, but the high stakes in this case make the problem especially poignant. Indeed, though we do not often stop to think about it, most of the desired effects of our actions—the goods that we seek to protect or promote by our actions—rely on a host of contingent factors over which we have no direct control.[4] Even a simple act such as taking a walk to get some exercise relies upon countless physical, biological, and chemical causes. Our ability to achieve the goods we seek is even more uncertain when the free cooperation of other human beings is required. To take an example likely to be familiar to many readers of this book: the success of a teacher's efforts in the classroom depends in no small part on the dispositions and choices of the students; on the other hand, the success of a student seeking to learn depends

---

2. Pettinger, "Biography of Maximilian Kolbe."

3. "Franciszek Gajowniczek."

4. I say "most" here because the effect of one's action on one's own character is not contingent on external factors, and is an important aspect of the type of future that one's action might bring about. I am grateful to Patrick Lee for pointing this out.

to a significant extent on whether the teacher explains the material in a clear, organized, and engaging manner.

Given all of these contingencies and uncertainties with regard to the fruits of our actions, one might easily be tempted to think: Is it really worth the effort to try to protect and promote human goods, acting in morally upright, virtuous ways, even when — as is often the case — this requires considerable toil and sacrifice? Can there be any assurance that our efforts and sacrifices will not be in vain?

Further, there are some cases in which it may seem that human goods might be more effectively promoted by violating moral norms rather than acting in accordance with those norms. In such cases, what can motivate us to act morally? What can assure us that, despite appearances to the contrary, violating moral norms is never truly compatible with integral human fulfillment?

My aim in this chapter is to consider how understanding God's relationship to human flourishing and morality can alleviate these problems, providing a deeper grounding for moral obligation and moral motivation. I will consider this primarily from the perspective of what can be known by rational reflection — as is fitting for a work of philosophical ethics — but at the end of the chapter I will venture a few reflections from the perspective of Christian revelation.

GOD AND MORAL OBLIGATION

In *The Brothers Karamazov*, Dostoyevsky (through one of his characters) famously poses the question, "Without God, are all things permitted?" The answer to this question is both yes and no, depending on how the question is understood. Throughout this book, I have argued that we can come to recognize the existence of moral principles and norms through rational reflection. Knowledge of these norms and principles — knowledge of natural law — is not logically dependent on knowledge of God's existence. Further, the moral force or obligatoriness of these norms is grounded on the directiveness of practical reason's first principles, which guide us to respect and pursue human goods. In other words, practical reason directs us toward integral human fulfillment, and this necessary connection between practical reason's directives and our flourishing gives moral force to those directives.

The answer to Dostoyevsky's question is no, therefore, insofar as one can know natural law, recognize its obligatoriness, and provide a sufficient rational justification for moral norms without knowledge of or reference to the existence or will of God.

At the same time, there are further questions about the moral order and moral obligation — questions related to the moral order's ultimate metaphysical foundations — that can only be fully answered by recognizing that God is the source of the moral order. Analogously, a physicist can discover and demonstrate the truth of Newton's laws of motion (for objects traveling below the speed of light) without adverting to the existence of God, but there are further questions about the source of the physical order and its intelligibility that cannot be fully answered without reference to God. The arguments for moral norms presented here, like the arguments for Newton's laws presented by a physicist, are sufficient within the order of knowledge to which they belong, but nonetheless fail to answer further metaphysical questions about the very foundations of that order. Of course, an important difference between physical laws of motion and moral norms is that we can choose whether or not to follow moral norms. And this is why understanding that God is the ultimate source of the moral order does have practical relevance insofar as it can deepen our sense of moral obligation and moral motivation.

It is beyond the scope of this book to present a full-fledged argument for the existence of God, but the very existence of a moral order and of human beings capable of knowing that order (along with the whole universe of other contingent beings whose existence does not explain itself) can be the starting point for several lines of reasoning leading to the conclusion that there must be a necessary (noncontingent) being who is the ultimate, uncaused cause of all that exists, and of its order and intelligibility.[5] Metaphysically speaking, therefore, the answer to Dostoyevsky's question is yes insofar as everything (including the moral order) depends on God as its ultimate cause, and without God we would not even be here to ask the question. Thus Aquinas, in considering the natural law from a metaphysical perspective, refers to the natural law as "the rational creature's participation

5. For a fuller version of an argument for the existence of God along these lines, see, e.g., Finnis, *Aquinas*, chap. 10; Grisez, *Beyond the New Theism*.

of the eternal law," which is God's governance of the universe as a whole.[6] And though on Aquinas's view we can know the natural law and recognize its obligatoriness even without adverting specifically to God, recognizing God as natural law's ultimate source can deepen our understanding of that law and of why we ought to follow it.[7]

Once we recognize that the principles and norms by which practical reason directs us toward our good have their ultimate source in God, we can then recognize those principles and norms as guidance from God, who knows and seeks what is good for us. Grisez, Boyle, and Finnis explain that if God is the transcendent source of the directiveness of our practical reason, this implies that God is "a person anticipating human fulfillment and leading human persons toward it."[8] Further, we also recognize that our actions in pursuit of human goods depend for their fulfillment on countless causes outside our direct control. For example, in pressing on various keys to type this sentence, I am relying on the proper functioning of my muscles, on the laws of physics, on the various electrical and chemical reactions necessary for the keyboard to transmit information to the computer and for the computer to function correctly. Yet all of these causes upon which I rely also ultimately depend on God as their transcendent source. And so I can understand that the fruitfulness of my actions depends in a very real sense on God's cooperation, thus seeing all of my actions as part of a cooperative endeavor with God.

This recognition can deepen our sense of moral obligation in several ways.[9] First, if we understand moral norms as guidelines for flourishing

6. Aquinas, *Summa theologiae* I-II, q. 91, a. 2.

7. "Compliance with the law is necessary, first of all, simply in order that one's conduct be right, or at least not wrong, and therefore good, or at least not bad. . . . [T]his necessity, necessity for the sake of rectitude, is what the obligation of the law chiefly consists in. There are passages that show clearly that this is Thomas's view" (Brock, *The Light That Binds*, 190; see also 244–49). Thus, on Brock's interpretation, "natural law does appear to be a full-fledged law" even for those who do not recognize God as its ultimate source. At the same time, Brock argues that on Aquinas's account, "the ultimate explanation of [natural law's] binding force would still be its derivation from the eternal law" (214).

8. Grisez, Boyle, and Finnis, "Practical Principles," 142.

9. In developing this point, I am drawing broadly on insights from the work of other new natural law theorists, especially Grisez, Boyle, and Finnis, "Practical Principles"; Grisez, "Natural Law and the Transcendent Source," 443–56; Finnis, *Aquinas*, chap. 10; Tollefsen, "Morality and God."

given to us by a benevolent God, who is the source of our existence and nature and thus knows what our good is and how to promote it better than we do, our trust in the reliability of these norms increases. Consider, by comparison, the way in which small children trust the guidelines given to them by loving parents, because they trust that their parents know and want what is good for them. Of course, this analogy has limits, because parents—who, unlike God, are imperfect—can err in their judgment about what is good for a child, or impose rules for their own benefit rather than for the benefit of the child. But the comparison nonetheless helps to illustrate how our sense of moral obligation deepens when we identify the source of moral guidelines as a person who knows and seeks our good.

Second, if we see moral norms not as impersonal rules, but as personal invitations to cooperate with God in the promotion of human flourishing, our sense of moral obligation becomes *personal.* Even in cases when there is no other human being to whom we are directly accountable for the fulfillment of a particular moral obligation, we are always accountable to God. To put the same point slightly differently, even when no human relationship is likely to be damaged by our failure to act in a morally upright way, our relationship with God is still on the line. Again, thinking about parent–child relationships can be helpful here. Just as children's desire to be in harmony with their parents provides an overarching reason to follow their guidelines, fostering and maintaining right relationship with God becomes an overarching reason to act morally when we recognize that God is the ultimate source of the moral order.

Third, and relatedly, if we know God is the source of our existence, of all the goods from which we benefit, of the practical principles and norms that guide us toward our flourishing, and of our capacity to know those principles and norms, then we can also recognize that all of these things are God's gift to us, and that we owe God a profound debt of gratitude that we can never fully repay. One way of expressing this gratitude is to make proper use of these gifts by pursuing genuine goods in line with the moral guidelines that God has made accessible to us through practical reason (and also, as many believe, through divine revelation). We show our gratitude to other human beings in this way all the time. A woman might, for instance, wear a necklace given to her by her husband not only because she likes the necklace, but also to show her gratitude for the gift (and thus to foster and maintain a loving relationship with him). And she might take special care not to lose or damage the necklace for the same reason. Her gratitude — and related desire to strengthen their relationship — therefore gives her a reason to take care of the gift and use it in line with the giver's intentions, a reason that she would not have if she had simply bought the necklace for herself. Similarly, our gratitude to God gives us an additional and overarching reason to pursue human goods in line with moral norms, thus deepening our sense of moral obligation.[10]

10. The account of the relationship between God and moral obligation given in the preceding two paragraphs may help to respond to Mark Murphy's concern that standard natural law theories (including the new natural law theory) fail to provide a sufficiently immediate role for God in the explanation of morality. Murphy's concern rests on his argument that any account of morality in which God fails to play an explanatory role is incompatible with God's sovereignty: "To hold that there is something explanation-eligible [e.g., morality] that is not explained by God, something not dependent on and controlled by God, is to hold that God is not perfectly sovereign" (Murphy, *God and Moral Law*, 11). Murphy later goes on to specify that the only kind of explanation that suffices is one in which facts about God play an immediate role (61–68). According to Murphy, the account provided by Finnis and other new natural law theorists is insufficient, because on this account answers to questions about moral normativity "bottom out in the basic goods" (82). God is acknowledged as creator of those goods, and of human nature as directed to and fulfilled by those goods, but God's role remains in the background, for the goods themselves do all the immediate explanatory work. Yet the second and third explanations provided above of how God relates to moral obligation arguably do have the sort of immediacy Murphy believes is necessary. For instance, in the example of the necklace given to a woman by her husband, the woman wears and takes care of the necklace not only because she likes it, but because she wants to please and show gratitude to her husband. The husband and his purposes thus do seem to play an immediate role in the wife's valuing of this particular necklace and of her decision to wear it. Christopher Tollefsen provides a similar example of buying a game for his children in order "to further [his] relationship with them by giving them an opportunity to act in a way that relates their play to [him]" (Tollefsen, "Morality and God," 52–53). He argues that even though play is a basic good, worthy of pursuit for its own sake, "the goodness of *this* game cannot be fully explained without reference to [him] and [his] purposes." Thus, Tollefsen and his purposes play an immediate explanatory role in how his children value the game and in their choice to play it, for they "choose to play this game both for its own sake and in order to please [him], and thus foster the relationship" (53). Analogously, the second and third explanations provided above show how God and his purposes can play an immediate explanatory role in all of our choices to pursue genuine goods in morally upright ways.

GOD AND MORAL MOTIVATION

The topic of moral motivation is not entirely separable from the topic of moral obligation, for on the account I have offered here, moral obligation is based on the connection between moral norms and human goods, and human goods are what provide us with a rational motivation to act. All the points made in the previous section therefore already tell us something about how recognizing God as the source of moral principles and norms strengthens our motivation to follow them, for a deeper and stronger sense of moral obligation corresponds directly to a deeper and stronger sense of moral motivation. Nevertheless, there is still more to be said about God and moral motivation, particularly when considering the difficulties for moral motivation presented at the beginning of this chapter. In particular, how can we have sufficient motivation to protect and promote human goods when doing so requires considerable effort and sacrifice, and/or when the desired fruits of our actions are far from guaranteed? Or, conversely, how can we be motivated to follow moral norms when violating them seems to promise great benefits? Recognizing that God is the source of the moral order helps to ameliorate these difficulties, but I do not think that the problem can be *fully* overcome unless we look beyond what we can know through rational reflection alone and consider the resources offered by Christian revelation. In this section I will consider how we can respond to these difficulties for moral motivation from a purely philosophical perspective, and then in the next section I will consider how Christian theology can offer a fuller resolution to these problems.

When we understand that God is the source of human goods, wants us to respect and promote them (because he wants us to flourish), and cooperates with us in our efforts to do so, this strengthens our moral motivation in at least two ways. First, if the various contingent factors on which we rely for the fruitfulness of our actions are aspects of an orderly, intelligible universe governed by the providence of a benevolent God, we can have greater confidence in the dependability of these factors, and greater hope that even if things do not turn out as we had planned, the unseen hand of providence will enable some good to come from our efforts. This hope in providence becomes much clearer and stronger when the promises of Christian revelation are added, but even without these additional promises, a reason-based belief in a benevolent and provident God is sufficient to give us at least a vague hope that our efforts to protect and promote human flourishing will not be in vain.

Second, and relatedly, if fostering and maintaining right relationship with God provides an overarching reason to act morally, this provides a source of moral motivation that is immune to the contingencies and uncertainties that affect our efforts to protect and promote other human goods. It is true that the good of personal integrity—most fully achieved through the cultivation of moral virtue—also provides one with a reason to act morally that does not depend on the external effects of our actions. Yet if one's moral judgments are not bolstered by the conviction that moral norms are guidelines for human flourishing given to us by a benevolent and provident God, and by the recognition that our relationship with God is itself at stake in our decision to act in accordance with those judgments, it can be extremely difficult to resist the temptation to compromise one's personal integrity in order to preserve or promote other goods that seem more tangible.

Imagine, for instance, that your country is in a just war, and that bombing civilian targets seems likely to bring a swift end to what would otherwise be a protracted conflict, on balance saving many lives for those on both sides. If you are a political leader, refusing to authorize such bombing because you believe that targeting noncombatants violates the moral prohibition on intentional destruction of basic human goods might even seem selfish, as if you were immorally prioritizing your integrity over the common good.[11] This is, of course, a misleading and inaccurate way of framing the choice, for integrity consists in loving and respecting all the goods involved, and it is precisely this love and respect for the good in all of its basic dimensions that is the ground for refusing to intentionally destroy any basic human good. In other words, violating a moral norm is always contrary to integral human fulfillment, and thus contrary to the genuine common good. Yet in a situation such as this one, this consideration may seem too intangible, too difficult to believe in the face of the more tangible calculations about how many lives the bombing will save. Recognizing that what is on the line in this situation is not only one's personal integrity, but also one's relationship with God, and also recognizing that God seeks our good and knows better than we do how to promote it, can powerfully bolster one's motivation to act morally even in the midst of such a difficult situation.

11. Such a (false) framing of the choice one faces in such circumstances seems to be exemplified in the provocative and much-discussed article by Walzer, "Political Action."

CHRISTIAN REVELATION AND
THE PROMISE OF THE KINGDOM

The considerations offered in the previous sections show how a purely reason-based belief in a benevolent and provident God can help to deepen our sense of moral obligation and bolster our moral motivation, in large part by strengthening our conviction that acting morally does ultimately protect and promote human flourishing. Yet the reassurances that rational reflection alone can provide in this regard are relatively vague and weak. Further, although the claims made in the previous sections can in principle be known through philosophical reflection, in practice this knowledge can be quite difficult to attain through reason alone. Thus, even though this is a book about natural law—about what we can know about ethics and morality through natural reason—it nonetheless seems helpful to close by briefly considering how Christian revelation can more fully resolve the difficulties for moral motivation that were outlined above.

Because it is beyond the scope of this book to present (let alone defend) an account of Christianity's core tenets, my discussion here presumes familiarity with the basic claims of Christianity, and focuses only on one element of Christian revelation that is particularly relevant for the problem of moral motivation. That element is Jesus's proclamation of the Kingdom of God and his promise that those who believe in him and follow his teaching (summarized in the dual commandment to love God and neighbor) will ultimately enjoy fullness of life in the Kingdom.[12] The promised Kingdom is not presented as an abstraction or as a purely spiritual reality, but is presented as a city, a heavenly Jerusalem, in which the saints, with glorified bodies, like that of the resurrected Jesus, will live in perfect communion with God and each other, and flourish in every dimension of their being.[13]

12. A fuller account of Jesus's proclamation of the Kingdom can be found in Grisez, "Natural Law and the Transcendent Source," 451–56. The brief account I offer here is indebted to Grisez's presentation. Note that the view presented here comes from the Catholic tradition, but nothing in this presentation is meant to be specific to Catholicism or incompatible with the beliefs of other Christian traditions.

13. See, e.g., Rev 21; 1 Cor 15:12–28, 35–58. That the Kingdom will include both bodily and spiritual fulfillment, and that it will involve a perfect communion among all persons, is also suggested by the fact that the Kingdom is often likened to a banquet or feast, and especially to a wedding banquet (see, e.g., Lk 14:15, 22:29–30; Mt 8:11–12, 22:2; Rev 3:20, 19:7–9).

This Kingdom is not to be understood as an extrinsic reward that lacks any intrinsic connection to our choices and actions in this life; rather it is a Kingdom that is in some respect already present, a Kingdom that we can contribute to and participate in through our morally upright choices and actions, and that we can reject and exclude ourselves from through immoral choices and actions (or failures to act).[14]

The inherent connection between the promised Kingdom and the moral norms discussed in this book can be seen by recalling natural law's master moral principle as articulated in chapter 2: Choose and act only in ways that are compatible with a will toward integral human fulfillment.

14. See, e.g., Lk 17:21; Mt 5, 25:31–46; Rev 14:13. For an in-depth discussion of how Christian moral teaching relates to natural law, see Grisez, *Christian Moral Principles*, chaps. 25–27. On Grisez's account, Christian teaching neither negates nor replaces natural law, but specifies it in certain respects by revealing the condition of humankind as fallen and redeemed, and proposes new options for choice that would lack sufficient appeal in the absence of Jesus's example and promise of the Kingdom. For example, Maximilian Kolbe's heroic self-sacrifice seems difficult to fully account for except as an emulation of Jesus's sacrificial death on the cross and as a fulfillment of Jesus's new commandment to love one another *as he has loved us*, a command that goes beyond the requirements of the Golden Rule (Jn 13:34–35). The Christian requirement to be merciful and generous, serving others in ways that go beyond strict obligations of justice, corresponds to the recognition that in a fallen world, many will fail to act justly. The only way to compensate for this (and ensure that the vulnerable are protected and cared for) is for some to give more than justice requires (Grisez, *Christian Moral Principles*, chap. 26.H). Similarly, Jesus's teaching on forgiveness indicates that we should sometimes forgo our just claims to retribution, for in a fallen world this may be the only way to avoid perpetuating conflict and achieve peace (26.H). It is beyond the scope of this book to offer a detailed account of how Christian revelation specifies the natural moral law, but a helpful summary is provided by Finnis, Boyle, and Grisez: "In the fallen world, men and women can fully discern and faithfully follow the law written by God in their hearts [i.e., the natural law] only by following the Lord Jesus. That way of life is rich in truly worthwhile goods, but it puts those who really follow it in a vulnerable position. They approach enemies, call attention to wickedness by offering reconciliation, and decline to explain away sin as error, disease, breakdown, abstract structure, or product of impersonal forces; they avoid resort to force, since it hinders trustful communication and cannot heal sin and its consequences. Reliance upon God, submissiveness to one's role in his plan, simplicity of life, self-denial, religious single-mindedness, forgiveness of offences, beneficence towards the suffering, love of enemies, patient conciliation, and readiness to suffer evil rather than do it, even to the point of accepting death out of fidelity, as Jesus did: these are the specific standards and marks of a life which takes Jesus as its model, seeing him as the key and centre of human history" (Finnis, Boyle, and Grisez, *Nuclear Deterrence*, 375–76).

Integral human fulfillment is the all-around fulfillment of human beings within a perfectly harmonious community. In other words, what makes choices and actions morally upright is their compatibility with membership in an ideal community, a community in which all members are flourishing in all of the dimensions of their being, and live together united in perfect peace and harmony. Morally upright choices and actions maintain openness to all human goods and to community with all human beings; thus morally upright choices and actions are an implicit participation in and contribution to the ideal community to which the term "integral human fulfillment" refers.

From the perspective of what we can know through reason alone, integral human fulfillment is an ideal, not an achievable goal. This is not only because of the moral obstacles to the achievement of this ideal in a world of imperfectly virtuous human beings, but also because of the inherent limitation of human mortality—for the ideal community would, in principle, be open not just to those human beings who are currently alive, but to all human beings, past, present, and future. From the perspective of reason alone, therefore, we can act with hope that our actions will contribute to the approximation of this ideal insofar as is possible, and this hope will be bolstered if we recognize that there is a benevolent and provident God, but there are no assurances that even this more limited hope will be fulfilled.

Christianity's promise of the Kingdom, however, indicates that integral human fulfillment can and will be realized through God's action and with our cooperation. Indeed, the promise of the Kingdom surpasses the ideal of integral human fulfillment insofar as it includes a promise of more-than-human fulfillment—of a type of communion with God that goes beyond the human good of religion, and that we are made capable of participating in through the gift of grace.[15] Here, however, I will focus on the Kingdom

15. This more-than-human fulfillment is often referred to as the beatific vision, the gift of seeing God face-to-face (1 Cor 13:11–12; see also Mt 5:8, 1 Jn 3:2, Rev 22:4). Some theologians—following Aquinas—claim that the true ultimate end of human beings consists essentially in the beatific vision (Aquinas, *Summa theologiae* I-II, q. 3, a. 8). However, Grisez argues that Aquinas's argument for this position is inherently flawed (Grisez, "The True Ultimate End"; see also Finnis, "Action's Most Ultimate End"). Grisez argues for a reformulation of the first principle of morality requiring that every choice be made for the ultimate end of "integral communal fulfillment," which he defines as "divine good together with the well-being and flourishing of created persons in respect to all of

as a realization of the ideal of integral human fulfillment, a perfect community in which we will flourish on all dimensions of our being. This fullness of life in the Kingdom is not an extrinsic reward, but is prepared by and in continuity with our morally upright pursuit of human goods during our earthly life.[16] By acting morally—maintaining openness to all human goods and to community with all human beings, which is equivalent to loving all persons by loving their good in all of its dimensions—we are thus at least implicitly preparing ourselves for membership in the Kingdom.[17] And all of the morally upright acts by which we have sought to protect and promote human goods will come to full fruition in the Kingdom, even if those efforts appear to fail here on earth, in line with Saint Paul's promise that "in the Lord your labor is not in vain."[18] "After we have promoted on earth . . .

---

their fundamental goods" (Grisez, "True Ultimate End," 57). In this book I have retained the earlier formulation of the first principle of morality and its reference to "integral human fulfillment," because I believe that, when acting on the basis of our natural human capacities, we can only be motivated to act for human goods, and the term "integral communal fulfillment" can give the impression that we act for the divine good in itself. Finnis also expresses reservations about the term "integral communal fulfillment" insofar as it "*seems* . . . to refer to a willed and effected fulfillment of the divine person(s) as it refers to the willed and effected fulfillment of human persons in that community," and thus "can grate against our apprehension of the transcendence, otherness and inherent perfection of God" (Finnis, "Reflections and Responses," 580–81; emphasis original).

16. This claim about the basic continuity between our pursuit of the good in this life and our fulfillment in the Kingdom is compatible with the recognition that there are also some elements of discontinuity. Grisez explains: "The basic principle of continuity between Christian life in this age and everlasting life is that the goods in which we participate now will be included in the fulfillment for which we hope. But there is also discontinuity, of two sorts: the discontinuity of maturation (goods shared in imperfectly now will be shared in more perfectly) and radical discontinuity (evil will be eliminated)" (Grisez, *Christian Moral Principles*, chap. 34, summary).

17. Because my aim here is only to briefly indicate how the Christian promise of the Kingdom complements the reason-based account of ethics I have offered in this book, it is beyond the scope of my argument to consider theological questions regarding the extent to which, in our fallen human condition, we need the aid of divine grace in order to know and do what is morally right. Nothing that I say here should be taken to imply that we can "earn" our entrance to the Kingdom through our own efforts alone.

18. 1 Cor 15:58.

the goods of human dignity, fraternal communion, and liberty—that is to say, all the good fruits of our nature and effort—then we shall find them once more, but cleansed of all dirt, illuminated, and transformed, when Christ gives back to the Father an eternal and universal kingdom," states the Second Vatican Council in *Gaudium et spes*.[19]

This reassurance that our labor is not in vain, that our good deeds will ultimately bear fruit, can powerfully strengthen our motivation to undertake difficult projects or make great personal sacrifices to promote human flourishing, even when the success of our efforts on this earth seems highly uncertain. Further, knowing that the heavenly Kingdom is constituted by our love for God, for one another, and for all the goods that constitute our flourishing helps us to resist the temptation to try to promote the good through immoral means, for such immoral means close us off from and undermine the Kingdom by closing us off from and undermining love of some person or good. Recognizing that moral norms are God's guidelines for integral human flourishing and for building up the Kingdom where that flourishing will be fully realized, we are also assured that immoral means will never actually be effective in promoting integral human flourishing. Indeed, it would be hubris to judge that we know better than God does how best to promote human flourishing, but if we understand that God is the author of the moral law, such a judgment is implicit in any choice to use immoral means in order to achieve a good end.[20] The Christian promise of

---

19. Second Vatican Council, *Gaudium et spes*, 39 (my translation from the Latin).

20. Finnis, Boyle, and Grisez explain: "God assigns everyone some role in his plan, not because he requires human help . . . but because he wishes to ennoble human persons. . . . One knows enough of the plan to do one's own work well, but not enough to revise and improve upon the design for human life provided by the law written in our hearts and by the Gospel." They go on to explain that this view also helps us to recognize the limits of our own responsibility: "Everyone knows that people are not responsible for everything, but only for what is within their power. Not everyone remembers that people are not even responsible for everything within their power. Men and women really are responsible only for those things which pertain to their various morally upright commitments and roles, and which can be promoted or prevented without doing evil." They summarize their argument: "When one contemplates the hardest cases . . . one simply cannot judge according to the maxim: Trust your feelings and follow them. For, while feelings respond to what one remembers, experiences, foresees, and imagines, human providence

the Kingdom therefore provides the fullest solution to the difficulties for moral motivation that arise from uncertainties about the fruitfulness of our actions, or from the apparent probability that violating moral norms will more effectively promote the human good than following them.

CONCLUSION

The overarching theme of this book, reflected in its title, has been to high-light the intrinsic connection between morality and human flourishing. Ultimately, morality matters because human flourishing matters, and we should want to be moral because we want to flourish. Acting morally, fol-lowing the moral norms outlined in chapter 2, protects and promotes our flourishing by contributing to and making possible our membership in the perfect human community where our human flourishing (which, as I em-phasized in chapters 3 and 4, is inherently social) would be complete. This connection between morality and human flourishing is sufficient to justify moral norms and ground our obligation to follow them. Yet from the per-spective of reason alone, this perfect human community — corresponding to the concept of integral human fulfillment — is an unrealizable ideal. The Christian concept of the Kingdom transforms this ideal into a promised re-ality, strengthening us with the sure hope that our morally upright efforts to protect and promote human goods will ultimately bear fruit.

---

cannot reach so far nor comprehend so much that one could ever have a rational ground for judging that less evil will come if one violates a moral absolute than if one respects it. Therefore, in such hard cases, one must remember that human responsibility can be rightly fulfilled only in co-operation with God's providence. If one faithfully refuses to do evil that good may come, God will bring about the greater good and permit only the lesser evil" (Finnis, Boyle, and Grisez, *Nuclear Deterrence*, 381–82).

A P P E N D I X

Annotated Resource
Bibliography

HISTORY OF NEW NATURAL LAW THEORY:
NOTABLE EARLY WORKS

See https://twotlj.org/other_works.html for links to these and other early works, which are precursors to the mature theory, along with commentaries explaining the context, importance, and limitations of each work. NB: In this history section references are listed chronologically, but elsewhere they are alphabetical by author.

Grisez, Germain. "Kant and Aquinas: Ethical Theory." *The Thomist* 21 (1958): 44–78. https://twotlj.org/EarlyEssays.html.
    This very early work did not contribute directly to the development of Grisez's natural law theory, but it is noteworthy because many criticize the theory as Kantian. This article makes clear that Grisez recognizes the fundamental differences between Kant's and Aquinas's accounts of the principles of practical reason, and that he agrees with Aquinas.
———. "The First Principle of Practical Reason: A Commentary on the *Summa Theologiae*, 1–2, Question 94, Article 2." *Natural Law Forum* 10 (1965): 168–201.
    Although this is a commentary on Aquinas's account of the first principle of practical reason, not an attempt to develop his own ethical theory, Grisez's interpretation of this principle is foundational for the new natural law account.

————. *Contraception and the Natural Law*. Milwaukee, WI: Bruce, 1964. See chapter 3.

After explaining and criticizing what he calls "conventional natural-law theory" and "situationism," Grisez presents an early version of his theory—a "more adequate theory of moral law," which he believes "is to be found in the later works of Thomas Aquinas" (60). However, he presents his approach not as a historical study, but "for consideration on its own rational merits" (60). See notes in the next entry on the article summarizing the book's main argument.

————. "A New Formulation of a Natural-Law Argument against Contraception." *The Thomist* 30 (1966): 343–61.

Highlights the importance of recognizing that ethics is a third-order, practical inquiry, and thus that moral norms cannot be derived directly from first-order speculative knowledge of human biology, psychology, and so on. After criticizing both Kantianism and consequentialism, Grisez presents his own theory, outlining an initial list of basic goods and offering an early formulation— which is later revised—of the most basic standard of morality. Note that the argument against contraception is updated in the coauthored article, "Every Marital Act Ought to be Open to New Life." *The Thomist* 52 (1988): 365–426, with slight additional revisions in Grisez and Boyle, "Response to Our Critics and Collaborators" (listed below).

————. *Abortion: The Myths, the Realities and the Arguments*. New York: Corpus Books, 1970.

Chapter 6 includes arguments against relativism, utilitarianism, Kantianism, and Protestant situationism, and a somewhat refined—but still not fully mature—explanation of basic goods, of the most basic standard of morality, and of intermediate moral principles that specify that basic standard. It presents a slight reformulation of the principle of double effect (and argues against proportionalist reformulations that deny the existence of intrinsically evil acts). Many of these arguments are incorporated into Grisez, "Toward a Consistent Natural-Law Ethics of Killing." *American Journal of Jurisprudence* 15 (1970): 54–96. Note that Grisez's action theory—his account of how to distinguish what is intended from what is accepted as a side effect—is immature in these works. Grisez's mature action theory can be found in Finnis, Grisez, and Boyle, "'Direct' and 'Indirect': A Reply to Critics of Our Action Theory." *The Thomist* 65 (2001): 1–44.

Grisez, Germain, and Joseph Boyle. "A Response to Our Critics and Collaborators." In *Natural Law and Moral Inquiry*, edited by Robert George, 213–21. Washington, DC: Georgetown University Press, 1998.

Provides insight into the history/context of the theory's development.

MATURE PRESENTATIONS OF NEW NATURAL LAW THEORY

General Expositions of New Natural Law Theory

See "Explanations and Defenses of the Natural Law Theory Developed by Germain Grisez, Joseph Boyle and John Finnis," https://twotlj.org/EthicalTheory.html.

Finnis, John. *Natural Law and Natural Rights.* 2nd ed. Oxford: Oxford University Press, 2011[1980]. See chapters 2 to 5.
Note that it is crucial to read the second edition, published in 2011, which has a postscript that comments on the book's argument section by section, adding important substantive clarifications and updates to the original.
———. *Fundamentals of Ethics.* Washington, DC: Georgetown University Press, 1983.
———. *Aquinas: Moral, Political, and Legal Theory.* Oxford: Oxford University Press, 1998.
Although this book is a presentation of Aquinas's thought, not a presentation of new natural law theory as such, it is helpful for understanding the theory because Finnis and other new natural law theorists see the theory as being in continuity with Aquinas's thought, but not in agreement with Aquinas on every point.
———. *Collected Essays of John Finnis.* Vols. 1 to 5. Oxford: Oxford University Press, 2013.
Finnis, John, Joseph Boyle, and Germain Grisez. *Nuclear Deterrence, Morality and Realism.* Oxford: Clarendon Press, 1987. See chapters 9 to 11.
Grisez, Germain. *Christian Moral Principles.* Vol. 1 of *The Way of the Lord Jesus.* Chicago: Franciscan Herald Press, 1983. See chapters 2–10. https://twotlj.org.
Note that Joseph Boyle and John Finnis made significant contributions to the development of the moral theory presented here, and to the drafting of *The Way of the Lord Jesus* more generally. For more details, see the biographical sketches of Grisez's collaborators at https://twotlj.org/grisez_collaborators.html.
Grisez, Germain, Joseph Boyle, and John Finnis. "Practical Principles, Moral Truth, Ultimate Ends." *American Journal of Jurisprudence* 32 (1987): 99–151.
This is a relatively mature account of the theory, but the account of the ultimate end has been updated in later works, especially Grisez, "Natural Law, Religion, God and Human Fulfillment," and Grisez, "The True Ultimate End of Human Beings: The Kingdom, Not God Alone" (listed below). For scholars interested in reading the essential primary sources that provide a full account of the mature moral theory, I would recommend reading this article, together with the

aforementioned articles on the ultimate end, the coauthored 2001 article on action theory ("Direct and Indirect," listed below), and Grisez's 1965 article on the first principle of practical reason in Aquinas (listed above). These articles are, however, quite dense, and need to be read with great care to be properly understood.

Grisez, Germain, and Russell Shaw. *Beyond the New Morality*. 3rd ed. Notre Dame, IN: University of Notre Dame Press, 1988.
This presents a nontechnical version of the theory aimed at a popular audience.

Theological Works

Finnis, John. *Moral Absolutes: Tradition, Revision and Truth*, Washington, DC: Catholic University of America Press, 1991.
This work focuses primarily on defending moral absolutes against proportionalist trends in moral theology.

Grisez, Germain. *The Way of the Lord Jesus*. Vols. 1 to 3. https://twotlj.org/index.html. Chapters 2–10 of volume 1 outline Grisez's natural law theory and are therefore largely philosophical; the rest of volume 1 and the remaining volumes are theological, integrating the theory with Christian revelation. Note also that the monograph-length draft first chapter of volume 4, dealing with the theological presuppositions for a sound theology of clerical and consecrated life, is available at http://twotlj.org/G-4-V-4.html.

May, William. *An Introduction to Moral Theology*. 2nd ed. Huntington, IN: Our Sunday Visitor, 2003.

See also Finnis's theological articles, listed at https://twotlj.org/Finnis.html, and the work of E. Christian Brugger (mostly related to bioethics), listed at https://twotlj.org/brugger.html.

Short Overviews

Finnis, John. "Natural Law." In *Reason in Action*, Vol. 1 of *Collected Essays*, 199–211. Oxford: Oxford University Press, 2011.

Lee, Patrick. "The New Natural Law Theory." In *The Cambridge Companion to Natural Law Ethics*, edited by Tom Angier, 73–91. Cambridge: Cambridge University Press, 2019.

———. "The New Natural Law Theory." *Lyceum* 10 (2008): 1–17.

Moschella, Melissa. "The New Natural Law Theory." In *Natural Law: Five Views*, edited by Andrew Walker and Ryan Anderson. Grand Rapids, MI: Zondervan Academic, 2025.

Moschella, Melissa, and Robert P. George, "Natural Law." In *International Encyclopedia of the Social and Behavioral Sciences*, 2nd ed., 320–24. Elsevier, 2015. https://doi.org/10.1016/B978-0-08-097086-8.86084-5.

Tollefsen, Christopher. "Natural Law and Modern Meta-Ethics: A Guided Tour." In *Natural Law and the Possibility of a Global Ethics*, edited by Mark Cherry, 39–56. Dordrecht: Kluwer, 2004.

Specific Aspects of the Theory

On Action Theory

Finnis, John, Germain Grisez, and Joseph Boyle. "'Direct' and 'Indirect': A Reply to Critics of Our Action Theory." *The Thomist* 65 (2001): 1–44.

Girgis, Sherif. "The Wrongfulness of Any Intent to Kill." *National Catholic Bioethics Quarterly* 19 (2019): 221–48.

Lee, Patrick. "Distinguishing between What Is Intended and Foreseen Side Effects." *American Journal of Jurisprudence* 62, no. 2 (2017): 231–51.

Tollefsen, Christopher. "Is a Purely First Person Account of Human Action Defensible?" *Ethical Theory and Moral Practice* 9 (2006): 441–60.

———. "Terminating in the Body." *National Catholic Bioethics Quarterly* 19 (2019): 203–20.

On the Ultimate End

Finnis, John. "Action's Most Ultimate End." In *Reason in Action*, Vol. 1 of *Collected Essays*, 159–72. Oxford: Oxford University Press, 2011.

Grisez, Germain. "Natural Law, God, Religion, and Human Fulfillment." *American Journal of Jurisprudence* 46 (2001): 3–36.

———. "The True Ultimate End of Human Beings: The Kingdom, Not God Alone." *Theological Studies* 69 (2008): 38–61.

Lee, Patrick. "Germain Grisez's Christian Humanism." *American Journal of Jurisprudence* 46 (2002): 137–52.

On Natural Law and Human Nature

Finnis, John. "Is and Ought in Aquinas." In *Reason in Action*, Vol. 1 of *Collected Essays*, 144–55. Oxford: Oxford University Press, 2011.

Girgis, Sherif. "Subjectivity without Subjectivism: Revisiting the Is/Ought Gap." In *Subjectivity: Ancient and Modern*, edited by R. J. Snell and Steven McGuire, 63–88. Lanham, MD: Lexington Books, 2016.

Lee, Patrick, and Robert George. *Conjugal Union: What Marriage Is and Why It Matters*. Cambridge: Cambridge University Press, 2014. See chapter 2, "Human Nature and Morality."

Matava, R. J. "'Is,' 'Ought' and Moral Realism: The Roles of Nature and Experience in Practical Understanding." *Studies in Christian Ethics* 24 (2011): 311–28.

Moschella, Melissa. "Sexual Ethics, Human Nature, and the 'New' and 'Old' Natural Law Theories." *National Catholic Bioethics Quarterly* 19 (2019): 251–78.

Tollefsen, Christopher. "Aquinas's Four Orders, Normativity and Human Nature." *Journal of Value Inquiry* 52 (2018): 243–56.

On Metaphysical and Anthropological Presuppositions

Electronic copies of Grisez's works on these topics, with helpful commentaries explaining the context and importance of each work, can be found at https://twotlj .org/Metaphysics.html.

Boyle, Joseph, Germain Grisez, and Olaf Tollefsen. *Free Choice: A Self-Referential Argument*. Notre Dame, IN: University of Notre Dame Press, 1976.

Grisez, Germain. *Beyond the New Theism*. Notre Dame, IN: University of Notre Dame Press, 1975; reprinted with a new preface as *God? A Philosophical Preface to Faith*. South Bend, IN: St. Augustine's Press, 2005.

————. "Free Choice and Divine Causality." Lecture at Franciscan University of Steubenville. March 29, 2000. https://twotlj.org/Metaphysics.html.

Lee, Patrick. "Human Beings Are Animals." In *Natural Law and Moral Inquiry: Ethics, Metaphysics and Politics in the Work of Germain Grisez*, edited by Robert P. George, 135–51. Washington, DC: Georgetown University Press, 1998.

Lee, Patrick, and Robert P. George. *Body-Self Dualism in Contemporary Ethics and Politics*. New York: Cambridge University Press, 2008.

Tollefsen, Christopher, and Robert P. George. *Embryo: A Defense of Human Life*. 2nd ed. Princeton, NJ: The Witherspoon Institute, 2011.

Political Philosophy

John Finnis not only collaborated with Grisez in developing the new natural law theory, but also did independent work in legal and political philosophy. The new natural law theory has political implications, but when moving to political philosophy and especially to practical political questions, there are a range of positions that could be compatible with the theory's basic principles. For example, there is a disagreement between Finnis and Robert George—who was Finnis's student—about whether purely paternalistic legislation is, in principle, beyond the legitimate scope of political authority.

Finnis, John. *Natural Law and Natural Rights.* 2nd ed. Oxford: Oxford University Press, 2011.

———. "Public Good: The Specifically Political Common Good in Aquinas." In *Natural Law and Moral Inquiry*, edited by Robert P. George, 174–209. Washington, DC: Georgetown University Press, 1998.

George, Robert P. *The Clash of Orthodoxies: Law, Religion and Morality in Crisis.* Wilmington, DE: ISI Books, 2001.

———. *In Defense of Natural Law.* New York: Oxford University Press, 1999.

———. *Making Men Moral: Civil Liberties and Public Morality.* Oxford: Clarendon Press, 1995.

Grisez, Germain. *Living a Christian Life.* Vol. 2 of *The Way of the Lord Jesus.* Quincy, IL: Franciscan Press, 1993. See chapter 11, available at http://twotlj.org/G-2-V-2.html.

Moschella, Melissa. *To Whom Do Children Belong? Parental Rights, Civic Education and Children's Autonomy.* New York: Cambridge University Press, 2016.

Tollefsen, Christopher. "Pure Perfectionism and the Limits of Paternalism." In *Reason, Morality and Law: The Philosophy of John Finnis*, edited by John Keown and Robert George, 204–18. Oxford: Oxford University Press, 2013.

On Religion/Church-State Relations

Boyle, Joseph. "The Place of Religion in the Practical Reasoning of Individuals and Groups." *American Journal of Jurisprudence* 43 (1998): 1–24.

Bradley, Gerard, ed. *Challenges to Religious Liberty in the Twenty-First Century.* New York: Cambridge University Press, 2012.

Finnis, John. "Does Free Exercise of Religion Deserve Constitutional Mention?" *American Journal of Jurisprudence* 54 (2009): 41–66.

George, Robert, and William Saunders. "*Dignitatis humanae*: The Freedom of the Church and the Responsibility of the State." In *Catholicism and Religious Freedom*, edited by Kenneth L. Grasso and Robert P. Hunt, 1–17. Lanham, MD: Rowman and Littlefield, 2006.

Moschella, Melissa. "Beyond Equal Liberty: Religion as a Distinct Human Good and the Implications for Religious Freedom." *Journal of Law and Religion* 32, no. 1 (2017): 123–46.

Tollefsen, Christopher. "Conscience, Religion and the State." *American Journal of Jurisprudence* 54 (2009): 93–116.

Responses to Critics

Bradley, Gerard. "Natural Law as Real 'Law': Response to Hittinger." *American Journal of Jurisprudence* 39 (1994): 33–34.

Bradley, Gerard, and Robert P. George. "The New Natural Law Theory: A Reply to Jean Porter." *American Journal of Jurisprudence* 39 (1994): 303–15.

Finnis, John, and Germain Grisez. "The Basic Principles of Natural Law: A Reply to Ralph McInerny." *American Journal of Jurisprudence* 26 (1982): 21–31.

George, Robert P. "A Defense of the New Natural Law Theory." *American Journal of Jurisprudence* 41 (1996): 47–61.

———. "Does the 'Incommensurability Thesis' Imperil Common Sense Moral Judgments?" *American Journal of Jurisprudence* 37 (1992): 185–95.

———. "Recent Criticism of Natural Law Theory." *University of Chicago Law Review* 55 (1988): 1371–1429.

Matava, R. J. "On *Knowing the Natural Law*: A Response to Steven Jensen." *American Journal of Jurisprudence* 61 (2016): 237–527.

Moschella, Melissa. "Sexual Ethics, Practical Reason, and the Magisterium: A Response to Irene Alexander." *National Catholic Bioethics Quarterly* 22 (2022): 99–127.

See also the articles in *The National Catholic Bioethics Quarterly* 19, no. 2 (2019) (special issue dedicated to new natural law theory in response to recent criticisms).

APPLICATIONS TO SPECIFIC MORAL QUESTIONS

Note that both philosophical and theological works are included here.

Grisez, *Difficult Moral Questions*. Vol. 3 of *The Way of the Lord Jesus*. Quincy, IL: Franciscan Press, 1997. Addresses a wide variety of topics.

Abortion

Curlin, Farr, and Christopher Tollefsen. *The Way of Medicine*. Notre Dame, IN: University of Notre Dame Press, 2021. See chapter 7.

Grisez, Germain. *Abortion: The Myths, the Realities and the Arguments*. New York: Corpus Books, 1970. https://twotlj.org/other_works.html.

Lee, Patrick. *Abortion and Unborn Human Life*. Washington, DC: Catholic University of America Press, 1996.

———. "The Pro-Life Argument from Substantial Identity: A Defense." *Bioethics* 18 (2004): 249–63.

Lee, Patrick, and Robert P. George, *Body–Self Dualism in Contemporary Ethics and Politics*. New York: Cambridge University Press, 2008. See chapter 4.

May, William. *Catholic Bioethics and the Gift of Human Life*. 3rd ed. Huntington, IN: Our Sunday Visitor, 2013. See chapter 5.

Tollefsen, Christopher. "Abortion and the Human Animal." *Christian Bioethics* 10 (2005): 105–16.

———. "Whose Body?" In *Agency, Pregnancy and Persons: Essays in Defense of Human Life*, edited by Nicholas Colgrove et al., 70–86. New York: Routledge, 2023.

Biomedical Ethics

Boyle, Joseph. "Personal Responsibility and Freedom in Health Care: A Natural Law Perspective." In *Persons and Their Bodies: Rights, Responsibilities, Relationships*, edited by Mark Cherry, 111–41. Dordrecht: Kluwer Academic, 1999.

Curlin, Farr, and Christopher Tollefsen. *The Way of Medicine*. Notre Dame, IN: University of Notre Dame Press, 2021.

May, William. *Catholic Bioethics and the Gift of Human Life*. 3rd ed. Huntington, IN: Our Sunday Visitor, 2013.

Moschella, Melissa. "A Natural Law Account of Biomedical Ethics." In *Explorations in Ethics*, edited by David Kaspar, 269–86. Cham, Switzerland: Palgrave Macmillan, 2020.

Capital Punishment

Bradley, Gerard. "No Intentional Killing Whatsoever: The Case of Capital Punishment." In *Natural Law and Moral Inquiry: Ethics, Metaphysics, and Politics in the Work of Germain Grisez*, edited by Robert P. George, 155–73. Washington, DC: Georgetown University Press, 1998.

Brugger, E. Christian. *Capital Punishment and Roman Catholic Moral Tradition*. Notre Dame, IN: University of Notre Dame Press, 2003.

———. "Catholic Moral Teaching and the Problem of Capital Punishment." *The Thomist* 68 (2004): 41–67.

———. "Rejecting the Death Penalty: Continuity and Change in Catholic Tradition." *Heythrop Journal* 49 (2008): 388–404.

Grisez, Germain. "Toward a Consistent Natural-Law Ethics of Killing." *American Journal of Jurisprudence* 15 (1970): 54–96.

Tollefsen, Christopher. "A Philosophical Case against Capital Punishment." *Public Discourse*, November 13, 2017. https://www.thepublicdiscourse.com/2017/11/20393/.

See also additional *Public Discourse* articles on this topic by Tollefsen, by John Finnis, and by Christian Brugger.

Embryonic Stem-Cell Research/The Moral Status of the Embryo

Lee, Patrick, and Robert P. George. "The First Fourteen Days of Human Life." *New Atlantis* (Summer 2006): 61–67. https://www.thenewatlantis.com/publications /the-first-fourteen-days-of-human-life.

Lee, Patrick, Christopher Tollefsen, and Robert P. George. "The Ontological Status of Embryos: A Reply to Jason Morris." *Journal of Medicine and Philosophy* 39 (2014): 483–504.

May, William. *Catholic Bioethics and the Gift of Human Life*. 3rd ed. Huntington, IN: Our Sunday Visitor, 2013. See chapter 6.

Tollefsen, Christopher. *Biomedical Research and Beyond*. New York: Routledge, 2008. See chapter 5.

———. "Embryos, Individuals, and Persons: An Argument against Embryo Creation and Research." *Journal of Applied Philosophy* 18 (2001): 65–78.

Tollefsen, Christopher, and Robert P. George. *Embryo: A Defense of Human Life*. 2nd ed. Princeton, NJ: The Witherspoon Institute, 2011.

End-of-Life Issues

Boyle, Joseph. "Medical Ethics and Double Effect: The Case of Terminal Sedation." *Theoretical Medicine and Bioethics* 25 (2004): 51–60.

———. "Towards Ethical Guidelines for the Use of Artificial Nutrition and Hydration." In *Artificial Nutrition and Hydration: The New Catholic Debate*, edited by Christopher Tollefsen, 111–21. Dordrecht: Springer, 2008.

Grisez, Germain. "Should Nutrition and Hydration Be Provided to Permanently Unconscious and Other Mentally Disabled Persons?" *Issues in Law and Medicine* 5 (1989): 165–79.

Lee, Patrick. "Personhood, Dignity, Suicide, and Euthanasia." *National Catholic Bioethics Quarterly* 1 (2001): 329–44.

Lee, Patrick, and Robert P. George. *Body–Self Dualism in Contemporary Ethics and Politics*. New York: Cambridge University Press, 2008. See chapter 5.

May, William. *Catholic Bioethics and the Gift of Human Life*. 3rd ed. Huntington, IN: Our Sunday Visitor, 2013. See chapter 7.

Gender/Transgender

Anderson, Ryan T. "Sex Change: Physically Impossible, Psychologically Unhelpful, and Philosophically Misguided." *The Public Discourse*, March 5, 2018. https:// www.thepublicdiscourse.com/2018/03/21151/.

———. *When Harry Became Sally*. New York: Encounter Books, 2018.

Moschella, Melissa. "Sexual Identity, Gender and Human Fulfillment." *Christian Bioethics* 25 (2019): 192–215.

———. "Trapped in the Wrong Body? Transgender Identity Claims, Body–Self Dualism and the False Promise of Gender Reassignment Therapy." *Journal of Medicine and Philosophy* 46 (2021): 782–804.

Tollefsen, Christopher. "Gender Identity." *The Public Discourse*, July 14, 2015. https://www.thepublicdiscourse.com/2015/07/15308/.

———. "Sex Identity." *The Public Discourse*, July 13, 2015. https://www.thepublic discourse.com/2015/07/15306/.

Lying

Boyle, Joseph. "The Absolute Prohibition of Lying and the Origins of the Casuistry of Mental Reservation: Augustinian Arguments and Thomistic Developments." *American Journal of Jurisprudence* 49 (1999): 43–65.

Tollefsen, Christopher. *Lying and Christian Ethics*. New York: Cambridge University Press, 2014.

———. "Lying: The Integrity Approach." *American Journal of Jurisprudence* 52 (2007): 253–71.

———. "Why Lying Is Always Wrong." *The Public Discourse*, February 14, 2011. https://www.thepublicdiscourse.com/2011/02/2547/.

Marriage/Sexual Ethics/Contraception

Finnis, John. "The Good of Marriage and the Morality of Sexual Relations: Some Philosophical and Historical Observations." *American Journal of Jurisprudence* 42 (1997): 97–134.

———. "Marriage: A Basic and Exigent Good." *The Monist* 91 (July-October 2008): 388–406.

Girgis, Sherif. "The Historic Christian Teaching against Contraception: A Defense." *The Public Discourse*, August 10, 2016. http://www.thepublicdiscourse.com/2016/08/17559/.

Girgis, Sherif, Ryan Anderson, and Robert P. George. *What Is Marriage? Man and Woman: A Defense*. New York: Encounter Books, 2012.

Grisez, Germain. *Living a Christian Life*. Vol. 2 of *The Way of the Lord Jesus*. Quincy, IL: Franciscan Press, 1993. See chapter 9. http://twotlj.org/G-2-V-2.html.

Grisez, Germain, Joseph Boyle, John Finnis, and William May. "'Every Marital Act Ought to Be Open to New Life': Toward a Clearer Understanding." *The Thomist* 52 (1988): 365–426.

Lee, Patrick, and Robert P. George, *Body–Self Dualism in Contemporary Ethics and Politics*. New York: Cambridge University Press, 2008. See chapter 6.

———. *Conjugal Union: What Marriage Is and Why It Matters*. Cambridge: Cambridge University Press, 2014.

May, William, Ronald Lawler, and Joseph Boyle, ed. *Catholic Sexual Ethics*. 3rd ed. Huntington, IN: Our Sunday Visitor, 2011.

Moschella, Melissa. "Sexual Ethics, Human Nature, and the 'New' and 'Old' Natural Law Theories." *National Catholic Bioethics Quarterly* 19 (2019): 251–78.

Property/Distributive Justice

Boyle, Joseph. "Catholic Social Justice and Health Care Entitlement Packages." *Christian Bioethics* 2 (1996): 280–92.

———. "Fairness in Holdings: A Natural Law Account of Property and Welfare Rights." *Social Philosophy and Policy* 18 (2001): 206–26.

Finnis, John. *Natural Law and Natural Rights*. Oxford: Oxford University Press, 2011. See chapter 7.

Grisez, Germain. *Living a Christian Life*. Vol. 2 of *The Way of the Lord Jesus*. Quincy, IL: Franciscan Press, 1993. See chapter 10. http://twotlj.org/G-2-V-2.html.

Tollefsen, Christopher. "Disability and Social Justice." In *Philosophical Perspectives on Disability*, edited by D. C. Ralston and J. Ho, 211–27. Dordrecht: Springer, 2009.

Reproductive Technologies

Finnis, John. "On Producing Human Embryos." In *Intention and Identity*. Vol. 2 of *Collected Essays*, 293–301. Oxford: Oxford University Press, 2011.

May, William. *Catholic Bioethics and the Gift of Human Life*. 3rd ed. Huntington, IN: Our Sunday Visitor, 2013. See chapter 3.

Moschella, Melissa. "Reproductive Technologies and Human Dignity." *The Public Discourse*, November 17, 2019. https://www.thepublicdiscourse.com/2019/11/57961/.

———. "Rethinking the Moral Permissibility of Gamete Donation." *Theoretical Medicine and Bioethics* 35 (December 2014): 421–40.

———. "The Wrongness of Third-Party Assisted Reproduction: A Natural Law Account." *Christian Bioethics* 22 (2016): 104–21.

Tollefsen, Christopher. "In Vitro Fertilization Should Not Be an Option." In *Contemporary Debates in Bioethics*, edited by R. Arp and A. Caplan, 451–59. New York: Wiley-Blackwell, 2013.

War

Boyle, Joseph. "Just and Unjust Wars: Casuistry and the Boundaries of the Moral World." *Ethics and International Affairs* 11 (1997): 83–98.

———. "Just War Doctrine and the Military Response to Terrorism." *Journal of Political Philosophy* 11 (2003): 153–70.

———. "Traditional Just War Theory and Humanitarian Intervention." In *Humanitarian Intervention: Nomos XLVII*, edited by M. Williams and T. Nardin, 31–57. New York: New York University Press, 2006.

Finnis, John. "The Ethics of War and Peace in the Catholic Natural Law Tradition." In *The Ethics of War and Peace*, edited by Terry Nardin, 15–39. Princeton, NJ: Princeton University Press, 1996.

Finnis, John, Joseph Boyle, and Germain Grisez. *Nuclear Deterrence, Morality and Realism.* New York: Oxford, 1987.

Grisez, Germain. "Toward a Consistent Natural-Law Ethics of Killing." *American Journal of Jurisprudence* 15 (1970): 54–96.

Bibliography

Amato, Paul. "The Impact of Family Formation on the Cognitive, Social, and Emotional Well Being of the Next Generation." *The Future of Children* 15, no. 2 (2005): 75–96.

Andersson, Gunnar. "Children's Experience of Family Disruption and Family Formation: Evidence from 16 FFS Countries." *Demographic Research* 7 (2002): 343–64.

Aquinas, Thomas. *Commentary on Aristotle's "De Anima."* Translated by Kenelm Foster and Sylvester Humphries, O.P. New Haven, CT: Yale University Press, 1951.

———. *Commentary on the "Nicomachean Ethics."* Translated by C. I. Litzinger, O.P. Chicago: Henry Regnery, 1964.

———. *De regno.* Translated by Gerald Phelan, revised by I. Th. Eschmann. Toronto: The Pontifical Institute of Medieval Studies, 1949. https://isidore.co/aquinas/DeRegno.htm.

———. *The Summa Theologiae of St. Thomas Aquinas.* 2nd and rev. ed., 1920. Translated by the Fathers of the English Dominican Province. https://www.newadvent.org/summa/.

Aristotle. *The Complete Works of Aristotle.* Edited by Jonathan Barnes. Princeton, NJ: Princeton University Press, 1984.

Beeson, Diane R., Patricia K. Jennings, and Wendy Kramer. "Offspring Searching for Their Sperm Donors: How Family Type Shapes the Process." *Human Reproduction* 26, no. 9 (2001): 2415–24.

Bellah, Robert, et al. *Habits of the Heart.* Berkeley: University of California Press, 1985.

Bloomfield, Paul, ed. *Morality and Self-Interest.* Oxford: Oxford University Press, 2007.

Bohman, James, and Henry Richardson. "Liberalism, Deliberative Democracy, and 'Reasons that All Can Accept.'" *Journal of Political Philosophy* 17, no. 3 (2009): 253–74.

Boyle, Joseph. "Free Choice, Incomparably Valuable Options, and Incommensurable Categories of Good." *American Journal of Jurisprudence* 47 (2002): 123–41.

———. "On the Most Fundamental Principle of Morality." In *Reason, Morality and Law: The Philosophy of John Finnis*, edited by John Keown and Robert P. George, 56–72. Oxford: Oxford University Press, 2013.

———. "Reasons for Action." In *Natural Law Ethics in Theory and Practice: A Joseph Boyle Reader*, edited by John Liptay and Christopher Tollefsen, 38–60. Washington, DC: Catholic University of America Press, 2020.

———. "Toward Understanding the Principle of Double Effect." *Ethics* 90, no. 4 (1980): 527–38.

Boyle, Joseph, Germain Grisez, and Olaf Tollefsen. *Free Choice: A Self-Referential Argument*. Notre Dame, IN: University of Notre Dame Press, 1976.

Brewer, Talbot. *The Retrieval of Ethics*. Oxford: Oxford University Press, 2009.

Brock, Stephen. *The Light That Binds*. Eugene, OR: Pickwick, 2020.

Carney, Timothy. *Alienated America*. New York: HarperCollins, 2019.

Chappell, Timothy. "The Polymorphy of Practical Reason." In *Human Values*, edited by David Oderberg and Timothy Chappell, 102–25. New York: Palgrave Macmillan, 2004.

Chappell, Timothy, and David Oderberg. *Human Values: New Essays on Ethics and Natural Law*. New York: Palgrave Macmillan, 2004.

Chetty, Raj, et al. "The Opportunity Atlas: Mapping the Childhood Roots of Social Mobility." National Bureau of Economic Research, October 2018. https://doi.org/10.3386/w25147.

Child Welfare Information Gateway. *The Impact of Adoption*. Washington, DC: U.S. Department of Health and Human Services, Administration for Children and Families, Children's Bureau, 2019.

Condic, Samuel, and Maureen Condic. *Human Embryos, Human Beings: A Scientific and Philosophical Approach*. Washington, DC: Catholic University of America Press, 2018.

Crisp, Roger. "Finnis on Well-being." In *Reason, Morality and Law: The Philosophy of John Finnis*, edited by John Keown and Robert P. George, 24–36. Oxford: Oxford University Press, 2013.

Curlin, Farr A., and Christopher O. Tollefsen. "Conscience and the Way of Medicine." *Perspectives in Biology and Medicine* 62, no. 3 (2019): 560–75.

———. *The Way of Medicine: Ethics and the Healing Profession*. Notre Dame, IN: University of Notre Dame Press, 2021.

Duke, George. "The Distinctive Common Good." *Review of Politics* 78, no. 2 (2016): 227–50.

Dunkelman, Marc. *The Vanishing Neighbor*. New York: W. W. Norton, 2014.

Dworkin, Ronald. *A Matter of Principle*. Cambridge, MA: Harvard University Press, 1986.

———. *Taking Rights Seriously*. Cambridge, MA: Harvard University Press, 1978.

Eldridge, Sherrie. *Twenty Things Adopted Kids Wish Their Adoptive Parents Knew.* Bantam Dell, 1999.

Ellison, Katherine. *The Mommy Brain: How Motherhood Makes Us Smarter.* New York: Basic Books, 2005.

Felbab-Brown, Vanda. "Somalia's Challenges in 2023." Brookings, May 15, 2023. https://www.brookings.edu/articles/somalias-challenges-in-2023/.

Feser, Edward. *Neo-Scholastic Essays*. South Bend, IN: St Augustine's Press, 2005.

Finnis, John. "Action's Most Ultimate End." In *Reason in Action*, Vol. 1 of *Collected Essays*, 159–271. Oxford: Oxford University Press, 2011.

———. *Aquinas: Moral, Political, and Legal Theory.* Oxford: Oxford University Press, 1998.

———. *Fundamentals of Ethics*. Washington, DC: Georgetown University Press, 1983.

———. "Human Acts." In *Intention and Identity*, Vol. 2 of *Collected Essays*, 133–51. Oxford: Oxford University Press, 2011.

———. "Marriage: A Basic and Exigent Good." *The Monist* 91 (July-October 2008): 388–406.

———. *Moral Absolutes: Tradition, Revision, and Truth.* Washington, DC: Catholic University of America Press, 1991.

———. *Natural Law and Natural Rights*. Oxford: Oxford University Press, 2011.

———. "Reflections and Responses." In *Reason, Morality and Law*, edited by John Keown and Robert George, 459–584. Oxford: Oxford University Press, 2013.

———. "Religion and State: Some Main Issues and Sources." *American Journal of Jurisprudence* 51 (2006): 107.

Finnis, John, Joseph Boyle, and Germain Grisez. *Nuclear Deterrence, Morality and Realism.* Oxford: Clarendon, 1987.

Finnis, John, Germain Grisez and Joseph Boyle. "'Direct' and 'Indirect': A Reply to Critics of Our Action Theory." *The Thomist* 65 (2001): 1–44.

"Franciszek Gajowniczek." Wikipedia. https://en.wikipedia.org/wiki/Franciszek_Gajowniczek.

Fuller, Lon. *The Morality of Law*. New Haven, CT: Yale University Press, 1969.

Garbarino, James. *Lost Boys*. New York: The Free Press, 1999.

George, Robert P. "The Concept of Public Morality." *American Journal of Jurisprudence* 45 (2000): 17–32.

———. "Does the 'Incommensurability Thesis' Imperil Common Sense Moral Judgments?" *American Journal of Jurisprudence* 37 (1992): 185–95.

———. "Making Children Moral: Pornography, Parents and the Public Interest." *Arizona State Law Journal* 29 (1997): 569–80.

———. *Making Men Moral: Civil Liberties and Public Morality.* Oxford: Clarendon, 1995.

———. "Reason, Freedom and the Rule of Law." *American Journal of Jurisprudence* 46 (2001): 249–56.

———. "Recent Criticism of New Natural Law Theory." *University of Chicago Law Review* 55, no. 4 (1988): 1371–1429.

Gettleman, Jeffery. "The Most Dangerous Place in the World." *Foreign Policy* (March/April 2009): 62–69.

Girgis, Sherif, Ryan T. Anderson, and Robert P. George. *What Is Marriage? Man and Woman: A Defense.* New York: Encounter Books, 2012.

Grisez, Germain. *Beyond the New Theism: A Philosophy of Religion.* Notre Dame, IN: University of Notre Dame Press, 1975.

———. *Christian Moral Principles.* Vol. 1 of *The Way of the Lord Jesus.* Chicago: Franciscan Herald Press, 1983.

———. *Difficult Moral Questions.* Vol. 3 of *The Way of the Lord Jesus.* Quincy, IL: Franciscan Press, 1997.

———. "The First Principle of Practical Reason: A Commentary on the *Summa Theologiae* 1–2, q. 94, a. 2." *Natural Law Forum* 10 (1965): 168–201.

———. "Kant and Aquinas: Ethical Theory." *The Thomist* 21 (1958): 44–78.

———. *Living a Christian Life.* Vol. 2 of *The Way of the Lord Jesus.* Quincy, IL: Franciscan Press, 1993.

———. "Natural Law and the Transcendent Source of Human Fulfilment." In *Reason, Morality and Law: The Philosophy of John Finnis,* edited by John Keown and Robert P. George, 443–56. Oxford: Oxford University Press, 2013.

———. "Natural Law, God, Religion and Human Fulfilment." *American Journal of Jurisprudence* 46, no.1 (2001): 3–36.

———. "The True Ultimate End of Human Beings." *Theological Studies* 69 (2008): 39–61.

Grisez, Germain, Joseph Boyle, and John Finnis. "Practical Principles, Moral Truths, Ultimate Ends." *American Journal of Jurisprudence* 32 (1987): 99–151.

Haidt, Jonathan. *The Anxious Generation: How the Great Rewiring of Childhood Is Causing an Epidemic of Mental Illness.* New York: Penguin, 2024.

Hall, Elena. *Through Adopted Eyes: A Collection of Memoirs from Adoptees.* Wordrobe Media, 2018.

Haskins, Ron. "Combating Poverty: Understanding New Challenges for Families." The Brookings Institution, June 5, 2012. https://www.brookings.edu/articles/combating-poverty-understanding-new-challenges-for-families/.

Hittinger, Russell. *A Critique of the New Natural Law Theory.* Notre Dame, IN: University of Notre Dame Press, 1987.

———. "The Three Necessary Societies." *First Things: A Monthly Journal of Religion and Public Life*, June 2017. https://www.firstthings.com/article/2017/06/the-three-necessary-societies.

Jargon, Julie. "The School Took Away Smartphone. The Kids Don't Mind." *Wall Street Journal*, November 5, 2022.

Jensen, Steven. "Causal Constraints on Intention: A Critique of Tollefsen on the Phoenix Case." *National Catholic Bioethics Quarterly* 14, no. 2 (2014): 273–93.

———. *Knowing the Natural Law: From Precepts and Inclinations to Deriving Oughts*. Washington, DC: The Catholic University of America Press, 2015.

John Paul II. *Centesimus annus*. May 1, 1991. https://www.vatican.va/content/john-paul-ii/en/encyclicals/documents/hf_jp-ii_enc_01051991_centesimus-annus.html.

Kaczor, Christopher, and Jennifer Kaczor, *The Seven Big Myths about Marriage*. San Francisco: Ignatius, 2014.

Kaplan, Seth. *Fragile Neighborhoods: Repairing American Society, One Zip Code at a Time*. New York: Little, Brown Spark, 2023.

Kearney, Melissa. *The Two-Parent Privilege: How Americans Stopped Getting Married and Started Falling Behind*. Chicago: University of Chicago Press, 2023.

Keller, Simon. *Partiality*. Princeton NJ: Princeton University Press, 2013.

Keown, John. *Euthanasia, Ethics and Public Policy*. Cambridge: Cambridge University Press, 2002.

Kershnar, Stephen, and Robert Kelly. "The Right-Based Criticism of the Doctrine of Double Effect." *International Journal of Applied Philosophy* 34 (2020): 215–33.

Knobel, Angela. *Aquinas and the Infused Moral Virtues*. Notre Dame, IN: University of Notre Dame Press, 2021.

Korsgaard, Christine. "Two Distinctions in Goodness." *The Philosophical Review* 92, no. 2 (1983): 169–95.

Lee, Patrick. "Distinguishing between What Is Intended and Foreseen Side Effects." *American Journal of Jurisprudence* (2017): 1–21.

———. "The Specific Common Good of the Political Community." Paper delivered at the Romanell Center Workshop at the University of Buffalo, March 19, 2022.

Lee, Patrick, and Robert P. George. *Body-Self Dualism in Contemporary Ethics and Politics*. Cambridge: Cambridge University Press, 2009.

———. *Conjugal Union: What Marriage Is and Why It Matters*. Cambridge: Cambridge University Press, 2014.

———. "The Nature and Basis of Human Dignity." *Ratio Juris* 21 (2008): 173–93.

Lee, Patrick, and Melissa Moschella. "Embryology and Science Denial." *The Public Discourse*, November 8, 2017. https://www.thepublicdiscourse.com/2017/11/20449/.

Levin, Yuval. *The Fractured Republic*. New York: Basic Books, 2016.

———. *A Time to Build*. New York: Basic Books, 2021.

Lewis, V. Bradley. "Is the Common Good an Ensemble of Conditions?" *Archives of Philosophy* 84 (2016): 121–32.

Liao, S. Matthew. *The Right to Be Loved.* New York: Oxford University Press, 2015.

Locke, John. *Second Treatise of Government.* Edited by C. B. Macpherson. Indianapolis: Hackett, 1980.

Long, Steven. "Fundamental Errors of the New Natural Law Theory." *National Catholic Bioethics Quarterly* (Spring 2013): 105–31.

MacIntyre, Alasdair. *After Virtue.* 3rd ed. Notre Dame, IN: University of Notre Dame Press, 2007.

———. *Dependent Rational Animals: Why Human Beings Need the Virtues.* London: Duckworth, 2009.

———. *Edith Stein: A Philosophical Prologue.* New York: Rowman and Littlefield, 2006.

———. *Ethics in the Conflicts of Modernity.* Cambridge: Cambridge University Press, 2016.

———. "A Partial Response to My Critics." In *After MacIntyre: Critical Perspectives on the Work of Alasdair MacIntyre,* edited by John Horton and Susan Mendus, 283–304. Cambridge: Polity, 1994.

———. "Plain Persons and Moral Philosophy: Rules, Virtues, Goods." *American Catholic Philosophical Quarterly* 66 (1992): 3–19.

Mackie, J. L. *Ethics: Inventing Right and Wrong.* Harmondsworth: Penguin, 1977.

Manning, Wendy. "Cohabitation and Child Well-being." *The Future of Children* 25, no. 2 (2015): 51–56.

Marquardt, Elizabeth, Norval D. Glenn, and Karen Clark. *My Daddy's Name Is Donor: A New Study of Young Adults Conceived through Sperm Donation.* New York: Institute for American Values, 2010.

McInerny, Ralph. "The Primacy of Theoretical Knowledge: Some Remarks on John Finnis." In *Aquinas on Human Action: A Theory of Practice,* 184–92. Washington, DC: Catholic University of America Press, 1992.

McIntyre, Alison. "Doing Away with Double Effect." *Ethics* 111 (2001): 219–55.

McLanahan, Sara, and Isabel Sawhill. "Marriage and Child Wellbeing Revisited: Introducing the Issue." *The Future of Children* 25 no. 2 (2015): 3–9.

McMahan, Jeff. *The Ethics of Killing.* New York: Oxford University Press, 2002.

Moberg, Uvnäs Kerstin. *The Oxytocin Factor: Tapping the Hormone of Calm, Love and Healing.* 2nd ed. London: Printer & Martin, 2011.

Moore, Kristin Anderson, et al. "Marriage from a Child's Perspective: How Does Family Structure Affect Children, and What Can We Do about It?" Child's Trend Research Brief, June 2002. https://www.childtrends.org/publications

/marriage-from-a-childs-perspective-how-does-family-structure-affect-children
-and-what-can-we-do-about-it

Moschella, Melissa. "Beyond Equal Liberty: Religion as a Distinct Human Good and the Implications for Religious Freedom." *Journal of Law and Religion* 32, no. 1 (2017): 123–46.

———. "Contextualizing, Clarifying and Defending the Doctrine of Double Effect." *Journal of Ethics and Social Philosophy* 26 (2023): 297–324.

———. "Defending the Fundamental Rights of Parents: A Response to Recent Attacks." *Notre Dame Journal of Law, Ethics and Public Policy* 37, no. 2 (2023): 397–443.

———. "Integrated but Not Whole? Applying an Ontological Account of Human Organismal Unity to the Brain Death Debate." *Bioethics* 30, no. 8 (2016): 550–56.

———. "Practical Reason, Sexual Ethics and the Magisterium: A Reply to Irene Alexander." *National Catholic Bioethics Quarterly* 22, no. 1 (2022): 99–127.

———. "Sexual Ethics, Human Nature, and the 'New' and 'Old' Natural Law Theories." *National Catholic Bioethics Quarterly* 19, no. 2 (2019): 251–78.

———. "Social Contract Theory and Moral Agency." In *Caring Professions and Globalization*, edited by Ana Marta Gonzalez and Craig Iffland, 87–115. London: Palgrave Macmillan, 2014.

———. *To Whom Do Children Belong: Parental Rights, Civic Education and Children's Autonomy.* New York: Cambridge University Press, 2016.

Murphy, Mark. "The Common Good." *Review of Metaphysics* 59 (September 2005): 133–64.

———. *God and Moral Law.* New York: Oxford, 2001.

Murray, Charles. *Coming Apart.* New York: Random House, 2012.

Myers, Evan. "Taking the Postman Pledge." *The American Conservative*, December 2, 2022. https://www.theamericanconservative.com/taking-the-postman
-pledge/.

Nozick, Robert. *Anarchy, State, and Utopia.* New York: Basic Books, 1974.

Oderberg, David. *Moral Theory: A Non-Consequentialist Approach.* Oxford: Blackwell, 2002.

Pakaluk, Michael. "Is the Common Good of Political Society Limited and Instrumental?" *Review of Metaphysics* 55, no. 1 (2001): 57–94.

Perry, Bruce, and Maya Szalavitz. *The Boy Who Was Raised as a Dog.* New York: Basic Books, 2006.

Pettinger, Tejvan. "Biography of Maximilian Kolbe." Biography Online, August 3, 2014. https://www.biographyonline.net/spiritual/maximilian-kolbe.html.

Popeneo, David, and Barbara DaFoe Whitehead. *Should We Live Together? What Young Adults Need to Know about Cohabitation before Marriage: A Comprehensive Review of Recent Research*. 2nd ed. New Brunswick, NJ: National Marriage Project, Rutgers University, 2002.

Porter, Jean. "'Direct' and 'Indirect' in Grisez's Moral Theory." *Theological Studies* 57, no. 4 (1996): 611–32.

———. "Does the Natural Law Provide a Universally Valid Morality?" In *Intractable Disputes about Natural Law: Alasdair MacIntyre and Critics*, edited by Lawrence S. Cunningham, 53–96. Notre Dame, IN: University of Notre Dame University Press, 2009.

———. *Nature as Reason: A Thomistic Theory of the Natural Law*. Grand Rapids, MI: Eerdmans, 2005.

———. "Reason, Nature, and the End of Human Life: A Consideration of John Finnis's *Aquinas*." *Journal of Religion* 80, no. 3 (2000): 476–84.

Putnam, Robert. *American Grace*. New York: Simon & Schuster, 2010.

———. *Our Kids*. New York: Simon & Schuster, 2015

Pruss, Alexander. *One Body: An Essay in Christian Sexual Ethics*. Notre Dame, IN: University of Notre Dame Press, 2012.

Rawls, John. *Political Liberalism*. New York: Columbia University Press, 1996.

———. "The Priority of Right and Ideas of the Good." *Philosophy and Public Affairs* 17 (1988): 251–76.

———. *A Theory of Justice*. Rev. ed. Cambridge, MA: Harvard University Press, 1999.

Raz, Joseph. *The Morality of Freedom*. Oxford: Oxford University Press, 1988.

———. *Practical Reason and Norms*. 2nd ed. Princeton, NJ: Princeton University Press, 1990.

Rhoades, Galena. "How Moving In Together Makes It Harder to Know If He's the One." *Institute for Family Studies* (blog), October 16, 2018. https://ifstudies.org/blog/how-moving-in-together-makes-it-harder-to-know-if-hes-the-one.

Richardson, Henry. "Incommensurability and Basic Goods: A Tension in the New Natural Law Theory." In *Human Values*, edited by David Oderberg and Timothy Chappell, 70–101. New York: Palgrave Macmillan, 2004.

Sandel, Michael. "The Procedural Republic and the Unencumbered Self." *Political Theory* 12 (February 1984): 81–96.

Scanlon, T. M. *Moral Dimensions: Permissibility, Meaning, Blame*. Cambridge, MA: Harvard University Press, 2008.

Schindler, D. C. *The Politics of the Real: The Church between Liberalism and Integralism*. Steubenville, OH: New Polity Press, 2021.

Second Vatican Council. *Dignitatis humanae* (*Declaration on Religious Liberty*). December 7, 1965. https://www.vatican.va/archive/hist_councils/ii_vatican_council/documents/vat-ii_decl_19651207_dignitatis-humanae_en.html.

———. *Gaudium et spes* (*Pastoral Constitution on the Church in the Modern World*). December 7, 1965. https://www.vatican.va/archive/hist_councils/ii_vatican _council/documents/vat-ii_const_19651207_gaudium-et-spes_lt.html.

Shanholtz, Caroline, Megan Irgens, and Connie Beck. "Are the Adults Alright? Reviewing Outcomes for Adult Offspring of Parental Divorce." *Journal of Family Trauma, Child Custody & Child Development* 18, no.1 (2021): 4–20.

Siegel, Deborah H. "Growing Up in Open Adoption: Young Adults' Perspectives." *Families in Society* 93, no. 2 (2018): 133–40.

Simon, Yves. *A General Theory of Authority.* Notre Dame, IN: University of Notre Dame Press, 1962.

———. *Philosophy of Democratic Government.* Notre Dame, IN: University of Notre Dame Press, 1993.

Singer, Peter. "Voluntary Euthanasia: A Utilitarian Perspective." *Bioethics* 17 (2003): 530.

Smith, Megan, et al. "Review of Benefits and Risks for Children in Open Adoption Arrangements." *Child & Family Social Work* 25 (2020): 761–74.

Smith, Steven. "Christians and/as Liberals?" *Notre Dame Law Review* 98, no. 4 (2023): 1497–1522.

"Somalia's Country Profile." BBC News, April 26, 2023. https://www.bbc.com/ news/world-africa-14094503.

Steinhoff, Uwe. "Wild Goose Chase: Still No Rationales for the Doctrine of Double Effect and Related Principles." *Criminal Law and Philosophy* 13 (2019): 1–25.

Sullins, Paul D. "The Case for Mom and Dad." *The Linacre Quarterly* 88, no. 2 (2021): 184–201.

———. "Emotional Problems among Children with Same-Sex Parents: Difference by Definition." *British Journal of Education, Society and Behavioural Science* 7, no. 2 (2015): 99–120.

Teresa of Avila. *The Book of Foundations of S. Teresa of Jesus of the Order of Our Lady of Carmel With the Visitation of Nunneries, the Rule and Constitutions.* Translated by David Lewis; rev. ed. by Rev. Benedict Zimmerman. London: Thomas Baker, 1913.

Thompson, Michael. "Forms in Nature." In *Reason in Nature: New Essays on Themes from John McDowell*, edited by Matthew Boyle and Evgenia Mylonaki, 40–80. Cambridge, MA: Harvard University Press, 2022.

Tocqueville, Alexis de. *Democracy in America.* Translated by Harvey S. Mansfield and Delba Winthrop. Chicago: University of Chicago Press, 2000.

Tollefsen, Christopher. "Aquinas's Four Orders, Normativity and Human Nature." *Journal of Value Inquiry* 52 (2018): 243–56.

———. "Basic Goods, Practical Insight and External Reasons." In *Human Values*, edited by David Oderberg and Timothy Chappell, 32–51. New York: Palgrave Macmillan, 2004.

———. *Biomedical Research and Beyond.* New York: Routledge, 2008.

———. "Disability and Social Justice." In *Philosophical Reflections on Disability*, edited by D. C. Ralston and J. Ho, 211–27. New York: Springer, 2010.

———. "Double Effect and Two Hard Cases in Medical Ethics." *American Catholic Philosophical Quarterly* 89, no. 3 (2015): 407–20. https://doi.org/10.5840/acpq20156455.

———. "Is a Purely First-Person Account of Human Action Defensible?" *Ethical Theory and Moral Practice* 9 (2006): 441–60.

———. "Morality and God." *Quaestiones Disputatae* 5, no. 1 (2014): 47–60.

———. "Pure Perfectionism and the Limits of Paternalism." In *Reason, Morality and Law: The Philosophy of John Finnis*, edited by John Keown and Robert George, 204–18. Oxford: Oxford University Press, 2013.

———. "Terminating in the Body: Concerning Some Errors of Action and Intention." *The National Catholic Bioethics Quarterly* 10, no. 2 (2019): 203–20.

———. "Torture: What It Is, and Why It Is Wrong." *Public Discourse*, April 28, 2009. https://www.thepublicdiscourse.com/2009/04/233/.

Tollefsen, Christopher, and Robert P. George. *Embryo: A Defense of Human Life.* 2nd ed. Princeton, NJ: The Witherspoon Institute, 2011.

Truffaut, Francois, dir. *The Wild Child.* Les Films du Carrosse, 1970.

Velleman, David. "Persons in Prospect." *Philosophy and Public Affairs* 36 (2008): 221–88.

Verrier, Nancy Newton. *The Primal Wound: Understanding the Adopted Child.* Baltimore: Gateway Press, 1993.

Walzer, Michael. "Political Action: The Problem of Dirty Hands." *Philosophy and Public Affairs* 2, no. 2 (1973): 160–80.

Weston, Jonah, dir. "Wild Child: The Story of Feral Children." YouTube, September 30, 2022. https://www.youtube.com/watch?v=n1yuUeaYE24.

Williams, Bernard. "Internal and External Reasons." In *Moral Luck: Philosophical Papers 1973–1980*, 101–2. Cambridge: Cambridge University Press, 1981.

Wright, R. George. "Does Free Speech Jurisprudence Rest on a Mistake? Implications of the Commensurability Debate." *Loyola of Los Angeles Law Review* 23 (1990): 763–90.

Yousef, Nancy. "Savage or Solitary? The Wild Child and Rousseau's Man of Nature." *Journal of the History of Ideas* 62, no. 2 (2001): 245–63.

Index

Extended Table of Contents

MELISSA MOSCHELLA

is a professor of the practice in philosophy at the
University of Notre Dame's McGrath Institute for Church Life.
She is the author of *To Whom Do Children Belong? Parental Rights,
Civic Education, and Children's Autonomy.*

RUSSELL HITTINGER

is the Executive Director of the Institute for Human Ecology
and co-founder of the Program on Catholic Political Thought
at the Catholic University of America.

9 780268 209261